The D....

The Director's Idea

The Path to Great Directing

Ken Dancyger
New York University
Tisch School of the Arts
New York, New York

ELSEVIER

AMSTERDAM • BOSTON • HEIDELBERG • LONDON
NEW YORK • OXFORD • PARIS • SAN DIEGO
SAN FRANCISCO • SINGAPORE • SYDNEY • TOKYO
Focal Press is an imprint of Elsevier

Acquisitions Editor: Elinor Actipis
Project Manager: Paul Gottehrer
Associate Editor: Becky Golden-Harrell
Marketing Manager: Christine Degon Veroulis
Cover Design: Alisa Andreola

Focal Press is an imprint of Elsevier
30 Corporate Drive, Suite 400, Burlington, MA 01803, USA
Linacre House, Jordan Hill, Oxford OX2 8DP, UK

 Recognizing the importance of preserving what has been written, Elsevier prints its books on
acid-free paper whenever possible.

Library of Congress Cataloging-in-Publication Data
Application submitted

British Library Cataloguing-in-Publication Data
A catalogue record for this book is available from the British Library.

ISBN 13: 978-0-240-80681-5
ISBN 10: 0-240-80681-6

For information on all Focal Press publications
visit our website at www.books.elsevier.com

05 06 07 08 09 10   10 9 8 7 6 5 4 3 2 1
Printed in the United States of America

Working together to grow
libraries in developing countries

www.elsevier.com | www.bookaid.org | www.sabre.org

ELSEVIER   **BOOK AID** International   **Sabre Foundation**

For Joshua and Malka

Contents

CONTENTS

xi

CONTENTS

Acknowledgments

The Director's Idea is a book that comes out of my teaching experience with production students at New York University and with professional producers and editors at the Maurits Binger Institute in Amsterdam. In earlier books I had examined the storytelling tools of the screenwriter as well as of the editor. Now students and professionals have pushed for an articulation of the storytelling tools of the director.

Needless to say, a book such as *The Director's Idea* needs and gets a lot of help from many quarters. At Focal Press I'd like to thank Elinor Actipis, the acquiring editor as well as Becky Golden-Harrell and Paul Gottehrer who each in their own way have helped move the book to completion. I'd like to thank my friend Maura Nolan who helped me prepare the proposal and Dave Wapner who helped in the preparation of the manuscript.

Above all I'd like to say that my wife Ida was immensely helpful in the manuscript preparation and as a constant on-site editor of my work. She proved tireless and invaluable.

I'd like to thank all the external reviewers, but would like to especially single out Warren Bass of Temple University. His review made this a better book. I appreciate his intelligence, acuity, and passion. I only wish I have made the book as good as his road map proved to be for me.

Finally this is a book about directing for directors and talented individuals who want to become directors. Although its shortcomings are my own, I hope the book has succeeded in conveying a passion for directing that for me has never dimmed. I wish as much for the readers of this book.

Ken Dancyger
New York
January 2006

ACKNOWLEDGMENTS

Part I

What the Director Does

Chapter 1

Introduction

Much has been written about the mystique of film directing, so much so that the craft and the art of directing have been submerged in a swell of adulation. The adulation is understandable. Film—celluloid or digital—is the art form of the twentieth century, and the director is given much of the credit for a film's success. Paradoxically, directing remains a vocation that has used its mystique to its advantage; consequently, less is understood about the means of directing than about the other key roles in production. So, one of the goals of this book is to develop an understanding of what the director does and, by doing so, to help the reader become a better director. The path to better directing is exploring the tools available to the director and understanding how those tools can be deployed to make the competent director a better director and the good director a great director.

Having stated my über-goal, permit me to step back a bit to contextualize the goal of the book. First, the book examines the role of directing in production. Filmmaking, more than most popular or elite art forms, is collaborative. Producers, cinematographers, art designers, sound designers, editors, composers, scriptwriters, and actors all contribute mightily to the power of a finished film. Many have used the analogy of the director as the conductor of an orchestra or the coach of a sports team. Such analogies are, on one level, good. The director must marshal a varied group of talented individuals into a winning team and a single voice, and the sum of the whole must always be greater than the sum of the parts. This is the directing challenge, and this is where directors distinguish themselves as good directors or great directors, as opposed to competent or less competent directors. To do so, however, the director must be a politician, technician, storyteller, and artist.

This book focuses on the director. That is not to say that producers, writers, or actors are less important. Indeed, all are critical to the success of a film, and their roles are clearly understood. The goal of this book is to make the role of the director equally clear.

What Does the Director Do?

The director is responsible for translating a script (words) into visuals (shots) that will be turned over to an editor to pull together into a film. Start and finish points, however, may well blur, as the director joins the project in the writing or pre-production phase and does not leave the project until post-production. Thus, the director may well be involved in all aspects of the editing phase, such as sound design, music composition, recording, and mixing into the overall sound, until the film is completed. In other words, the director is responsible for the creative supervision of the film from early in its conception to its completion. The director will work most closely with the producer, who is responsible for the organizational and financial supervision of the film from its conception to its conclusion.

In the pre-production phase, the director may either play a secondary role to the scriptwriter or partner with the writer. The exact nature of the role depends on the director's track record, influence, and interest. There is no such variability in the production phase, when the director is clearly in charge. Interpretation of the screenplay, blocking, breakdown of the script into specific shots, and modulation of the performances of actors are some of the specific responsibilities of the director in the production phase. In the postproduction phase, the director's interest or influence will either expand or reduce the director's involvement. Generally, directors are quite involved in this phase even though editors (picture and sound) are driving many decisions.

What should be emphasized, however, is that writers, directors, and editors share one goal—to tell the story as effectively as possible—but their contributions differ. Writers use words, directors use camera shots and performances, and editors use visuals and sound to tell the story.

Who Is the Director?

Directors, as with every other profession, come in all different shapes and sizes. Whether they are male or female, Western, Eastern, Spanish, or American, their uniqueness is a result of the mix of each director's beliefs, experiences, interests, and character. Some directors are playful (think of Federico Fellini). Some are deadly serious (think of Ingmar Bergman). Some prefer particular genres (think of Clint Eastwood). Some seem to thrive on a diversity of genres (think of Howard Hawks). Some are political (think of Sergei Eisenstein). Some are apolitical (think of Blake Edwards). Some prefer comedy (think of Woody Allen). And some try to alternate serious films with comedy (think again about Woody Allen as well as Billy Wilder).

My point here is that each director has a distinct personality that makes the work of that director different from the work of others. Part of the pleasure derived from films is their diversity, which contradicts the notion roaming around too many halls of film education institutes that there is one right way to make a film. My feeling is that there are many right ways, depending on the character, beliefs, and interests of the specific filmmaker.

How Did We Get Here?

Directors were not always the central figures they are today. As Hollywood developed into an industry, stars and producers were far more important than directors. David Selznick, a studio executive, became an important producer; consequently, he is the central creative figure associated with "Gone with the Wind." No one remembers the four directors and as many writers on the film. When one speaks about "Casablanca," it is Bogart and the Epstein brothers, the writers, who are remembered rather than Michael Curtiz, the director. Otto Preminger and Joe Mankiewicz both began their ascent in the film industry as producers. Both later made their mark as directors. Billy Wilder began as a writer, as did Preston Sturges. There were important directors in Hollywood (such as John Ford, Frank Capra, and Howard Hawks), but whenever possible they also acted as producers of their films. Even today, Jerry Bruckheimer and Brian Grazer are important producer figures in the industry. So, how did the director become so important?

The pivotal event occurred in France rather than in Hollywood. There, critics such as François Truffaut, Claude Chabrol, Eric Roehmer gathered around the journal *Cahiers du Cinema*, under the editorship of André Bazin. In post-war France, they studied and wrote about the creative genius of John Ford, Howard Hawks, Alfred Hitchcock, Anthony Mann, and Sam Fuller. They considered these American filmmakers to be the auteurs of their films, and they criticized the structure and output of their own French film industry. They began to make their own films—independent, low-budget films in the freer style characteristic of American cinema. The effect of their adulation was revolutionary, as directors came to be widely regarded as the auteurs or creative kingpins of their films. This concept was seized by cinephiles in England, where Karel Reisz and Lindsay Anderson wrote about film in the same spirit and began to make their own films in the freer, more personal style of the French "New Wave" filmmakers.

In America, the notion of auteurism was quickly adopted by John Cassavetes, Arthur Penn, Mike Nichols, and Sidney Lumet. Also, an intellectual–journalistic rationale was provided by Andrew Sarris; in his film reviews and later in his book *The American Cinema*, Sarris articulated and applied the auteur theory to all of American cinema. The auteur revolution had come to the United States, and film schools became a hotbed of auteurism. Graduates of the late 1960s (particularly Martin Scorsese, Francis Ford Coppola, and George Lucas) fueled in their early films the idea that the revolution was going to take over Hollywood.

In fact it did not, as studios, agents, and actors became more important even as the director's status was rising. Everyone in film—actors, editors, writers, musicians—became superstars right along with the directors. As the commercial stakes rose, so too did the superstar population of Hollywood. Globalization and technology have deepened these trends, but today the director is at the pinnacle of the film hierarchy.

Where Are We Today?

Film today is one of the most important global industries. For many Hollywood films, most of the revenue can come from outside of the United States. A tentpole film such as "Troy" can expect to earn two thirds of its revenue offshore. In the United States, film and television are key export industries. In so fluid and lucrative a milieu, it is no wonder that directors are superstars the world over.

Wong Kar-wai of Hong Kong, Tom Tykwer of Germany, Luc Besson of France, and Steven Soderbergh of the United States are all at the peak of industry and public attention. In one sense, they are part of a continuum begun with Charlie Chaplin and Alfred Hitchcock 70 years earlier, but today is different. In addition to the industry being more global, there are other reasons for the increased importance of directors.

One reason is financial. George Lucas ("Star Wars"), Steven Spielberg (the "Indiana Jones" series, "Jurassic Park," "Jaws"), and Peter Jackson ("The Lord of the Rings" trilogy) have created financial empires within the Hollywood industry. Their scale is unprecedented. Another reason is critical recognition, that is to say, the attention of the critics. Francis Ford Coppola ("The Godfather" series, "Apocalypse Now"), Martin Scorsese ("Raging Bull," "Goodfellas," "Kundun"), and Spike Lee ("Do the Right Thing," "25th Hour") are not runaway commercial hit directors (indeed, the works of Scorsese and Lee are rarely commercially impressive); nevertheless, they are critically embraced and valued far beyond their commercial viability (or lack thereof).

Yet another reason is the director's willingness to experiment. Steven Soderbergh experiments with clashing style and content ("The Limey," "Traffic"). David Mamet, a well-known playwright, experiments with very filmic plot-oriented genres ("Heist," "Spartan," "The Spanish Prisoner"); Mike Figgis experiments with technology ("Time Code"); and Oliver Stone experiments with the MTV influence ("Natural Born Killers").

A number of filmmakers try to replicate their style and success as commercial and television video makers. The world of advertising has launched the careers of Tony Scott ("Man on Fire"), Michael Bay ("Bad Boys"), and McQ ("Charlie's Angels"). Their transition to filmmaking has worked and created yet another layer of directors in the industry.

Finally, some directors were something else before they became directors, such as the actors Robert Redford ("Ordinary People"), Clint Eastwood ("Mystic River"), Mel Gibson ("The Passion of Christ"), Diane Keaton ("Unstrung Heroes"), and Angelica Huston ("Bastard out of Carolina"). The theater directors Sam Mendes ("American Beauty"), Nicolas Hytner ("The Crucible"), and David Mamet ("The Winslow Boy") follow in the footsteps of Elia Kazan, and all do very good work.

Another consideration with regard to today's directors is that they are far more international than their predecessors. Many successful foreign directors (that is, directors who are successful in their own countries) are now working in English productions as well as those in their languages of origin. Istvan Szabo of Hungary ("Taking Sides," "Sunshine"), Luc Besson of France ("The Messenger,"

7

"Leon the Professional"), and Tom Tykwer of Germany ("Heaven") are among the best known of these filmmakers.

American directors are also taking a more flexible approach to their careers. Spike Lee makes documentaries and commercials between his feature films. Martin Scorsese also makes documentaries between his features. Steven Soderbergh occasionally jumps into digital video and small-scale features in between his more commercial projects. Barry Levinson takes on edgy television projects in addition to his more conservative (read commercial) feature films. Oliver Stone has moved from directing a low-budget HBO documentary about Castro to directing a $200 million feature about Alexander the Great. In Europe, Lars von Trier continually experiments with the style of his films. Roger Michell jumps from film to television to theater with great frequency.

One of the most interesting career paths exhibiting this flexibility is that of Ang Lee. Lee has moved from ethnic family comedies ("Eat Drink Man Woman") to Jane Austen family comedy ("Sense and Sensibility") to Chinese-language action adventure ("Crouching Tiger, Hidden Dragon") to American action adventure ("The Incredible Hulk"). And I have not even mentioned his Western or nonlinear films! This degree of diversity keeps the director challenged and in risk-taking rather than risk-aversion mode.

What I am suggesting is that today the director is a superstar, but the means of becoming such a superstar as well as sustaining one's superstardom have grown far more complex.

The Structure of the Book

This book is divided into two parts. The first focuses on the question "What is directing?" and discusses how a director arrives at the director's idea. The first half of Part I defines the director's idea and differentiates competent or technical directing, good directing, and great directing. I realize that *competent*, *good*, and *great* are loaded, subjective words. They are hierarchical, and my use of such terminology and my taste may not match those of the reader; nevertheless, I am going to use these terms to capture the sense that there is a distinct path to improved directing and that the path requires a premise, a director's idea, to guide the choices the director makes.

8

Those choices—the direction of the actors, the shot choices, the proximity of the camera to the action, deciding when to switch to a stationary camera, and finally text or script interpretation—are the substance of the second section of this first part. Approaches designed to reach the director's idea of the reader are provided in an appendix that appears at the end of the book.

The second part of the book is comprised of 14 case studies of the work of individual directors. The case studies are organized as follows:

1. Articulation of the director's idea.
2. Application of the director's idea.

Scenes from each director's work have been chosen to examine their approach to directing. The discussion of these scenes includes:

1. A summary of the narrative content of the scene
2. The performances (how they are adapted to orchestrate emotionally the director's idea)
3. The camera work or visualization utilized to achieve the director's idea
4. Lighting, sound, and, if applicable, art direction and how they contribute to the director's idea
5. A summary of how these elements work together to further the director's idea

How I Came to Write This Book

I have already pointed out that this book presents a hierarchy of directing. Understanding the genesis of my biases will allow readers to either give in to my views or to temper their views with mine. First and foremost, I hope that the reader will come to share my excitement for great directing and to appreciate how to reach for those stars. Second, I must say that I have always been smitten with the directing bug. From the very first time I made a film I knew that I had experienced a singular pleasure of the act. Of course, I instantly associated that effort with those of my idols, the poetic John Ford, the vigorous Raoul Walsh, and the epic Anthony Mann.

Although I had not yet navigated the emotional depths of, for example, Charlie Chaplin, I felt certain that doing so lay just ahead.

The joy of directing has never left me, but in short order it was joined by a drive to write, and nothing proved more pleasurable than editing my own work. Indeed, the process of discovery I experienced in the editing process is quite unmatched in all of my film experiences. I began to teach and quite enjoyed that, also. I have never thought of myself as pollyannaish. I simply enjoy every aspect of the form. It is all about telling a story, about having—and giving to the audience—a thrilling experience. This has not changed, even after thousands of films viewed and even more thousands of students taught. In the past 15 years of my career, I have been writing books about scriptwriting, editing, and production.

In 1988, an editor at Focal Press, Karen Speerstra, asked me to evaluate a book proposal on directing. I did so, and in the course of that evaluation I shared with her that the best directing book I ever encountered was Karel Reisz's *The Technique of Film Editing*. First written in the early 1950s, that book was for me the bible of directing, and I said as much to Karen. Her response was to ask me if I wanted to write the third update of the Reisz book. Of course I did, but it did not come to pass. What did result is what I call the cousin of the Reisz book, my 1993 book, *The Technique of Film and Video Editing*. That book, now in its third edition, has given me the opportunity to flesh out Reisz's subtextual idea: What do directors need to know about shots to make a strong film? Much has changed—styles (*e.g.*, MTV), pacing, types of documentaries, elaborate nonlinear films—but the ideas of Griffith and Vertov and Eisenstein and Pudovkin remain the fundamentals for the shot organization and selection that create powerful film experiences. And those ideas are at the core of the Reisz book.

Flash forward to 2003. I am teaching a workshop in Amsterdam on the history of editing. Attending are working editors and producers. To a person, the attendees express their regret that directors have not come to the workshop. They should be your audience, I am told again and again. Thus, the idea for this book took form.

I would like to end this chapter with the following ten ideas about directing that I would like to share with the reader:

1. Writing, directing, and editing are all about storytelling. The writer uses words, the director uses the camera and the

performance, and the editor uses shots and sound. The means differ but the goal is the same: Tell the story as clearly and as strongly as you can.

2. Making a film is both a creative and organizational challenge, akin to setting up, operating, and shutting down a small (or mid-size) business; consequently, the director needs a creative team (actors, cinematographers and crew, sound and crew, art director and crew, editor and crew), as well as an organization team (producer, production manager, script supervisor, assistant director), and must get along with both teams. Think of this role as a mix of general and captain.

3. Many different styles of leadership can be effective.

4. Making a film requires making hundreds of decisions each day.

5. Directors can never be over-prepared.

6. Directing is technical, intellectual, emotional, and creative. The more layers operating for the director, the more likely the film will be lively and engaging.

7. Actors are critical to the success of a film; they are the front line, the great risk takers in a production. Because of the risks they take, they deserve the respect of their directors.

8. Character matters. Good and great directing is fueled by the character of the director. By character I mean that vague mix of ethics and behavior that make each of us who we are. False character, conversely, does not make for good directing.

9. The story, whether 30 seconds or 3 hours, can be told in many ways. The emphasis or interpretation of a director will depend on that director's interests, intuition, and belief system. One interpretation is not necessarily better than another. It is simply different. And herein lies another pathway to viewing directing as a unique expression of the director (as opposed to an objective view of the work).

10. Technology is not a solution to the directing challenge. Technology is just technology. Directing is the human factor in the directorial equation.

And now let us begin.

Chapter 2

The Director's Idea

- The director's idea is a deep subtextual interpretation that unifies the production. Using an aspect of the main character and his goal, the director finds an existential, relational, or physical dimension that relates to the main character in the deepest fashion. Using the subtextual idea, the director articulates a complementary approach to the performances and to the camera. It is the quality of the director's idea that differentiates the competent from the good and great director. The director's idea drives all the many decisions a director makes in the course of the production.

HOLLYWOOD

PRODUCTION

DIRECTOR

CAMERA

DATE   SCENE   TAK

In this book, I am going to say many things about technique, about directors, and about directing. To persuade the reader that what follows is not simply esoteric, abstract, and academic, I would like to use this chapter to demonstrate that the views presented in this book are conceptual in their framing but practical in their goal. The goal is to help readers become better directors by utilizing the concept of the director's idea. What needs to be said at the outset is that there are all kinds of directors: intuitive directors, self-conscious directors, dictatorial directors, laissez-faire directors, directors whose agendas are political, and directors who are utterly commercial and exploitative in their intentions.

In order to develop our understanding of directing, we must consider three broad areas of decision making that are critical to defining the type of director: (1) text interpretation, (2) attitude toward directing actors, and (3) how the camera is used (*e.g.*, shot selection, camera angle, shape of the shot, point of view of the shot). Beyond those areas is the issue of whether the director's decisions add value to the project. What I am proposing in this book is that there are three categories of such decision making: competent, good, and great. To understand directing, each level of decision making must also be clearly understood; accordingly, the next three chapters address the concepts of competent, good, and great directing.

In each case, the consciousness of the director's idea is where progress begins. The competent director conveys a singular attitude about the script, be it romantic, violent, or victorious. The good director conveys a more complex, layered vision of the narrative. The great director transforms the narrative into something surprising and revelatory. Each of these options exists. Only the ambition of the director can elevate the audience's experience.

The goal of this book is to illuminate the pathway from basic to great. We can assume that the director consciously chooses a director's idea, which implies an awareness about the directorial choices that must be made and a sense of what constitutes better directing. This is not a matter of intellect or personality. It is far more about conscious goal setting and moving along a pathway to achieve that goal. The opposite view, which has its proponents, is that art (including directing) is mysterious, subconscious, intuitive, and therefore impossible to articulate. My approach in the book is to embrace what I believe to be the source of art making: consciousness. The

THE DIRECTOR'S IDEA

greater the consciousness of the director with regard to what the director's idea is and how to apply it, the better, the clearer, and the more powerful the outcome.

The tools that the director uses are text interpretation, directing the actors, and directing the camera shot selection. The director can value one of these tools over the other or use them equally. Whichever he chooses, these three tools are the prism through which he filters the thousands of choices he will have to make in the course of a production. What I am suggesting is that a clear, articulated director's idea will help sharpen the focus and purpose of those thousands of decisions.

Here we come to the hierarchy that this book creates as its pathway to great directing. The presumption here, as elsewhere in life, is that some people are better at their jobs than others. In addition to our three categories of competent, good, and great, we could add another for those who misunderstand directing or are unable to function as directors. Let us call them ill-suited and unsuccessful in their goal of directing. Of course, our categories of competent, good, and great are subjective, so I put forward the following criteria.

The competent director tells a clear story, even an effective story, but the audience's experience of the film is single-layered and flat. A film directed by the competent director can be commercially successful and the director's career can be a rewarding one, but even from the directorial perspective the experience is flat. A competent director is technically competent and produces shots that are useful to a clear edit and performances that are credible within the parameters the director has set for the film. The competent director provides a kind of technical baseline for the purposes of this book.

The good director gives the audience a more complex experience, a layered experience. The layering may be generated from a more complex text interpretation, such as a modern main character in a classic Western, for example. The layering may arise from modulation of the actors' performances; Elia Kazan, the great director of performers, utilized this kind of strategy. Or the director might use a broader variety of shots, wide-angle foreground–background shots rather than mid two shots or extreme long shots rather than the anticipated close-ups. Whatever the choice, the good director seeks out a director's idea that will deepen meaning, add subtext, and complicate the narrative.

The great director not only adds value to the experience of the film but also provides a transformative experience. By transformative I refer to what all great art does: It gives us another way of seeing the ordinary. A man uses his bike for work. The bike is stolen. The economic future of his family is in jeopardy. The man steals a bike, and his son watches as he is caught. The boy shares his humiliation. Vittoria De Sica transforms an everyday story of survival into a story about poverty and fathers and sons. The shared humiliation of father and son will no doubt have an effect on the child. How will this boy grow up—a thief or a doctor? Will he be a caring or callous person? Such questions emanate from the directing of "The Bicycle Thief," in which De Sica transformed a simple story into something quite special about all of us. This is what the great director does. And the instrument is the director's idea. Because individual chapters are devoted to each of these categories, we will move on to a discussion of how a director's idea unifies a production.

The Unity of the Production

It is critical for the viewer that the film be experienced whole. By that I mean that the text interpretation, the performances of the actors, and the shot selection act together to build the viewer's experience. Imagine a jokey, superficial performance in a film such as *Ordinary People*, where the realism and emotional credibility of the characters are key to the experience of the film. Unity means the tools of directing are working together, and this is the purpose of a clear and strong director's idea, which promotes a unity of experience for the audience. A few examples will illustrate how. I have intentionally chosen two relatively simple narratives so it will be clear how the director's idea is operating.

The first example is Volker Schlondorff's "The Ninth Day" (2005). The story takes place over the course of nine days in 1942. A Catholic priest is held in Dachau, where he and his fellow priests are poorly treated but not as poorly as the rest of Dachau's inmates. He is given a leave of nine days to convince his bishop in Luxembourg to accept the primacy of Nazi rule. We learn that the priest is respected, scholarly, and pious and comes from an important family in Luxembourg. For eight days he visits with his family and the bishop's secretary. He sees his mother's grave. Everyone pressures him to make his life easier and not return to Dachau, but in the end he does return, unwilling to yield to the demands of the Nazis.

The story is simple, but Schlondorff's director's idea turns the film into an overwhelming experience. The director's idea is that the world in 1942 became a black and white world. For most people it was black—their lives, their dignity, everything could be instantly taken away. On the other hand, there was the white world, filled with privilege, power, and seeming immortality. In the black world, violence and cruelty knew no bounds; in the white world, indulgence and selfishness knew no bounds.

To work with this idea, we begin with the text interpretation. In Dachau, the focus is on death, cruelty, torture, humiliation. In Luxembourg, the settings are Father Henri's family apartment, Gestapo headquarters, the church, the bishop's office, and the cemetery. These latter environments seem untouched by what Dachau represents in the narrative.

Two people are specifically seen as spiritual: Father Henri and a priest from Norway, who commits suicide as a result of his personal suffering in Dachau. Father Henri too suffers but he maintains his humanity in spite of the suffering. Father Henri's brother is an industrialist who offers to save Henry by taking him to Paris. Father Henri's pregnant sister offers to use all her connections to get Henri to Switzerland. In spite of the implications for each of them, the siblings need him to survive, as if he is the spiritual center of the family.

Three other characters are important: the bishop, the power of the Church in Luxembourg; the bishop's secretary, keen to accommodate the Nazis; and a Gestapo official who almost became a priest but at the last moment saw more of a future with the SS. All are believers. All of these characters care, but self-interest in whatever form motivates them. All live in the white world of power and have no understanding of true powerlessness and the black that represents life and death in Dachau. The director's idea of black and white frames the events of the narrative such that we see each event and each character as residing in one world or the other. When Father Henri chooses to return to Dachau, he is remaining spiritually intact and embracing the blackness of the world he and his fellow priests occupy at Dachau. For him to accept the blackness means to never replace his spiritual wholeness with the material benefits of a world that is power oriented, the white world. As such, Father Henri represents the best values of the Church in the world, the spiritual values of piety and valuing others in life.

The performances are in keeping with the director's idea. The tormented Father Henri fluctuates between spiritual strength and human weakness. With the exception of the Norwegian priest, the other performers dwell in the material world where power is everything.

Schlondorff is very interesting in how he uses the camera to present the two worlds of the director's idea. The black world of Dachau is shot in telephoto lens, and the background is compressed, pushing the people in the images together such that they are less individualistic and more herd. We learn they are priests. The camera looks down upon the mass, and the camera angles rob the characters of individualism and dignity. They are victims and we watch as they are victimized. Intense close-ups bring Father Henri and the SS into emotional and cruel conflict. The intensity makes this black world threatening and devoid of humanity.

When Father Henri is in Luxembourg, long shots replace close-ups and wide-angle shots provide a clear context for the white world. The solid church, the powerful Gestapo headquarters, even the graveyard where Father Henri's mother is buried seem to belong to a different world than Dachau. Here, Schlondorff is deepening visually our sense that black and white live side by side, yet one is hell and the other is heaven, the powerless *versus* the powerful. His execution of the director's idea helps transform this simple story into an emotionally alive and vivid experience.

A second example is Cedric Kahn's "Red Lights" (2004). Again, the story is simplicity itself. A rather ordinary man has a successful wife—an attractive corporate lawyer. They have two children. The entire film is occupied with their setting out from Paris to pick up their children from a camp holiday in Bordeaux. The journey itself is the focus. The husband drinks, waiting for his wife and their journey to begin. Whether or not he is jealous and why he might be is unexplained, but he is troubled and alcohol empowers him. Driving like a wild man he becomes increasingly provocative. At his second drink stop, she abandons him for the train. He tries to catch the train but cannot. Again stopping for a drink, he picks up a young one-armed stranger who has asked him for a lift. The main character keeps stopping for alcohol and becomes quite drunk. Road blocks set up to catch an escaped convict do not encourage caution, just more bravado. When a tire bursts, the stranger pulls the car over and takes over. He changes the tire but then drives into the woods. When the stranger becomes more threatening, the main character smashes him with a liquor bottle, batters him, and runs him over with the car. Lost and again sober, the main character has the car towed to the local town for repair. There he learns that his wife never made it to Bordeaux. He finds out that she was raped and shot on the train by the previously mentioned escaped convict. Eventually, we learn that the stranger he killed was the convict. The film ends with husband and wife reconciled and continuing on to pick up their children.

Kahn's director's idea is that violence resides everywhere in the world and arises from expected sources (the escaped convict) and from the most unexpected (the normally rather timid main character). Violence complicates everything—relationships, vacations, and more. The director's idea regarding violence begins to take shape with the text interpretation. The main character is Antoine. His frequent calls to his wife are punctuated by glasses of beer. The alcohol illustrates his frustration; alcohol and coping will be further linked as we move through the film. His wife, Helene, is clearly a strong person. Her lack of tolerance for the drinking, together with its implications for his driving, illustrates her unwillingness to be victimized by her husband's behavior (his drinking as well as the way he is driving). Antoine's driving becomes increasingly violent as his risk-taking on the road becomes increasingly dangerous. The upshot of his driving will be two consecutive incidents of flat tires (separate scenes)—consider them as foreshadows of the consequences of the violence of his behavior on the road. Finally, we have the stranger, who is in fact a violent escaped convict. His silence and his actions imply bottled up, explosive violence. Physically, he is the opposite of Antoine, which also makes him a threat.

All of the actions—telephone calls, drinking, driving, talking to doctors and nurses—seem to be filled with the potential to be unpredictable and terrifying. Kahn regards all the actions and behaviors in the narrative as actions and behaviors that have violent potential, no matter how benign they might inherently be. Kahn's goal in the interpretation of the text is to convey violence and its revelation in all things.

THE DIRECTOR'S IDEA: *The Path to Great Directing*

The performances are also keyed away from the romantic aspects of relationships and encounters. Warmth consequently is totally absent from the performances until the last five minutes of the film. The emphasis is on anger, overt and suppressed, as well as on the inability or unwillingness of the characters to help one another. Even those who are helpful (the waitress in a small café, the nurse in the hospital) seem hesitant, as if they are deciding to help or harm a character in spite of the fact that their jobs are essentially to help the other.

Kahn's camera use is interesting. The road is photographed subjectively, but most of the time the characters are observed through more objective camera placements. The subjective road represents danger and the opportunity for violence, rather than the excitement or thrill of driving. Kahn also uses the jump cut to disrupt our sense of continuity. The disruptive jump cut introduces violence into our experience of the events and characters in the film. Kahn uses the jump cut extensively throughout the film to instill the director's idea into the emotional flow of the film (the edit).

Both of these simple stories, "The Ninth Day" and "Red Lights," illustrate how the director's idea works to focus and lead our experience of the film. This is how a director's idea adds value to the narrative but most importantly how the director unifies the production.

Directors use different strategies to find their director's ideas. Of course, personality, interest, and training are contextual elements that dispose a director to a particular set of choices, but specific aspects of a particular film can be considered that will help the director move toward a clear director's idea.

In order to articulate the director's idea it is first necessary for the director to understand his attraction to a particular script. Generally, directors are attracted to a script because of a particular character, usually the main character, as well as that character's life situation and how the character has chosen to deal with it. To move toward a director's idea, it is important to fully understand whether we want our main character to be a victim or a hero. Are we interested in their psychology, their surroundings, and the sociology involved, or are we more interested in the political dimension of their story? Every story has elements of all of these dimensions. What attracts us?

A second aspect is the importance of plot in the narrative. For some directors, such as Steven Spielberg and Ridley Scott, plot is very important. For others, such as Anthony Minghella or Steven Soderbergh, plot is far less important. If plot is critical, character flattens. If character is critical, psychology is central, and the plot becomes secondary.

The director also needs to clearly bring into the foreground his own values. What are his obsessions in life? The director's idea allows the director to highlight and articulate the values in the story that are important to him. All of us in a fashion are curious about the corners of ourselves. A director who wants to gain the audience's love will be charming and maybe funny as they tell the story. Another director might want the audience to be impressed and will seek the most complicated, challenging approach to telling the story. Yet another director will be attracted by the challenge of the project itself. The more challenging the project is, the more the director becomes vested in it. Directors of comedies want to earn the love of their audiences (think of a film such as "Meet the Fokkers"). Directors such as Steven Spielberg ("Schindler's List") want to earn both the audience's love and respect. In "2001: A Space Odyssey," Stanley Kubrick took up the challenge of dealing with human history and such philosophical issues as being and of man *versus* technology. For Kubrick, the challenge was his goal of creating a visual meditation on man and technology. These goals are important filters as directors create their director's ideas.

What I am suggesting is that the director must have a conscious personal and creative set of goals when choosing to commit to a story. I am also saying that such a commitment will require articulating how the director feels and wants us to feel about the main character.

The director begins developing a director's idea by interpreting the text. What is the basic concept or premise of the story? It is best to think of the premise in light of two opposing choices facing a main character. Love or money is the choice facing the main character in "Titanic." To be like the father, an immigrant, or to be different from the father is the premise in "Four Friends." To be an ambulance chaser for the rest of his life or to restore his dignity are the two choices for the main character in "The Verdict."

The premise is the key to both the film and to our relationship with the main character. Understanding the premise and being excited about exploring that premise lead to articulation of the

20

director's idea. How passionately does the director feel about the premise? How should he approach the premise? In "Mr. Smith Goes to Washington," Frank Capra wanted to overvalue the idealistic option of the premise for his main character, and he wanted to demonize the other option ("realpolitique") and its consequences for personal behavior. This means that his director's idea was to overdo both options of the premise. Such an over-the-top approach has its dangers (*e.g.*, caricature and farce), but it also enables Capra to be impassioned about his populist views.

An important tool for articulating a director's idea is creating backstories for characters and events in the film. The fact that Maximus and Commodus, the main character and antagonist, respectively, in "Gladiator," were raised virtually as brothers makes their current struggle more personal and more anguished. In Robert Aldrich's "Attack," a Battle of the Bulge World War II story, the main character and antagonist have a similar linkage. Back home in the south in the United States, the antagonist's father was the political boss. The main character was a capable, ambitious young man, recognized by the local political boss. The political boss asked the main character to look out for his wayward, less capable son. Again, the tension of two sons in conflict gives this war story deeper meaning. In both of these film examples, the Cain–Abel factor became the director's idea.

Another avenue toward developing a director's idea is to work with a specific subtext to the narrative. "The Bourne Identity" is a film with a big thriller plot about a CIA contract killer who has lost his memory and is being pursued by his employer, who intends to kill him. The subtext of the film is about loneliness, the deepest kind of loneliness a human being can experience—the belief that they have been abandoned. Director Doug Limans's director's idea was to work with the loneliness not only of the main character but also of other characters in the film. Remember the death scene of the other contract killers? Each scene bespeaks the effects of loneliness on the characters.

The subtext of "All about Eve," the great film about the theater and stardom, is ambition, which takes each of the film's characters to different places. Joseph Mankiewicz used ambition as his director's idea and explored the vanity, depth, even desperation of ambition and subsequent loss of dignity experienced by each of the characters. The greater the ambition, the greater the loss of dignity.

The subtext of the "Road to Perdition," directed by Sam Mendes, is paternal love. The subtext of "Zorba the Greek," directed by Michael Cacoyannis, is *eros*, or life force. In each of these films, the directors used the subtext as their director's ideas to deepen the classic gangster film and classic melodrama. For the director, the subtext can be the most overt path to his director's idea.

A coherent character arc can also be a useful vehicle for the director's idea, but for the arc to be genuinely animated by the director's idea it must be surprising. All screen stories, at least those that are character driven, are essentially stories of character transformation. Stories of adjustment, coming of age, or loss of innocence are not in and of themselves surprising. What make them surprising is the use of deeper themes as both the director's idea and the instrument of transformation. Two examples will illustrate how this works. William Wyler's "The Heiress" is an adaptation of the Henry James novel *Washington Square*. In a nutshell, the character arc introduces a main character who is plain but wealthy. Two relationships are key: a father who is judgmental and treats his daughter harshly and a suitor who is handsome and a fortune seeker. In the beginning, the main character is hungry for acceptance but at the end she rejects her suitor because her father was right. She is initially hopeful and young but ends up more mature, realistic, and embittered. The character arc can be viewed as a loss of innocence. The director's idea here is to show how disappointment plays a major role in the lives of all the characters and how those disappointments drive the outcome of the character arc. The father is disappointed that when his wife dies in childbirth he is left with his daughter; the daughter is disappointed by the absence of her father's love and is disappointed that her father was right about her suitor.

A second example is George Miller's "Lorenzo's Oil." A married couple has a child late in life. For the husband, it is his second family, as he has two grown children from the first marriage. The inciting incident of the film is the onset of an incurable disease in the child, who is five years old. The main character is the wife, who had the child when she was forty years old. The character arc is discovering motherhood relatively late in life and marveling at the state of motherhood. The onset of the child's disease threatens to rob this mother of her newly discovered state of motherhood. The character arc ends with the boy alive but essentially crippled by the disease.

The mother is humbled but not destroyed. She has grown in her understanding of what it means to be a mother. Love was always there, but now patience, empathy, and something almost intangible or spiritual complements the sense of love she experienced at the outset of the story. The character arc is a coming-of-age arc, as the woman has matured over the course of the story. We can view the plot as the progression of the disease and the efforts of the mother and father to work with doctors to find a cure for the disease. The director's idea in "Lorenzo's Oil" is the power of the will as a force of nature. The doctors say the child will die, but the son the mother waited so long for simply cannot die. She will not allow it. The presence of will in her behavior, in her husband's efforts, in the African people among whom the son grew up is a surprising and palpable force in the outcome of the film. And will is the surprise that in the end changes the plot and allows the discovery that saves Lorenzo, the child, thus altering the character arc. The character arc and the role of surprise can be vehicles for realizing the director's idea in a film. By exploring the character arc and what will provoke change, the director can discover the device that will become the director's idea.

When the director has found an idea in the text interpretations, this director's idea can then be used to shape the performances and organize shots to serve the idea. The design of the edit will use these shots to integrate the text interpretations and performances with the director's idea. Deciding on a director's idea can only be arrived at through conscious examination of script and an awareness of the director's own priorities as a storyteller. Using text interpretation as the vehicle for defining the director's idea will further articulate what the director needs from the actors and from the camera to realize the director's idea. (See the appendix at the end of the book.) Now that the director's idea has been conceptualized, it is time to consider how directors deploy these ideas, but first we must define what constitutes competent directing, good directing, and great directing.

Chapter 3

The Competent Director

- The competent director has a straightforward interpretation of the text. Character and narrative fall under that interpretation. There is no subtext. Directing the actors and camera choices support that interpretation. Competent directors often have a vigorous camera style, but that style does not deepen meaning.

HOLLYWOOD

PRODUCTION _____

DIRECTOR _____

CAMERA _____

DATE   SCENE   TAK

Here comes that loaded term again, the *competent director*. In these next three chapters I will chart the roadmap from competence in directing to value (the good director) to transformation (the great director). I know the term *competent* implies "not good enough," and I am willing to let that implication stand, even though it is not intended. What is intended is for readers to use this chapter as a baseline for determining what constitutes competent or good enough directing. I could have as easily used the term *technical directing*, but I did not want to confuse the subject of this chapter with the specific role in television known as the technical or studio director, the person who orchestrates the multicamera movements in a live or taped television show, from news to sitcom. Keep in mind, however, two other phrases—"technically proficient" and "imaginatively understimulated"—to obtain a more layered sense of what I mean by the competent director.

What the Audience Wants

Whether audiences visit movie theaters to be reassured or challenged, whether they seek the familiar or desire the unfamiliar, we know that when they see a film they want more than the "Dragnet" mantra of "just the facts, ma'am." Whatever the genre, surprise, subversion, subtext, and style all enhance the film experience for the film audience.

We can formulate a set of guiding expectations that go beyond the too general "escape from their own lives for two hours." First, I would suggest that audiences want a story well told. From the director's point of view that means narrative clarity. Two good examples of directors who tell a complex story very clearly are Fred Zinnemann in "The Day of the Jackal" (1977) and Robert Zemeckis in "Back to the Future" (1983). Even good directors have lapses when the story is far from clear. Sam Peckinpah loses narrative focus in "Bring Me the Head of Alfredo Garcia" and in "The Osterman Weekend." Both films exemplify what the audience does not want.

Genre acuity is the second goal for an audience. When they go to a thriller they want to see a thriller, and when they go to a situation comedy they want to laugh. Sidney Pollack's "Tootsie" (1982) represents the kind of movie that audiences are looking for when they attend a situation comedy. John Frankenheimer's "Ronin" represents the kind of thriller audiences are looking for when they attend a thriller. Francis Ford Coppola has made many great films, but he was missing in action when he made the situation comedy "Jack" (1995) and when he made the Grisham thriller "The Rainmaker" (1997). These represent the loss of acuity of genre that alienates an audience.

Audiences also are looking for a style that lifts up the narrative. Steven Spielberg understands this notion very well. His Indiana Jones films have a sense of playful fun, a tone that lifts the film experience from B movie plotting to a pleasurable sense of fun. Spielberg's "Empire of the Sun" (1984) creates an eccentric education for a young British boy in a Japanese prisoner of war camp; the sense of wonder that permeates the boy's sensibility sustains him through the greatest hardships. Spielberg shifts to a totally opposite extreme, a documentary style, in the ghetto clearance sequence in "Schindler's List" and in the D-Day landing that opens "Saving Private Ryan." Because Spielberg had goals for both films, these sequences elevate the power of the films. This sense of style is important for audiences when they attend a film.

Audiences want an emotional journey when they attend a film. That requires inviting the audience to identify with a main character and then articulating that person's inner struggle. An example will illustrate this point. In Patrice Chereau's "Queen Margot" (1996), the princess Margot, a Catholic, is forced by her mother, Catherine de Medici, to marry a Protestant, Henry Bourbon of Navarre. The time is 1572, and the Protestants and Catholics of France are struggling for power. A critical component of the plot is the St. Bartholomew's massacre—the state-sanctioned murder of Protestants by the Catholic rulers. The inner journey of Margot, the emotional core of the story, is Margot's love for her Protestant husband. Because of this love, she chooses to side with her husband Henry against her mother and brothers. By doing so, Margot gives up her safety net and risks everything. Her emotional journey brings the audience into her struggle and her transformation.

The same filmmaker made the film "Intimacy" (1999), a film about two strangers who meet for weekly sex in today's London. Although the main male character becomes obsessed with his lover, we are never privy to his inner life; consequently, the experience of the film, although sensational, is never emotionally affecting. In "Intimacy," the audience is left out in the cold, the opposite of the experience of Chereau's "Queen Margot."

Although the term *subtext* seems to carry a pompous theatrical resonance, film audiences who experience it are grateful for its ambition. Jonathan Demme's "Silence of the Lambs" (1994) is a plot-driven police story: Find the serial killer Buffalo Bill. But, it is also about Clarice's coming of age as an adult and as a professional person. Like the women who are victims of Buffalo Bill, Clarice may be victimized by men or she can avoid victimization. This is the subtext of "Silence of the Lambs." Peter Jackson's "The Lord of the Rings" (2002–2004) has a number of plots, but let us focus here on Frodo's journey to rid the world of the ring that involves his personal struggle with the power of good and evil that the ring represents. He succeeds in his quest but is forever changed by the inner struggle he has experienced while transporting the ring. Spiderman has to contend with the evil doings of Dr. Octavius in Sam Rami's "Spiderman 2" (2004), but he also has to deal with the inner struggle between his own personal goals and his sense of responsibility to his community. In each case, the existence of a powerful subtext raised a plot-driven genre film into a more powerful and meaningful film experience.

Finally, audiences want to be surprised. They want to be surprised by twists and turns of the plot and they want to be surprised by the behavior of characters. The notion that love of a sort (at least affectionate respect) develops between the serial killer Hannibal Lechter and his FBI protegé Clarice Starling is a delightful surprise for audiences, as is the vulnerability of the action hero Indiana Jones when he is in the company of his father in "Indiana Jones and the Lost Crusade" (1987). Surprise, in the form of dialogue or a behavioral twist or a plot shift, is valued by a film's audience.

Directors and Competence

Here I would like to qualify what will follow in the rest of the chapter. What do I mean by competence in directing? We can have two extremes of directing, with competence lying in between those extremes. At one extreme is directing so bad that it takes on a campy virtue. The films of Ed Wood are a good example of this extreme. At the other extreme are good filmmakers who clearly have added value to their projects but who occasionally lapse. John Frankenheimer, who made the great "Manchurian Candidate" (1962), also made "The Year of the Gun" (1985). William Friedkin, who made "The Exorcist" (1973) and "The French Connection" (1970), also made "The Hunted" (2003). Lapses such as these can be due to personal or professional problems. My point here is that even good directors fall down from time to time.

In between these two extremes lie some of the most commercial directors of all time. To make my point I will concentrate on three: Brett Ratner ("Red Dragon"), Chris Columbus ("Mrs. Doubtfire"), and Richard Donner ("Conspiracy Theory"). The example of "Red Dragon" will suffice for the moment. Based on Thomas Harris' *Hannibal* novel, the film is the second film version of the novel. This version by Brett Ratner focuses on the plot to find a serial killer. The Lechter character is a presence in the film but is not as central as he is in *Silence of the Lambs*, the follow-up Harris novel; nevertheless, the Lechter character dwarfs the protagonist, the FBI psychologist (Ed Norton), as well as the antagonist (Ralph Fiennes).

Turning to the earlier film version, Michael Mann's "Manhunter" (1986) used emotional instability and its inherent violent unpredictability as the director's idea. The protagonist, the antagonist, the reporter, and of course Hannibal Lechter all share an unsettled, unsettling instability or fear of it; consequently, their actions and their reactions come as a surprise to the character as well as to the audience, which becomes immersed in that instability. All the while Mann presents a very structured visualization that is clean and antiseptic. When violence does erupt (the murder scenes, the killing of the reporter), they are all the more shocking as they break up the ordered world Mann has visually presented. The result is the powerful, disturbing experience of "Manhunter" created by the use of the director's idea to add value to the narrative. It is this result that differentiates the competent director from the good director. The two case studies that follow provide creative profiles of two competent directors, Antoine Fuqua and Simon Wincer.

Case Study I. The Competent Director: Antoine Fuqua ("King Arthur," 2004)

Antoine Fuqua is best known for his 2001 film "Training Day," featuring Denzel Washington's Oscar-winning performance. "King Arthur" (2004) followed the Bruce Willis film, "Tears of the Sun" (2003). "King Arthur" is in scale and budget Fuqua's largest film. The King Arthur legend of early England and the knights of the Round Table has been a frequently used basis for films. Cornell Wilde's "The Sword of Lancelot" (1963) tells the story as Action Adventure. John Boorman's "Excalibur" (1981) tells the story as fable, and Joshua Logan's "Camelot" (1967) tells the story as a musical. Fuqua's presentation is pure action adventure.

Fuqua, working with a David Franzoni script, casts Arthur as part Roman, part Briton. His knights are Eastern cavalry Sarmatians from the plains adjacent to the Black Sea who are indebted to fight for Rome for 15 years. All have been sent to the Empire's most distant outpost, Britain. An added complication is that Rome is about to quit Britain. As we join the story, the knights are a day from discharging their duty to Rome, but there is one last assignment for Arthur and his knights: rescue an important Roman family north of Hadrian's Wall. They need to cross the forest of the Woats, pagan Britons who have never accepted Roman rule. Also complicating the story is the fact that the cruel Saxons have invaded Britain from the north. They pose a real threat as they destroy all and everyone in their path.

It is 450 A.D., and Rome is controlled by the Pope and the Church. The Woats and Arthur's knights are pagan. At the Roman villa, they find that the priests are torturing and killing the Woats. Arthur intervenes and saves the two Woats who are still alive, a young boy and a woman, Guinevere. This represents Arthur's first distancing from the authority of Rome, and for Arthur Guinevere will become the voice of Britain for the Britons. On the journey back to Hadrian's Wall, Merlin, the leader of the Woats, invites Arthur to lead all Britons against the common enemy, the Saxons. Lancelot, Arthur's friend and principal knight, urges self-interest—ride away, leave this place—but Arthur cannot just ride away as other Romans can. He leads the Britons to defeat the Saxons. A number of his knights, including Lancelot, die in the battle. Arthur becomes King, takes Guinevere as his Queen, and claims Britain as the last bastion of freedom, at which point the film ends.

The text as presented sidesteps the Pagan/Christian thread of the story which became so compelling an element in the narrative in Boorman's "Excalibur." Instead, the main thread is the plot: The Romans are leaving. The Saxons are coming. The Woats will fight for their land. What will Arthur do? What will his knights, who are not Britons, do? Although Arthur speaks about equality and freedom, he is presented for the most part as a gifted warrior, and his knights, although physically different from one another, are also attractive and gifted warriors. Some are more physically imposing than others but essentially they are the good guys, no mistake about it.

Guinevere, although she will be the love interest, is more con-science than lover, and she too is a gifted warrior. If I had to char-acterize this group of protagonists I would call them noble in their idealism and in their comradeship, but these characterizations are stereotypical rather than compelling, suitable to a plot-driven action adventure film. Fuqua used the same approach to characterize the military extraction team in "Tears of the Sun."

Just as the good are very good, the bad characters are very bad, suitable for the antagonists in an action adventure film. Stellan Skarsgård plays the leader of the Saxons, and he takes the meaning of cruelty to another level. I must admit that it's great fun to watch a good actor work with a stereotype.

The director's priority in "King Arthur" is the plot. The battle scenes begin early with the introduction of Arthur and his knights while fighting Woats who have attacked a Roman convoy. Later, the two set pieces involve combat with the Saxons, with the first being a battle on an iced-over lake. That battle pits eight bowmen against a thousand Saxons. A few days later the odds are no better. Thousands of Saxons face Arthur, the knights, and the Woats at Badon Hill inside Hadrian's Wall. Each battle proves that tactics and bravery and ferocious determination win the day.

Between battles is the time for characterization, but character is presented in shorthand. One knight has a falcon; the most daunting knight, physically, has a relationship with the Woat boy freed at the Roman villa. The second most physically daunting knight has eleven bastard children. Another is masterful with the bow, and yet another is an absolute cynic. The point here is that, for Fuqua, character is not as important as plot.

Although there are numerous plot twists in King Arthur, the story lacks a great deal of surprise. Fuqua's film is arresting visually, which we will turn to shortly, but the machinations of plot do not shock or thrill us, which brings us to the director's point of view, or lack of a point of view.

Few characters in history have conjured up more enthusiasm than King Arthur. Was he an idealist? Was he a man ahead of his time? Was Arthur a fool? Antoine Fuqua and Clive Owen have tried to present Arthur as idealistic and noble, yet what he seems to be above all else is a super leader. Fuqua's Arthur is militaristic, a hero. Fuqua's Arthur is the idealized hero rather than the idealist as hero. In this sense, he is a romanticized cartoon character, made all the more so for the cruelty of his antagonist. Fuqua's point of view as the director is to see the Arthur legend as an opportunity for visual excitement, an area that displays his own particular skill as a director. So, we should examine where Fuqua chose to place his camera. Those positions best serve to bring to life his singular view of the text: It is a struggle of good guys *versus* bad guys, and the heroes will overcome the villains, just as beauty always overcomes ugliness, at least in the plot-driven adventure genre.

With regard to the landscape, Hadrian's Wall defined the northernmost boundary of lands held by Rome. That land at various times in the film is heavily forested or has ice-covered mountains and lakes. The land is evocative as opposed to being geographically correct. That land is visually presented as heavily shadowed and menacing. The land is not so much a real place as an active environment that takes sides. Realism is far away; atmosphere is everything. Fuqua preferred the use of very low or very high angles and extreme long shots to present the land.

In terms of how he presents people, they too appear in extreme long shot, a dot on the horizon, or in extreme close-up. Fuqua used the land and the people (Arthur, Merlin, the knights, the Romans, and the Saxons) to evoke a particular atmosphere and feeling. It is as if each person is an icon, a superhero, or a supervillain. The intense close-ups establish the person. The extreme long-shots establish the opposition, which is so great that surviving makes each character a superhero. The rapid pace at which characters and their

31

adversaries are juxtaposed only heightens the sense that a hero is being created as we watch. Fuqua almost fetishizes the struggle between these opposites.

Because so much of the plot is battle, the moving camera, whether a steadicam or camera mounted on a helicopter or crane, is important. Movement gives a majestic aesthetic to battle and scale to the opposing sides. Editing on action and specific violence to individuals adds to the fetishizing of violence, a key factor to being victorious. Consequently, the dynamic of battle becomes central to Fuqua as action director. Although his battle scenes are not as emotionally loaded as Kubrick's nor as aesthetic as Ridley Scott's battle sequences in "Gladiator," Fuqua nevertheless manages to make the battles compelling. The settings become critical—the battle on the ice is beautiful to watch as are all the fires and smoke during the battle on Badon Hill. The scenes are devoid of logic, but the look of the battles is every bit as evocative as the dance sequences in Adrian Lyne's "Flashdance." I am suggesting that, for Fuqua, the look of the battle was as important as who is fighting or who is winning. The battles are dynamic and exciting, but do not probe too deeply for their logic because that is not what Fuqua is interested in.

"King Arthur," like the work of Adrian Lyne or Tony Scott, is easy on the eyes and has an MTV pace, but it lacks subtext and a layered character arc. Instead, the film is enjoyable as a linear entertainment populated by beautiful people. Its director, Antoine Fuqua, exemplifies the competent director.

Case Study II. The Competent Director: Simon Wincer ("The Lighthorsemen," 1987)

Simon Wincer's "The Lighthorsemen," a war film set in World War I, is about the desert campaign in the Middle East and the role played by the Lighthorsemen, mounted infantry from Australia. At the beginning of the film, Danny, a young man in Australia, expresses an interest in joining the Lighthorsemen, and the film follows him to the British campaign against the Turks to take Jerusalem. The film focuses on one battle in the campaign, the battle for Beersheba. Danny replaces a veteran who has been injured. Three battle-hardened Lighthorsemen comprise the core relationships for Danny. They are judges and jury as Danny discovers he cannot shoot a man. Rather than endanger his mates, he joins the ambulance corps. At the battle for Beersheba, he saves one of his three mates while another dies in battle. Danny falls in love with a nurse, meets an eccentric intelligence officer, and generally wrestles with his conscience while the Lighthorsemen save the day, win the battle, and go on to national glory in Australia.

The film is an Australian production, but it differs considerably from the earlier "Gallipoli" (1982), a film that condemns the war losses sustained by Australian units under British command. Wincer's approach is essentially entertaining, more action adventure than war film. Wincer is the director of the celebrated television film, "Lonesome Dove," and he remains very much in demand as a director of Westerns for television. I have chosen to discuss Wincer's work here because he is such a successful director and his work is so likeable that my remarks about him should be viewed as a positive take on the competent director as opposed to a critique. What I would like to suggest is that by the choices he has made Wincer has established himself as a competent director.

As to those choices, let us look at them through a prism of six specific criteria, the first five having to do with text interpretation and the sixth with the direction of the camera:

1. Simplicity or complexity of the narrative
2. Approach to characterization
3. How the director treats the narrative (literally or as a start point)
4. Issue of surprise
5. Point of view of the director
6. Where the director chooses to place the camera

Turning to the narrative of "The Lighthorsemen," we see this simplified narrative intent played out repeatedly. A nurse in the hospital attends to Danny's wounds. Very quickly they move from a caregiver–patient relationship to would-be lovers. Earlier in the film, Danny has accompanied his colonel on a scouting patrol, during which they encounter a British officer parlaying with the local

Bedouins. They escort the major, who may be a spy, to their headquarters. Quickly we learn that he is the intelligence officer for General Allenby, who will shortly take command of the allied army in the region. The spy quickly becomes the indispensable hero of the upcoming campaign against Beersheba. But, to do so, the major enlists the nurse mentioned earlier to write the forged love letter of a wife to her officer husband, a letter that is in short order planted to mislead the Turks about the location of the upcoming offensive. This narrative turn of events is as rapid and simplified as all the other narrative events in the film.

Wincer's approach is to tell the narrative in a simplified and rapid manner, an approach that will not undermine the overall intent—to present the romantic heroism of the Australian Lighthorsemen regiment. None of the narrative events should distract us from this intent. As we look at Wincer's approach to characterization, a similar pattern emerges. Danny is shy and young. Having lost a brother in the war, he wants to prove he is as worthy and committed to family and country as was his brother. His problem is that, although he is a good rider and shot, he simply cannot kill another human being. This is his dilemma. No such dilemma for his three mates. They are rugged and manly and they miss their families, but they have no problem killing. We know little else about them.

Officers tend to fall into two categories: The English officers are rigid or eccentric, and the Australian officers are able and risk-taking, feeling and pragmatic, which the English and German officers are not. Only the Turkish officers among the enemy are portrayed as able and honorable. The Germans are rigid and not able or smart. The only woman in the film, the nurse, is compassionate and serious and beautiful—what we would all like our nurses to be. Wincer's approach to characterization, then, serves the simplified narrative approach.

To take this discussion to the next level, we need to look at whether the director keeps the narrative simple or departs from this strategy. Is the simplified narrative a start point or is it the end point? I would have to say that competent directors tend to view the narrative as the start *and* end points. The narrative in "The Lighthorsemen" is a good example. The literal treatment of the story as a romantic revisitation of a historical event suggests and makes for a noneditorial experience of a chapter in Australia's military history. Even from the perspective of Australian films, "The Lighthorsemen" differs from two earlier Australian films dealing with war. Bruce Beresford's "Breaker Morant" (1980) deals with an incident in the Boer War, and Peter Weir's "Gallipoli" (1982) deals with the Gallipoli landing in 1915. Both films humanize the main characters who will be sacrificed in the course of acting as soldiers during war, and both films characterize the British command of Australian troops as the reason for those sacrifices. Both films, in this sense, view war as cruel and the killer of the innocents, those Australian sons, who for various reasons found themselves fighting for king and country and then needlessly sacrificed not for country but for king. The enemy is not the Boers or the Turks or the Germans. In both films, the enemy is much closer: It is the colonial rule of the British.

Returning to narrative intent, "Breaker Morant" and "Gallipoli" do tell a clear story but each tells a layered story and not simply because they offer up an anti-war position. Rather, in the case of "Breaker Morant," the narrative about atrocities against the Boers and the consequences for three participating soldiers reveals atrocities on both sides. Indeed, the implication of the narrative is that war breeds atrocities, and the British making peace with the defeated Boers required sacrifices—in this case, three human sacrifices. In the case of "Gallipoli," the focus is on the sacrifice of a beautiful, idealistic Australian generation in a battle that was ill conceived by the Admiralty in London. The film is an argument against colonialism, as it illustrates that the colonized (Australia) can only be destroyed in service of the colonial relationship. Although each film has a romantic layer, neither dwells exclusively on that layer, as in the case of Wincer's "The Lighthorsemen."

I now turn to the issue of surprise. As I mentioned earlier, audiences want to be surprised by plot and the behavior of the characters. The characters in "The Lighthorsemen" are not surprising. Only the intelligence officer (Anthony Andrews) twists away from expectations. Initially, we are led to believe he may be a German spy. That twist is short lived, and the best we can say about his characterization is that he is eccentric, although that eccentricity and affectation are part and parcel of intelligence officers, a profession that traffics in subterfuge. Beyond this character, there are no surprises in the characterization.

Turning to the plot, even its twists and turns are continually telegraphed in the story. The plot twist that will save the day and win the battle at Beersheba is that the Lighthorsemen are mounted infantry. They are expected to ride to battle, dismount, and fight the enemy. That is what we are told from the beginning of the film, and we do see them dismount to fight. Certainly the Turks expect them to dismount as they charge the city, and when they do the Turkish artillery will decimate their ranks. But, we know that in *this* battle the Lighthorsemen have been ordered to ride into battle. They do, and they win the day and the town. Plot is treated in just this way throughout the film. There are twists and turns, but not the kind of narrative twist found in two of the great narratives of 2003: Pedro Almodovar's "Talk to Her" and Denys Arcand's "The Barbarian Invasions." In those films, surprises and revelations of deeper narrative intentions have delighted audiences all over the world and raised to almost mythic levels the reputations of these two writer–directors.

Finally, we turn to the point of view of the director. Sometimes referred to as voice, point of view can be best considered as a counterpoint to the narrative. That voice can be articulated around a character or the plot, and it can be expressed in irony or in the direction of performance. Whatever strategy the director chooses, point of view will and should surprise the audience. For example, in Stanley Kubrick's "Full Metal Jacket" (1987), the first half of the film presents the sergeant in basic training as the enemy. In the second half of the film, set in Vietnam, the critical sequence is a sniper attack. At the end of the sequence, we discover that the sniper is a teenage girl. Dying, she begs for death as the members of the patrol debate whether they should kill her or let her bleed to death. In the end, the most pacifist member of the unit, Joker, kills her. Ironically, this scene is the most humane in the film. Kubrick is displaying a point of view at odds with the narrative. Life is precious. Even death can be precious if it is intended to end suffering. Here, in the midst of a killing field, Kubrick finds humanity. His subversive voice is a distinct and distinctive point of view.

No such irony or subversion is at play in "The Lighthorsemen." Wincer's point of view is romantic, just as the characters and events are romantic. Such a direct approach supporting the narrative typifies the work of the competent director. Wincer has chosen to view the soldiers and their plight (survival) through a romantic prism; consequently, the camera generally photographs the action from a low angle looking upward. This creates a heroic image of the four principal characters. He also uses the alternative of extreme long shots of the Lighthorsemen marching across the desert. Such images, shot at daybreak or dusk, provide a powerful impression of unity, strength, even fortitude with regard to the group as a whole. When photographing the Lighthorsemen in battle, Wincer uses various lenses, including telephoto (to compress the visual context) and extreme close-ups of the enemy or of a Lighthorseman responding to the enemy. This alternating between extreme long shots with extreme close-ups supports the romantic sense of the Lighthorsemen. As a battle proceeds, the increased pace or tempo of the editing adds a certain dynamism to the scene. Wincer never varies, however, from his romantic view of the characters or their actions.

Singularity of visualization is a choice that consistently implies the intent of the director. Two extreme examples from other war films will help contextualize the director's intent. At one extreme is the bombing of Pearl Harbor in Michael Bay's film "Pearl Harbor" (2000). Bay's purpose in the film, like Wincer's, is to romanticize the heroism of the American airman in the film. The attack on Pearl Harbor is not so much horrific in its presentation as it is romantic. At one point, there is a shot of a bomb falling toward the ships that will be destroyed in the harbor. The shot, from the point of view of the bomb, illustrates the precision, even the beauty of the bombing. No tragedy here, just bombs doing their work. At the other extreme is the shot of Slim Pickens riding a nuclear bomb down toward its target in the USSR in Stanley Kubrick's "Dr. Strangelove" (1991). Pickens rides the bomb as if he is a cowboy riding a bronco. Here, too, we follow the bomb toward its intended target, but the image is intended to editorialize an American airman's view of attacking the enemy. It is cavalier, even insane in its dissociation from the intent of the bomb: to kill hundreds of thousands of Russians. The image reverberates with director Kubrick's voice. Nuclear war is insane, an act of madness born of a cowboy mentality. Here, the image is complex and troubling.

Returning to the bombing in "The Lighthorsemen," bombs fall and men die, particularly Lighthorsemen, but their deaths are romantic deaths. The camera placement records the moment of death more closely to Bay's interpretation of dying in war, and in this sense the camera placement supports a simplified visual intention.

In this discussion of Wincer's "The Lighthorsemen" I have tried to present a positive portrait of competent directors, whose approach is straightforward, singular, and consistent when presenting a narrative that is clear, engaging, and implicitly entertaining rather than thought provoking. That is not to say that competent directors are not ambitious in their selection of material. Turning to the work of another competent director, Adrian Lyne, we can compare his treatment of a particular subject matter to the treatment accorded the same material by another director. Both Kubrick and Lyne directed a version of Nabokov's novel *Lolita*. Kubrick's version (1962) of an older man falling for an underage nymphet is filled with irony, humor, and a subversive point of view. Lyne's version (1994) is a literal treatment of an older man falling in love with a teenager. Lyne's version has neither humor nor irony. It is a melodrama, straight and simple, and a tragic one at that, whereas the Kubrick version is a commentary on 1950s America and its morality. The Kubrick version is as troubling today as it was when it first appeared.

In 2002, Lyne remade the Claude Chabrol film "Une Femme Infidele" (1976) as "Unfaithful." Again a comparison is revealing. Chabrol's film is the tale of a jealous husband who believes his wife is cheating on him. He hires a detective and discovers that she is cheating. When he visits the lover, he finds the man likeable but is overcome by his anger and kills him. The film then explores his guilt and his punishment (he is arrested by the police in the last shot). The film is rife with irony. This plain man with a beautiful wife just cannot believe that she is devoted to him in the way he is to her. His obsession overtakes his life. Perhaps it pushed her away; we are not told, but our empathy is with him. We understand him. We even forgive his transgressions.

Adrian Lyne exhibits no such irony in "Unfaithful." The film is shifted to a melodrama about the wife, a woman looking for the excitement and thrill of a sexual encounter. She finds it with a Frenchman (an indirect reference to Chabrol's film), and eventually the husband finds him and kills him. What is the couple to do? Go on as if nothing happened? Confess to the police? We never find out. Lyne leaves us in doubt about their fate. There is no humor, only confusion, in this titillating treatment of unfaithfulness in marriage. The absence of irony or subversion leaves us with the narrative and no editorial view of the subject from the director.

One last example will illustrate how the competent director differs from our subject of the next chapter, the good director. Rob Marshall, the director of the Oscar-winning film "Chicago" (2002), exemplifies the competent director, while Bob Fosse, the director of "Cabaret" (1972), offers us something more. If a director's idea is floating around in "Chicago," it is that films about wannabe performers should be fun; consequently, the performances and visualization of the story are charming and energetic—in short, fun. Although "Cabaret" is also about performers and would-be performers, the performances move beyond fun. Fosse's director's idea is that Berlin in the 1920s was a desperate place and in that environment all barriers fell. Sensuality, anxiety, living in the moment, violence—all become the new reality. When Fosse directed the performances of the master of ceremonies and the other characters he was directing for that subtext. The master of ceremonies is ironic, Sally Bowles is sensual, and so on. When he presents the Nazi song in the beer garden, he focuses on the youthful innocence of the singers (in contrast to the implications of the lyrics). The consequence is a musical that is fun but also one that has gravitas. This is the result of Fosse's director's idea. Fosse is a good director, while Marshall remains an example of the competent director. We turn next to the director that adds value to the project, the good director.

Chapter 4
The Good Director

- The good director uses text interpretation to find a layered interpretation of the story.
- The interpretation makes the narrative more complex.
- The interpretation may generate from the director's approach to characterization—for example, the goal of the character may differ from expectations or the director can use the surprise of plot to promote the transformation of the character in the character arc.
- The director can also use a specific subtext to alter the meaning of the narrative.
- The point of view of the director is more pronounced in the case of the good director.
- Directing the actor and the camera supports the director's idea regarding the subtext or creates a deeper sense of the main character.

HOLLYWOOD
PRODUCTION
DIRECTOR
CAMERA
DATE   SCENE   TAKE

The competent director presents a straightforward narrative, clearly and cleanly focusing on a style of performance, text reading, and camera execution that delivers the narrative without subtext. The intent of the director is in this case explicit, and he may be very successful as a result. The good director is more ambitious and employs strategies to add value to the project. Our task in this chapter is to explore and exemplify how that value is added. The three major areas of activity for the director are text reading, performance, and visual interpretation. And, of course, the impetus for making useful, effective choices is the director's idea. What exactly is the director's idea and how does it work?

How the Director's Idea Works

Two versions of "The Manchurian Candidate" offer us the opportunity to look at two directors applying two different director's ideas to essentially the same story. Both versions are based on George Axelrod's screenplay of the Richard Condon novel, and both focus on the plot of creating an assassin via brainwashing—an assassin who is trained to kill a presidential candidate at a political convention. The killing would allow the antagonists and their backers (the Communists in the 1962 version, a transnational corporation in the 2004 version) to control the presidency and consequently to exploit the most powerful country in the world for its own purposes. In this sense, both versions are "paranoid" political thrillers.

The 1962 version, directed by John Frankenheimer, focuses on Raymond Shaw, who is the assassin brainwashed in Manchuria. His mother, a conservative political powerhouse, is the American agent who controls him on behalf of the Communists. Her husband is a U.S. senator who, as the vice presidential candidate, would become the presidential candidate when the assassination takes place. Bennett Marco, Raymond's commanding officer in Korea, is a man with bad dreams. He keeps dreaming that Raymond killed members of their patrol in Korea rather than saving the platoon, as Raymond's Medal of Honor commendation reads. These dreams drive Marco to discover the truth about Raymond Shaw and to try to stop him.

In this version of "The Manchurian Candidate," Raymond is the main character, and the Cold War context gives this 1962 film a frighteningly believable quality. The Axelrod script bristles with irony about Cold War politics as well as the domestic divide on race—a black soldier dreams of the Communists as black church ladies and Marco, a white man, dreams of the Communists as white church ladies (pillars of their community). The Frankenheimer version also has humor—the newspaper columnist who sleeps in his dead wife's nightgown; the costume party where Senator Jordan's daughter, the lost love of Raymond Shaw, appears wearing a Queen of Hearts costume. The Queen of Hearts is the visual cue to put Raymond into a hypnotic state. This time instant obedience is to a good purpose—to advance his relationship with the woman he loves.

The Frankenheimer version also has daring scenes, such as the seductive train conversation between Marco, in the midst of a panic attack, and Rosie, the woman who becomes his love interest. Another such scene is the Raymond Shaw confessional scene ("I know I'm not loveable"), where Raymond recounts his relationship with Jocelyn Jordan at a time when he was loveable. The scene ends with his mother stepping in to destroy the relationship.

The irony, the humor, and the audacious scenes are characteristic of the first version of the film but are absent in the later version. Frankenheimer's director's idea was to focus on power and powerlessness: political power and powerlessness, personal power and powerlessness. This idea arises from a less conscious substrata of the plot, the creation of an assassin for political purposes. To articulate how the director's idea works, we must look first at the characterizations. Raymond is powerless with regard to his relationship with his mother and his Communist handlers. Bennett Marco is also powerless and is a victim of his dreams. He is powerless as a military man subjected to political authority, and he is even more powerless as a troubled military man within the structure of the military. Power, on the other hand, is embedded in the Communists' scientific ruthlessness (evaluating the brainwashing apparatus by carrying out a murder at each stage of testing), in Raymond Shaw's mother's political power, and in Communist influence via Raymond's mother over her Senator husband and through his nomination as vice president and candidate for his party.

Visually, the theme of power and powerlessness is created by Frankenheimer's camera choices. He often used a moving camera and wide-angle or deep-focus images to create a sense of power.

When we see Raymond in his mother's home, the depth of focus of the images of her home conveys her power. Her dominance in the foreground of those images tells us who is at the top of this pyramid of power. Rarely has a matriarch been as evocatively captured visually.

Powerlessness, on the other hand, is presented in the middle or background of the frame, where Raymond Shaw and Bennett Marco are so often found, as are Raymond's victims, his newspaper employer, Senator Jordan, and Jocelyn Jordan. And, by using a moving camera to approach the victims, the ultimate outcome of powerlessness, death, is all the more vividly presented.

If the original "The Manchurian Candidate" is about externalized power and powerlessness, Jonathan Demme's 2004 version is about something far more internal. Whether he is portraying a descent into madness or madness run amok in the political–industrial complex, Demme's concerns are all the more personalized. In this version, Bennett Marco is the main character, and Raymond Shaw occupies the plot position the Marco character occupied in the first version. In this version, both Shaw and Marco have been implanted with devices to make them compliant to the wishes of the corporation—to assassinate the President. In this version, Vice President Raymond Shaw will become the corporation's President rather than the President of all the people. The Jordans, who played such personal roles in the first version, are now relegated to being political adversaries. Rosie, the love interest for the Marco character in the first version, is now an FBI agent investigating Marco's allegations. She pretends to be interested in Marco romantically and, although she echoes Janet Leigh's dialogue from the first version, plays a far more central role in this version.

Demme's director's idea was that paranoia when it is real is not madness, but he works with an inner sense of madness and paranoia, particularly for Marco. Although Shaw and Al Melvin (Jeffrey Wright) are both played off center (troubled, disturbed), in fact the majority of the inner madness is left to Marco to portray. To deepen this idea, Demme used many more close-up and medium-range shots than is typical. Long shots and wide-angle shots tend to contextualize, and Demme was trying to take away rather than create context. He also used a camera placement that crowds the Marco character, again creating a sense of disturbance and that all is not right. The pace of shots and scenes, particularly early in the film, also suggests disruption, that the circuits are not all working.

What works less well here are the actors' performances feeding this sense of madness and paranoia. The performances tend to be too realistic. Perhaps an example from a director's idea keyed to performance will illustrate my point here. Elia Kazan, in his direction of performances in "Splendor in the Grass," perfectly captured his director's idea. "Splendor in the Grass," set in 1928 Kansas, tells the story of two teenagers in love. Deenie is beautiful and poor. Bud is handsome and rich. Both are overflowing with sexual desire and both are mindful of their parents' admonitions. Her mother tells her that boys don't respect girls who go all the way. His father tells him that he has plans for him (to go to Yale and take over the business), and if he gets Deenie pregnant he will have to marry her (and ruin his life).

Kazan begins the film in mid shot. The two main characters, Deenie and Bud, are kissing passionately in his convertible, parked adjacent to a waterfall. The sensuality at the core of the scene is powerful, but the scene ends with Bud frustrated at Deenie's resistance to go any further than petting. The next scene is between Deenie and her mother after Bud has dropped her at home. The scene that follows is Bud's return home and his encounter with his father. Both Deenie and Bud try to articulate their feelings but neither parent allows those feelings to be acknowledged. Deenie and Bud are clearly overwhelmed by their desire, and the parents warn their children about the consequences of that desire. Here is the point where Kazan's brilliance with actors deepens the director's idea. Kazan's director's idea is that sexuality is tactile and good but to censor it is destructive.

In the scene between Deenie and her mother, the mother states her position. Deenie asks about whether she, the mother, ever felt (as Deenie does about Bud) desire for Deenie's father, her husband. Deenie at this point embraces and holds on to the mother, as the mother tells her that women do not like sex and they give in to their husbands' sexual desires only after they are married. When the mother is not being held by her daughter she is munching away at a sandwich. The tactile quality, the physical need of each character is pronounced and central here; it overrides what is being said. For Kazan the need to touch is more important than the words spoken.

We find a parallel in the scene between Bud and his father. What Bud is trying to say is that he loves Deenie, but the father pummels Bud verbally with his ambitions for his son. All the while the father also physically pummels Bud, punching him with a mix of pride and aggression. As he punches Bud's shoulders, again we are aware of how much each of these characters needs a physical connection. Again, Kazan used his direction of the performances to illustrate the primacy of the physical. Indeed, for Kazan, desire and physicality are life itself, while control and censorship imply a life half lived and worse, as the tragedy that befalls these two lovers suggests.

Returning to Jonathan Demme's treatment of the performances in "The Manchurian Candidate," I have suggested that overall they were too realistic. Although Raymond Shaw and his mother are presented as narcissistic and political, we do not sense any madness here nor is there madness to be found in the Marco character. Because Rosie is there not as a bystander drawn to Marco in the midst of a panic attack (as in the first version) but rather as an FBI plant, she gives credibility to Marco's eccentric behavior. Consequently, only Wright's portrayal of Al Melvin's character suggests the madness that is necessary to make the director's idea work as effectively as does his early camera placements. The realism of the performances suggests that the political–industrial complex has an agenda that is credible and feasible. And, in good thriller fashion, the audience is saved when Marco kills Shaw and his mother, preventing them from highjacking the presidency. Were the performances keyed to the director's idea as they were in Kazan's "Splendor in the Grass," this remake of "The Manchurian Candidate" would have been as unnerving as the original.

Having looked at how a director's idea shapes choices for the director and how those choices either deepen the outcome or, in the case of "The Manchurian Candidate," differentiate two treatments of the same story, we should now return to our central topic of the good director.

I hope that I have not suggested that there is a single approach to being a good director. On the contrary, how good a director will be depends upon how far the director goes in his realization of the director's idea. Before providing a case study of the good director, I would like to address the diversity among good directors.

First not all directors are exceptional in every area. Essentially, the areas of opportunity are performance, visualization, and text

THE GOOD DIRECTOR

interpretation. As I mentioned earlier, Elia Kazan's strength lies in his direction of the performances of his actors. I would add that he is also a powerful interpreter of text. His film "America America" (1962) offers a good example. The director's idea in "America America," an epic journey of a young man from Turkey to America, is that in life everyone is either master or slave; consequently, in every scene—whether involving a father and son, husband and wife, employer and employee, or simply fellow travelers—the director's idea determines the shape and outcome and the level of the performance within the scene. The visualization in "America America" is strong but secondary to the director's text interpretation.

Visualization on the other hand, goes to the core of Ridley Scott's work. His director's idea in "Gladiator" is "What is a man?" Scott is interested in all aspects of manhood—son, father, friend, lover, leader. His visualization of the main character, Maximus, is Scott's idealization of what it is to be a man—assertive, aggressive, yet tender and moral. The antagonist, Commodus, on the other hand, is less than a man. He becomes Caesar by killing his father. He is cowardly, a man in need of constant attention and jealous of rivals, a man who needs his sister's comfort to have a night's sleep. Scott's visualization of manhood is always powerful. Maximus is foregrounded and photographed in movement. Low angles suggest his heroism. Commodus, on the other hand, appears mid-frame or toward the back. Mid shots instead of close-ups make him appear less of a man. Ridley Scott relied on visualization to articulate his director's idea.

The Coen brothers had a very different director's idea in "O Brother, Where Art Thou?" Their idea is that the American odyssey is less noble than the original. It is all about self-interest and religion, sin and repentance. This fable-like idea requires exaggerated performances, exaggerated text readings, and a visual style that connotes the opposite of realism—let's call it the fabulous.

What I am suggesting is that to be a good director, the director must have a director's idea that he executes using the tools of directing—text interpretation, performance, visualization in balance with the director's interests and skills. Now, let's turn to a case study of good directing.

A Case Study in Good Directing: Michael Mann's "Collateral"

Michael Mann films cross numerous genres and seem to test the core values of their main characters, whose very existence depends on their behavior in a crisis. The lone thief, Frank, in "Thief" (1981); Hawkeye in "The Last of the Mohicans" (1994); Neil, the criminal, and Vincent, the detective, in "Heat" (1996); and Jeffrey, the informer and Lowell, the producer, in "The Insider" (1998) are all tested, and each gives up a great deal in order to survive, if indeed the character does survive. Director Mann's efforts to lay bare the primal or true character of his main characters and their antagonists reflect his director's idea of viewing life as a test. Whether a character is honest or dishonest, professional or amateur, capitalist or environmentalist, the narrative is set up to test his beliefs and the depth of those beliefs. Only in the test can we measure the man. This is Mann's director's idea. In this, Mann is closest to Howard Hawks, as each used genre to explore the man.

What this means in a film such as "Collateral" (2004) is that Mann sets up the main character as someone who has reached stasis in his life and has both dreams and fears; all is in balance. Mann uses an antagonist and plot to challenge the main character. The environment in Mann's films is never neutral and is not enabling for the main character; if anything, it makes the challenge all the greater.

In "Collateral" the narrative is simple. The main character, Max, is a black man who has been cabbing in Los Angeles for 12 years and dreams of owning his own luxury limousine company. The evening begins simply with a young attorney as his fare. She is concerned about how long it will take to reach her office. Max remains low key and confident, and by the end of the ride the two have formed a bond. The next fare is far more direct when he asks Max if he wants to make $600. All he has to do is drive him to five meetings. Max agrees and the night from hell begins. His fare, Vincent, is a hit man, and as Max will learn target number five is the young attorney who will be prosecuting a case against a drug kingpin the next day. The others are the witnesses, and the hit man must kill them all.

The plots and the murders, particularly the threat to the prosecuting attorney, rouse Max to stand up and be tested. His relationships with the prosecuting attorney and the hit man are key. If Max is a mild human being, a dreamer, the hit man is intense and aggressive—a man on a clock. If Max seems kind to others, the hit man is indifferent and cold to feelings or needs. The only thing these two men have in common is the cab, Max's livelihood and the killer's transportation of choice to get through a hard night. The subtext of this film is what will rouse a mild man, perhaps even a meek man, to action? The answer is clear—survival—as well as Max's need to save the life of the prosecuting attorney.

Plot and character, then, are important dimensions of testing what kind of man Max is, but Los Angeles at night also plays a role. As presented, Los Angeles is all highways and sleek sky-scrapers. The few times Max seeks help from Angelinos he is either mugged or ignored. Mann's presentation of the environment is that it is cold and hostile. So many people, and yet they pass each other in the night and leave Max to his own devices. If he does not stand up for himself, no one else will. This is the Los Angeles Mann presents in "Collateral," and it makes the test that much harder.

Finally, we need to address the camera style Mann adopts in "Collateral." Max and the hit man are often shown in close-up with the camera placed close to them, as if they were the only two men in the world. The environment, on the other hand, is objectified, the camera distant. Mann used helicopter shots to look down on the city. He also used long shots to track the cab. The point of view only shifts when Vincent is doing his job or during an impending crash of the cab. At those points, Mann shifted into subjective motion and camera placement.

Even in the climactic scene when the hit man tries to kill the attorney but Max rescues her and they attempt to escape via the new subway system, Mann alternates close-ups and extreme long shots to objectify the confrontation. It is as if the environment (long shots) does nothing to help or harm those (close-ups) who pass through it. By doing so, Mann is suggesting that, if you can make it through a night in Los Angeles, you can and will survive anywhere. And Max does.

Adding Value to a Project

The good director moves beyond the choices made by the competent director with regard to:

1. Complexity of the narrative
2. Approach to characterization
3. Approach to the narrative
4. Issue of surprise
5. Point of view of the director
6. Camera placement

Whereas the competent director takes a singular approach to camera placement (*e.g.*, romantic, as in the case of Simon Wincer, cited in the previous chapter), the good director utilizes more varied camera placement. Anthony Mann directed film noirs, Westerns, and epics and is well known for his powerful visualization. Mann would enhance the dramatic tension and power by alternating between close-ups and extreme long shots. He also tended to place the camera close to the action to establish tension between a foreground character (the main character) and a character in the background (the antagonist). In other words, he used the image itself to create tension rather than relying on editing and pacing to create the tension (as Wincer does). This use of visual context for dramatic intensity is also typical of other good directors, such as John Frankenheimer, whom we discussed earlier in this chapter, as well as Roman Polanski and George Stevens, both of whom will be discussed in later chapters.

In terms of complexity of the narrative, I suggested in the previous chapter that the narrative is simplified in both Wincer's "The Lighthorsemen" and Michael Bay's "Pearl Harbor." Everything is sacrificed to serve the plot, and the plot provides the same romantic view of the main character as the camera placement does. Again turning to Anthony Mann as an example of going further with the narrative, we look at his first Western, "Winchester '73" (1950). The plot follows the fate of a rifle, a Winchester '73. The rifle is a much sought after weapon, and it is the prize for the marksmanship competition that begins the film. The best marksman, the main character, wins the competition, but the gun is stolen by his rival, the antagonist, who in turn loses the gun to a gambler. Indians seeking to buy guns from the gambler instead kill him and steal the rifle. When the Indians' chief is killed in battle, the gun passes to a ne'er-do-well. His pathological partner kills him for the gun, and he in turn is killed by the main character, who retrieves the rifle and uses it to kill the antagonist in a climactic shootout at the end of the film.

"Winchester '73" is anything but a romantic story. In fact, it is about constant betrayal. The power the rifle represents is elusive and temporary; those who come into possession of the powerful weapon end up losing it because the way in which they acquired it was immoral or unethical. In short order, they are destroyed for their greed and their immorality. The narrative is made even more murky when we learn that the antagonist, whom the main character is pursuing with the intent to kill, is his own brother. He seeks to kill his brother because the brother killed their father. What at first seems to be a story about a gun has instead become a Cain-and-Abel story, a revenge story with a tragic core. The narrative is very complex, with a subtext of unleashed sibling rivalry working its way toward a horrible climax, where one brother kills the other brother, his only living blood relative.

With regard to characterization, note how the characterizations of "Winchester '73" differ from those in "The Lighthorsemen." Again, the characterizations in "The Lighthorsemen" are romantic and simple—men are either brave or cowardly. The Australians are straightforward, and the British are eccentric or rigid. In "Winchester '73," only the main character, Lyn McAdam, is straightforward. He is a great marksman filled with a rage that drives him to avenge the death of his father.

All of the other characters are interesting. The antagonist, Dutch Henry, is aggressive but he is also impulsive and immature. His two companions have to keep him on track. Wyatt Earp, who oversees the competition at the outset, is a lawman, but he is also a civic enthusiast and something of a caregiver. Lyn's companion and friend, he is a father figure and something of a philosopher. He has to keep the main character from imploding due to his rage. The dance hall girl is honest, expressive, and funny, given the dangerous situations in which she constantly finds herself. Steve, her fiancé, is a coward trying to become a person who deserves respect, but he dies without achieving it. Waco, who kills him, is a romantic psychopath—a man who enjoys betraying others. All of these characters are complex and make the experience of "Winchester '73" one of witnessing absolute behavior in a world of considerable moral ambiguity. They make the story more complex, and their development as characters does not seem to slow down the busy plot.

Regarding the movie's plot deployment (pursuit of the Winchester '73) and its relationship to the character layer of the story, the plot was designed to mask the deeper character layer, particularly the protagonist–antagonist relationship. Initially, the plot highlights the intense rivalry between Lyn McAdam and Dutch Henry Brown. Initially, we believe the rivalry has something to do with a past grievance, but eventually it is revealed that Dutch Henry killed Lyn's father. Only late in the story do we learn they are brothers. Each revelation changes the story. In Act I, the story seems to be one of two rivals fighting to prove who is the top shot. In Act II, it becomes a revenge story. And, in Act III, the revelation that they are brothers changes the story yet again to one of fratricide. In a sense, the pursuit of the rifle (the plot) masks what the story is really about, but what the story is about keeps changing as the story unfolds. To put it another way, Mann's treatment of the story in "Winchester '73" yields considerable subtext and surprise. Thus, another mark of the good director is layered storytelling.

This brings us to Mann's point of view in the story. Here we reach an interesting point. Andrew Sarris viewed Mann as the ultimate craftsman or technician. Putting it another way, Mann did not have a personal voice, and he himself claimed to be a director for hire. Other directors have been damned with the same faint praise: Fred Zinnemann ("High Noon," "Day of the Jackal"), William Wyler ("Best Years of Our Lives," "Roman Holiday"), and Carol Reed ("The Third Man," "Odd Man Out"). I would include all of these directors in the category of good directors. I would like to suggest that these filmmakers excelled in the visualizations of their films, and each showed great strength in deploying an intricate mix of plot and character in a manner that raised the bar for the story in general. In the case of both Wyler and Reed, their use of the deep focus frame is as powerful as the work of Orson Welles in "Citizen Kane." Both Wyler's "Little Foxes" and Reed's "The Third Man" are classics with regard to the use of deep-focus foreground–background relationships to illustrate the core conflicts in their films.

Fred Zinnemann was able to make complex stories emotionally available ("A Man for All Seasons") or layered simple stories with complex subtext ("From Here to Eternity," "High Noon"). This intelligent director kept on story in one of the most complex narratives of the 1970s, "The Day of the Jackal." And, of course, Anthony Mann's capacity to tell a story powerfully, economically, and in a visually powerful fashion marks his work from "T-Men" to "El Cid" and "The Heroes of Telemark." All of these directors loved the visual power of the medium. They were not aesthetes, but their voices, in part, reflected the pleasure they found in playing with the medium. Today, directors such as Quentin Tarantino are celebrated for playing with the medium, but in an earlier time Anthony Mann, William Wyler, Fred Zinnemann, and Carol Reed were good directors who displayed an equivalent pleasure in visualizing their stories. This pleasure was an important component of their voices as directors.

The Director's Idea

I have discussed the many ways in which a good director's work differs from that of a competent director. What I have not yet added to the mix is the focal point of the director's skills—the director's idea, the magnifying lens that helps the director choose characterization, narrative, and visualization strategies that will elevate the work to another level.

In the case of Anthony Mann, his director's ideas arose first and foremost out of the genre in which he was working. Generally, the Western tends to be a genre where the main character and the antagonist represent certain values. The main character represents pastoral values, romantic individualistic values that are associated with the past, the West. These values do not differ from the romantic values of the knights of the court of King Arthur. The antagonist, on the other hand, represents civilization and material values. He wants all the cattle, all the land, or all the money. The main character and the antagonist do battle in the Western, ritualized battle, and the main character prevails. This romantic, even poetic notion infuses Wyler's "The Westerner," Ford's "My Darling Clementine," and Hawks' "Rio Bravo," all classic Westerns.

Mann, however, viewed the West differently. His is a more modern, far more ambiguous view of the West and of the characters that populate his films. Lyn McAdam is neurotically obsessed with killing his own brother, the antagonist. To call him morally ambiguous is to flatter the McAdam character. In a sense, he shares more values with his brother than he admits. The setting, the West, is beautiful, but given the narrative and its corruption of the traditional Western values it is ironic, unpredictable, and dangerous rather than poetic.

And now we come to Mann's director's idea. In Mann's take on the Western, the main character is not a hero, not a romantic character. He is all too human, and he is a man not unlike his antagonist. In the beautiful setting of the West, his behavior is ambiguous rather than idealized. In "Winchester '73," we view the main character's struggle as a modern one. He is obsessed and he has to survive to achieve his goal—in this case, revenge against his brother. When we look at the visualization, we can see that the Lyn McAdam character is crowded by the very close camera placement. He is foregrounded. In the background is his adversary, Dutch Henry Brown, his brother. This conflict, internal and deep, ties him to his brother. The two men are visually linked together but are adversaries. The intense close-ups alternate with extreme long shots. The intensity of the close-ups contrasts with the breathtaking beauty revealed in the extreme long shots. The beast is in the close-up, and the beauty is in the extreme long shot. The irony in this juxtaposition again and again reminds us of the madness of the main character. If he is heroic, he is at best a tortured hero. This pattern is repeated in the relationships of the main characters in "The Naked Spur," "The Man from Laramie," and "Men in War." In each case, the visual landscape plays the same role: to make ironic and modern the choices the main character must make. We see the same pattern in Mann's noir classics "He Walks by Night" and "Raw Deal." Mann's director's idea is to examine the moral compromises of his main characters, and the beauty of his long shots, whether of the West or Korea or a modern-day main street, deepens that moral ambiguity.

Chapter 5
The Great Director

- The great director looks for a deep subtextual interpretation of the text.
- The great director is passionate about character and narrative.
- The great director prefers a direct approach to the material, a simple approach, an economical approach.
- The subtextual interpretation drives performance and camera choices.
- The audacity of the interpretation transforms the experience from simple to surprising.
- The great director is very assertive about expressing his voice.
- The same can be said about the style of the film; it is unusually distinctive.

HOLLYWOOD

PRODUCTION

DIRECTOR

CAMERA

DATE   SCENE   TA

What differentiates the great director from the good director is the business of this chapter. To recap, the good director adds value to a project. Using the narrative tools of character, plot, and story form, the good director uses a counterpoint approach to give a layered reading to the text. We are surprised and delighted by surprises that deepen the story. Guided by his director's idea, the director orchestrates the visuals, performances, and text readings to create a subtext that again deepens the experience of the film for the audience.

The great director transforms the experience of the film when he utilizes his director's idea to add a powerful voice to the film. When the computer Hal becomes all too human and the human astronauts all too cold and mechanical in "2001: A Space Odyssey" (1968), Stanley Kubrick has told us something profound about our attachment to technology and human progress. Again and again in that film we are struck by this level of commentary on human progress through history. Kubrick uses irony to enhance his voice and in so doing challenges many of our beliefs about progress.

Thirty years earlier, Charlie Chaplin had made similar observations about human progress and human nature in "Modern Times" (1936). His focus, however, was more specific—the factory. Chaplin's ironic observations on the mechanization of production and how dehumanizing these progressive processes are veer into tragedy (and reveal his creative genius) when the main character is accidentally absorbed into the innards of a machine. Visually and spiritually, he is being consumed alive by the machine.

Both "2001: A Space Odyssey" and "Modern Times" are examples of great films made by great directors. Each transforms a narrative into a way of perceiving the world and the behavior of the people in it differently. This transformation is the mark of the great director. I should add that great films have been made by directors who have exceeded their previous work. In other words, great films have been made by good directors. "The Best Years of Our Lives" (William Wyler), "High Noon" (Fred Zinnemann), "Singing in the Rain" (Gene Kelly and Stanley Donen), and "West Side Story" (Robert Wise) are examples of this phenomenon. In this chapter, we will focus on great directors rather than great films, as our job is to understand how, through their work, directors become great.

Forty years ago, Andrew Sarris in his classic book, *American Cinema*, created a hierarchy of American directors and he referred to the top tier as the pantheon. This category included D.W. Griffith, Charlie Chaplin, Buster Keaton, Orson Welles, John Ford, Howard Hawks, Ernst Lubitsch, F.W. Murnau, and Fritz Lang. Excluded or relegated to a lower tier were directors such as Stanley Kubrick, George Stevens, Frank Capra, and Preston Sturges. It is not useful here to redefine the top tier with regard to great directors in an attempt to refute Sarris; rather, I want to focus on the development of an operational definition of the great director. We will examine the works of three contemporary directors to develop an operational definition; however, before doing so we must turn to the issue of voice.

Voice

I dealt extensively with the issue of voice in my book *Global Scriptwriting* (2001, Focal Press). Essentially, voice can be genre specific, or the director can use genres that enable his voice. Genres such as satire, docudramas, fables, experimental narratives, and nonlinear films require a distancing from character and structure so the voice is clear rather than embedded in a character. Irony is a favorite distancing device. When the voice is genre specific (for example, Joseph Mankiewicz in the melodrama "All About Eve"), it is usually expressed by the attitudes of the characters and the choice of words (dialogue) used to articulate those attitudes. The worldly theatricality of Addison DeWitt, the narcissism of Margo Channing (and the witty aggression that protects it), and the disingenuousness of Eve Harrington are all qualities that create the voice of Mankiewicz. He enjoys the energy and wit of the theater but none of the politics of stardom.

Voice, whatever the genre, is made powerful by the great director. It can reach its apogee in film noir, as in the case of Billy Wilder's "Sunset Boulevard," or it can join/be influenced by the choice of subject matter, as in the case of François Truffaut and his films about children—"The 400 Blows" (1966), "The Wild Child" (1970), and "Small Change" (1982). On the other hand, it may be subsumed by an attitude about being in the world, as in the case of Krystof Kieslowski, whose concern was always about existence, its quality, its containment, its need for the joining/affiliating with another human being—as revealed, for example, in "A Short Film about Loving."

In addition to the very strong voices of great directors are particular characteristics that mark their work. First, the work is marked by a level of passion that is unusual; a good example is Carl Dreyer in his silent film "The Passion of Joan of Arc" (1928). A second quality is the capacity to stake out a distinct position in the film; this capacity is notable in the work of Roman Polanski, who we will discuss later in the book. His film "A Knife in the Water" (1962) exemplifies this characteristic. A third quality is a simplicity in the director's approach to the subject. Ernanno Olmi's "Il Posto" (1965) is a good example of such simplicity and is enormously powerful. A fourth quality is an economy of narrative, or the ability to say a great deal in a single shot; Luis Bunuel's film "Belle de Jour" (1967) and Ernst Lubitsch's film "Ninotchka" (1939) are good examples. Finally, the great director has a distinctive style that may resemble a documentary, as in Roberto Rossellini's "The Rise of Louis XIV" (1968) and Gillo Pontecorvo's "The Battle of Algiers" (1968), or may be highly stylized, as in Luchino Visconti's "The Leopard" (1965) and Federico Fellini's "8 1/2" (1962). Whatever mix we find in a particular director, these qualities only serve to strengthen that director's voice.

Three Contemporary Great Directors in America

Although this section is about American directors, I must say I struggled with my choices. What is one to do with Peter Weir, the Australian who has been making films in America since "Dead Poet's Society" and "Witness"? And what of Sam Mendes, the British theater director who is responsible for two great American films "American Beauty" and "The Road to Perdition"? What needs to be said is that Hollywood has always been the creative home for immigrants and even temporary visitors. The first Academy Award went to a film called "Sunrise" (1927), which was directed by the German F.W. Murnau. Charlie Chaplin, Ernst Lubitsch, and Alfred Hitchcock all immigrated here, and the latter two were famous in their native countries (Germany and Great Britain, respectively). William Wyler, Fred Zinnemann, Billy Wilder, Milos Forman, and Paul Verhoeven all emigrated from Europe and each made significant American films.

When I look at the films made over the past 30 years (excluding the work of the directors we will discuss shortly), I can identify ten great films made by great directors: Bob Fosse's "All That Jazz" (1981), Robert Altman's "The Player" (1992), Steven Spielberg's "Schindler's List" (1994), Paul Anderson's "Boogie Nights" (1995), Spike Lee's "Do the Right Thing" (1998), Sydney Pollack's "Tootsie" (1983), Terence Malick's "The Thin Red Line" (1997), Oliver Stone's "Natural Born Killers" (1994), Michael Cimino's "The Deer Hunter" (1997), and Clint Eastwood's "Mystic River" (2003). All are great films by great directors.

My choice of directors to discuss here was based on their work over the last 30 years. Each director has, on an ongoing basis, used a director's idea that has powerfully amplified the experience of his work. We will look at each in turn: Francis Ford Coppola, Woody Allen, and Martin Scorsese.

Francis Ford Coppola's films "The Godfather" (1972), "The Godfather: Part II" (1975), and "Apocalypse Now" (1979) share a common director's idea: to view the narrative events of each film not as believable but rather as an opera, which requires an intensification of dramatic events. "The Godfather" and "The Godfather: Part II" each revolves around Michael Corleone as the main character. The choices Michael must make are between his career (professional) and his family (personal). In each film, Michael chooses the professional option and sacrifices his family. As in opera, where celebrations and crises are the focus, Connie's wedding, her husband battering her, the assassination attempt on Don Corleone, the assassination of Sonny, the baptism of Connie's baby, and the killings of all those responsible for acting against the Don and his business interests all mark the original "The Godfather." The assassination attempt on Michael on the day of his son's confirmation, the assassination attempt on Hyman Roth, the Cuban revolution, the discovery by Michael that his brother Fredo betrayed him, and the settling of all accounts, including the murder of Fredo, mark the sequel, "The Godfather: Part II." Both films treat these events as set pieces so there is a ritual feeling to these narrative events. The focus on the intensity of death, love, and life events supports the operatic feeling. Stylistically, Coppola takes a very deliberate, slow approach to all of these set pieces. The result is the antithesis of realism, a theatricality I suggest is more opera than film.

The "film as opera" director's idea is equally at play in "Apocalypse Now." War films tend to present realistically, with a focus on the main character's survival. Coppola's operatic approach posits the war as madness, and the main character from the outset struggles to hold onto his sanity. The soldiers' progression up the river to deliver an assassin to kill the rogue officer, Kurtz, approximates a series of set pieces on the river Styx. By the time we reach Kurtz's camp, the feeling is that we are in hell, and by the time the main character obeys his order to kill Kurtz we fully believe he may be a good soldier but is madder than a bat in hell. He has accomplished his mission but lost his mind. This is Coppola's view of the effect of the war in Vietnam on America. By using an operatic director's idea he has made even more extreme the narrative events of "Apocalypse Now" and created a film experience that functions as a war film on a narrative level but is transformed into an internalized psychodrama commenting on that war. Coppola's voice is loud and clear.

Woody Allen's director's idea is equally as powerful and enhances the film's voice just as it did for Francis Ford Coppola. Allen's director's idea is to be both a performer (stand-up comic) and a character in his films. When he is acting as stand-up comic, he speaks directly to the audience, breaking down the wall between the film's character and its audience. When he assumes the role of a character in the film, he remains in character and relies on the narrative strategies to invite the audience to identify and empathize with his character. In brief, Woody Allen's director's idea is as a writer/performer/director to step out of the film from time to time to comment on the ongoing narrative. In this sense, he is closer to the Marx Brothers as a comic persona/performer than he is to Charlie Chaplin, Buster Keaton, or Jerry Lewis.

Woody Allen is also profoundly influenced by the great filmmakers Ingmar Bergman and Federico Fellini. The consequence is a series of homages such as "September" (1987) and "Stardust Memories" (1980), and their influence can also be seen less directly in most of Allen's work, such as "Crimes and Misdemeanors" (1989) and "Broadway

Danny Rose" (1984). In "Crimes and Misdemeanors," the darkness of human behavior, so central a theme for Bergman, manifests itself in the ophthalmologist who gets away with commissioning the murder of his mistress. Faith, or the loss of it, is also addressed in the work of both filmmakers. A circus (or clown) theme is prevalent in the attitude and work of Fellini, just as it is in Allen's "Broadway Danny Rose." Closely related to the circus idea is the magic of the movie media, the theme of Allen's "The Purple Rose of Cairo," a film that echoes Fellini's "The White Sheik."

But it is in Allen's films about love and relationships that we see his director's idea most powerfully at play. Looking at "Annie Hall" (1977), "Manhattan" (1980), and "Hannah and Her Sisters" (1986), we can see that each focuses on different variations of relationships. First, in "Annie Hall," we see the relationship between a Jew and a Shiksah, a gentile very different from himself. In "Manhattan," the focus is on the relationship between an adult and a teenager, where age, not cultural background, is the barrier. Finally, in "Hannah and Her Sisters," the difficult relationship is between a married man and his sister-in-law. Allen plays a central role in the first two films and a more subsidiary role in the third. Each film explores the need for love (a relationship) in the ultra-urban, upper middle class society of modern New York. In each case the love is crucial and intense, but the relationships are doomed to failure, so the focus is on the bittersweet outcomes of the relationships. Two of Allen's later films, "Husbands and Wives" and "Deconstructing Harry," focus on lonely characters, survivors of doomed love relationships.

To examine more closely how the director's idea works, we turn first to "Annie Hall" (1977), in which Allen assumes the role of narrator to comment on the narrative action, on being a Jew in a gentile society, on his relationship with his mother, or on other dimensions of feeling like an outsider. Allen feels free to intersperse such commentary freely throughout the narrative. Another strategy is to have the characters themselves address the audience directly, as he does when he introduces his classmates from junior high school to the audience. Visually, each is five years old, but they tell us what they are doing or have become as adults. The contrast between the angelic visuals and misanthropic futures—"I'm on methadone," "I'm a prostitute," etc.—is startling and makes the point that life disappoints and is not what it seems to be in one's childhood.

A third strategy Woody Allen uses to break down the wall between film characters and audiences is probably the most famous scene in "Annie Hall." Allen is in line to see Ophul's documentary, "The Sorrow and the Pity." Behind him two academics chatter on, the man trying to impress the woman with a flood of McLuhanesque observations and interpretations. Allen's character grows increasingly frustrated and eventually walks away, only to reappear with the real Marshall McLuhan, who proceeds to tell off the academic, after which he leaves the scene. This intervention in the narrative serves to bring the real world into the film.

The performer/character strategy is used to heighten the romanticism in "Manhattan" and to give the characters in "Hannah and Her Sisters" the opportunity to confess, in a therapeutic fashion, their desire and their guilt. In both cases, the strategy amplifies the narrative and transforms it from a love story to a commentary on a particular time and place—New York, today. In a sense the director's idea has made Allen not only an impassioned storyteller (Fellini) but also a modern philosopher on our lives and times (Bergman).

To understand the director's idea that operates in the work of Martin Scorsese, we need to review the films of Roberto Rossellini, Robert Bresson, and Yasujiro Ozu. In their films, characters who have an inner drive to be valuable and to be validated find the world a disappointing place. In "Open City" (Rossellini, 1945), the disappointment is in the realpolitique of fascism operating to corrupt a society and its individuals. In "Mouchette" (Bresson, 1970), it is found in the indifference and cruelty of communities and families to a simple, underprivileged young girl. In "Tokyo Story" (Ozu, 1953), it can be seen in the selfishness of one generation (children) toward another generation (parents). In each story, a character operates or lives by a moral code that simply does not help them. It is as if a character seeks or lives within a state of grace (spirituality) that the family or community or society does not share. The consequence is disappointing but on another level is tragic.

This tragedy, the gap between the inner life of a character and the lives of the character's surrounding family, community, or society, is the thread that runs through the work of Martin Scorsese. His characters seek a state of grace but what they find is a material world, a political world that cannot nurture them. Indeed, it is a world that does not accept them, and the results are often tragic. The search for a state of grace is Scorsese's director's idea.

This director's idea is clearly at play in Scorsese's "The Last Temptation of Christ" (1987) and "Kundun" (1999), his film about the life of the Dalai Lama. In a more subtle way, it is the subtext of Jake LaMotta's journey in "Raging Bull" (1980) and Travis Bickle's search in "Taxi Driver" (1976). The casting of Robert De Niro in both roles further underscores the restless, searching inner life that amplifies the director's idea.

Much has been made of the tone of Scorsese's films. Implicit in his director's idea is the clash between what the character wants and what the character gets. It has been said that Scorsese has a propensity for creating film noir, but I believe this not to be the case. The tone is dark in "Taxi Driver," "Mean Streets" (1973), and "Casino" (1995), but I believe that the darkness has more to do with the narrative outcomes than a deliberate attempt to produce film noir. In "Raging Bull," for example, LaMotta is no longer a champion. He has lost his family due to continual wife battering and is alone. We see him rehearsing a monologue for a nightclub routine and realize that he is a man exploiting his own fame and former glory to make money to pay off his debts. In this scene, Scorsese presents a man who has fallen from the state of grace he enjoyed within the aesthetic of combat in the ring. That was LaMotta's moment, and when he lost it he was set adrift in the material world. This is LaMotta's tragedy. He has fallen from that state of grace that allowed him to associate with something larger than life. The ring, the combat, and being the middleweight champion meant everything to him.

Another aspect of Scorsese's work needs to be addressed—his style. Scorsese uses an active, searching, moving camera, such as in the nightclub entry shot in "Goodfellas" (1990), the balletic tracking shots in "Raging Bull," and the dynamic preparation for battle shots in "Gangs of New York" (2002). Scorsese uses the camera, together with chiaroscuro lighting, to create energy and to imply the restless search. The energy is the desire, the moving camera the hope, and the lighting the anxiety that hope will be dashed and desire will be disappointed. This stylistic approach underpins the director's idea. It articulates how very much the character hopes he will find a state of grace, and the use of lighting indicates how difficult the goal truly is.

Each of these directors transforms his narrative into something bigger, deeper, and different through his director's idea. In the case of Coppola, his operatic approach turns a gangster story into a powerful evocation of immigrants (the Corleone family) who are steeped in family values at the outset but lose their way. Power corrupts Michael Corleone and he loses everything that he and his father valued. Under Coppola's direction, their saga becomes a tale of America as paradise lost.

In the case of Woody Allen, his performer/character director's idea allows Allen to comment on the importance of love and relationships to his characters and how, because they are outsiders (*e.g.*, Jewish or a writer), his characters remain outside the possible realm of enduring love. Consequently, his films capture the paradigm of contemporary American life—material success and spiritual ennui.

Martin Scorsese also is concerned with values in American life but by using his director's idea, the search for grace, he deepens the paradox. In this successful place, America, the divine is always elusive and the inevitable disappointment leads his characters to violence and self-destruction. They suffer the fate of living outside grace.

These dark perceptions of American life have powerfully countered the popular image of American life that includes success, material wealth, and power unprecedented in world history. These three great directors have asked important questions and provided alternatives to prevailing and popular views.

Three Contemporary Great Directors Outside America

Great non-American directors have concentrated on particular issues, with perhaps the most significant being the universal issue of tradition *versus* change. Particular filmmakers, such as India's Sajajit Ray ("Pather Panchali," 1955) and Japan's Yasujiro Ozu ("Early Spring," 1956), have implicitly advocated tradition, while others, such as Spain's Luis Bunuel ("Exterminating Angel," 1960) and France's Jean Luc Godard ("Weekend," 1968) have aggressively advocated change. Other filmmakers have represented creative movements—Italy's

Vittoria de Sica and neorealism, Germany's G.W. Pabst ("Pandora's Box") and expressionism. Others have decided their creative agenda should be reexamining the past in order to find a way toward a better future, such as Poland's Andrej Wajda ("Ashes and Diamonds," 1960) and Hungary's István Szabó ("Mephisto," 1982). Still others consider reconsideration of genres (based on their culture) as a way to introduce other cultures to their societies and introduce their societies to other cultures, such as Akira Kurosawa of Japan ("Seven Samurai," 1956) and Bille August of Denmark ("Pelle the Conqueror," 1986). Finally, some have used the fable to press their countries to embrace change, such as Germany's Werner Herzog ("The Enigma of Kaspar Hauser," 1984) and Michael Verhoeven ("The Nasty Girl," 1989), as well as France's Coline Serreau's ("Chaos" (2002)).

Whatever the approach, Europe and Asia have contributed mightily to the category of great directors. Before proceeding to discuss three directors in greater detail, I would like to mention a number of films and their filmmakers that represent great directing. If this book was solely about the subject of this chapter, the following directors would get the amount of space they deserve.

In the category of great directors, I would include Volker Schlondorff ("The Tin Drum," 1979) and Tom Tykwer ("The Princess and the Warrior," 2001) from Germany; Mike van Diem ("Character," 1998) from The Netherlands; Eric Zoncka ("The Dreamlife of Angels," 1998) from France; and Thomas Vinterberg ("The Celebration," 1997) from Denmark. "The Celebration" (or "Festen," as it was called abroad), the first of the Dogme films, is probably the single most influential European film of the 1990s. I would also include Elem Klimov ("Come and See," 1987) and Nickolai Michalkhov ("Close to Eden," or "Urga" in Europe, 1994) from the USSR; Bernardo Bertolucci ("Beseiged," 1999) from Italy; Krystof Kieslowski ("Red," 1995) from Poland; and Xiang Yimou ("Hero," 2002) from China. Each of these films transforms a narrative into a creative challenge to tradition or genre in unique and special ways. Having noted these great directors and their films, I will now take a more detailed look at three contemporary non-American directors.

The choices here are abundant. To choose just three, I identified a notion that would tie together three filmmakers. Rather than seeking a national, stylistic, or creative (*e.g.*, Dogme) commonality, I looked for filmmakers who exhibit a certain freedom in their choice of narrative tools to tell their stories. The directors I have chosen to discuss here—Pedro Almodovar, Denys Arcand, and Emir Kusturica—share the attitude that narrative tools should be driven by the directors' narrative ambition to tell a culturally specific story that nevertheless reaches beyond borders. These filmmakers are looking at the global themes of friendship, family, the roles of men and women, birth, death, love, and relationships to tell their stories in ways that have made each of them important throughout the world of film.

Pedro Almodovar has been making films for more than 20 years. Initially, he made melodramas about being gay. In the last few years, however, Almodovar has settled on a specific director's idea that has transformed his work. Almodovar's director's idea is that men and women exist in each of us, whatever our gender. The result is a male nurse and a female bullfighter in "Talk to Her" (2002) and a father who has become a woman with breasts and an actor who has also become a woman in "All About My Mother" (2000). In "All About My Mother," the story is essentially that of a mother who, at the outset of the story, loses her adolescent son in a car accident. She then returns to Barcelona to tell the father, her husband, only to discover that he has become a man with breasts. But he/she is as irresponsible a person as he/she was before the sex-change operation. The mother chooses to live with a friend, an actor who has also had a sex-change operation. The story is rounded out by the inclusion of a pregnant nun whose family has rejected her. The woman's husband dies of AIDS, the nun dies in childbirth, and a new family is formed when the female main character and her transsexual friend adopt the baby, albeit the new father is visually a female. The story sounds dark, but actually Almodovar's bright art direction and cinematography lighten the mood, which becomes one of acceptance of all these characters and their personal transgressions and gender blurring.

That blurring is more subtle in "Talk to Her." This film focuses on four characters and three relationships. The first relationship is between two men: a male nurse and a journalist. They are introduced to us at a dance performance just before they meet for the first time. The course of their relationship is the core of the story. The male nurse is rather feminine, while the more masculine journalist is gruff and mildly depressed. There is always the feeling that the male nurse hopes that this relationship might evolve into a love relationship (but it never does).

The second relationship in the film is between the male nurse and a comatose female dancer. He was so taken with her in life that he became a patient of her father, a psychiatrist, in order to see her. Later, after an accident, she becomes the nurse's patient. He is very happy to care for her. He is a man in love, but late in the narrative he rapes her. She becomes pregnant and eventually awakens from her coma. Prior to her awakening, the male nurse is imprisoned and, seeing no hope, commits suicide.

The third relationship is between the journalist and a female bullfighter he interviews. They begin an affair that is suddenly interrupted when she is gored by a bull. Her injuries are so severe that she remains in a coma for a long time. In this phase, the fact that both the journalist and the male nurse have someone they love in a coma brings the two men closer together. They have grown very close when the bullfighter dies. At this stage, the two men console one another. The film ends by suggesting the beginning of a fourth relationship—between the journalist and the now-awakened ballet dancer. They see each other at a dance performance, and the film ends where it began.

This story summary does not do justice to the director's idea. All aspects of being a man and of being a woman are explored. The performance helps blur gender distinctions. The caring exhibited by the male journalist for the male nurse, the emotionality of the male nurse, the cerebral character of the dancer, and the masculine professional aura and personal hysteria of the bullfighter all blur gender lines.

As in "All About My Mother," the art direction and camera choices in "Talk to Her" are sunny and lift the film away from the tragedy of the events in the film. In both films, Almodovar has challenged fixed ideas about men and women—cultural, sociological, and political. He has created characters that move us, and their stories help us redefine how we view gender in our own societies.

Denys Arcand is a Quebec filmmaker whose early work in documentary was quite political. For over 30 years he has been making feature films that increasingly have moved away from strictly political subject matter. Since 1987, with "The Decline of the American Empire" (essentially a comedy of manners), Arcand has focused on values rather than politics; yet, in some ways, his films since then have never been more political.

The characters in "The Decline of the American Empire" are adult intellectuals who want to fulfill their desires—sex, food, drink—and they are critical of a society that focuses on social organizations (family, church, state) rather than on the individual. This brings us to Arcand's director's idea. For him, the artist, who may be an academic or an actor, has an obligation to challenge society, to challenge all of the -isms. For the artist, values are a moral shield against materialism, against intellectual dogma, against political dogma. The artist represents the satisfaction of desire and a responsibility to care for another (lover or friend or fellow citizen). In his later films, such as "Jesus of Montreal" (1995) and "The Barbarian Invasions" (2003), Arcand's director's idea is presented full force. Because the latter is a sequel to "The Decline of the American Empire," we turn to it first.

The artist in "The Barbarian Invasions" is the same academic we met in "The Decline of the American Empire," but now he is dying of cancer, and the film ends shortly after his death. This is not a film about dying, though. The main character is his son, an economic success story. The son hates his father for leaving the marriage (at the end of the previous film). Upon his mother's urging, however, he comes back to see his father. The couple's other child, a young woman, has escaped to a sailing life in the South Pacific. The son returns to Canada to find a health system falling apart. He seeks an opinion from a childhood friend who is now a cancer specialist in the United States; however, the father refuses to die in the United States. He wants to die in Canada surrounded by friends—and sex, food, and wine. The son buys comfort for his father, bringing in his friends from abroad and providing heroin for his pain. By helping his father legally and illegally, the son discovers that there is more to life than economic success. We leave the son moved and perplexed about his own future (and his values).

What is interesting about this film is that Arcand takes a cue from Woody Allen. Arcand's characters speak to us directly as they criticize all the intellectual and political trends of the academic's life. By doing so, Arcand leaves us with the impression that the love that these friends (male, female, gay, heterosexual) have for one another is the real life, the worthwhile life, while the -isms of life are transitory and unimportant, just chatter in the overall scheme of things.

Whenever possible, Arcand presents the public face of a hospital or the police and then undermines this rule or that rule with a humane response or outcome. It is as if Arcand is saying that there are rules (about heroin, for example) that simply do not apply when a citizen who ordinarily lives by the rules is dying. The strategy then becomes a more moral one, a more humane one. As a result, in this film we see businessmen, nurses, and policemen transgress to help an academic die without pain and with dignity. This is the experience of "The Barbarian Invasions," which presents law and social order as barriers to what is best for the individual, and transgression is seen as moral and humane. This is Arcand's transformation.

The director's idea in "Jesus of Montreal" is even more pronounced and transgressive. The artist's role is taken by a radical actor who is asked to stage the Passion play. The play is to be performed in the open on a mountain in Montreal. The sponsor is the church, and the producer is a priest, who is having an affair with an acting school classmate of "Jesus." "Jesus" gathers a group of actors, among whom one has been lending his voice to dubbing foreign pornographic films and another has been "prostituting" herself in beauty commercials. When the cast has been assembled and the Passion play is performed, the roles ennoble the actors and they become the characters they are portraying. "Jesus" becomes the radical critic of all things materialistic. He disrupts the production of a commercial (an attack on the Temple clerics and their activities), and the actresses become Mary and Mary Magdalene. They have found grace and they turn against the lives they have led. This terrifies the priest who has produced the play. He shuts the play down mid-performance. Jesus is badly injured and is taken to the hospital by the two actresses, but he walks away only to die in the local subway station. He dies as Jesus did, for the sins of others—the priest, the "priests" of the media, and producers and directors who exploit their actors and the public.

As in "The Barbarian Invasions," it is difficult to distinguish between a play being performed by actors and the actors who become the characters they are portraying, and Arcand speaks directly to us about values. In "Jesus of Montreal," he gives us a classic and modern passion play in which "Jesus"/Arcand, the character/voice of the writer/director, forces us to question our values. For Arcand, the choice is clear: Modern material values must be seen as transient and as less important than deeper communal values and spiritual values. It is telling that Arcand positions a priest, society's bearer of spiritual values, as one of the antagonists in this film. Once again, the organizations of society have failed the individual. The artist as radical voice upholds the spiritual values that Arcand associates with Jesus in "Jesus of Montreal."

Emir Kusturica is a Muslim who has made the majority of his films in Serb Orthodox Serbia. Kusturica's director's idea is to portray the Middle Eastern male personality by exploring its vitality, its creativity, and its self-destructiveness. From "When Father Was Away on Business" (1986) through "Underground" (1999), Kusturica has explored all aspects of maleness, but probably no single film presents a more hopeful arc than his "Time of the Gypsies" (1992). "Time of the Gypsies" tells the story of Perhan, a gypsy adolescent raised by his grandmother. His choices are simple—to be a caregiver like his grandmother or to be a man like his uncle, a worker who has returned from Germany. All his uncle's relationships have failed and his compulsive gambling is all but ruining the family. The narrative follows Perhan through work and helping his crippled sister, marriage to a childhood sweetheart, his sexual paranoia about her, her death in childbirth, betrayal by his benefactor, his murder of his benefactor, and his own death at the hands of the benefactor's family. At the end, his son will be raised as he was by his grandmother.

Superstition, passion, and paranoia are mixed in with youthful idealism, and in the end Perhan succumbs to the male disease of jealousy, which leads to hatred and violence, thus destroying the idealism that was there in abundance when Perhan was an adolescent. It is as if Kusturica was trying to portray a life with a slow-release poison embedded in it. When enough poison is released, the life ends, a fate that is inevitable.

The director's idea is presented in such a way that, as the narrative unfolds, Kusturica gives full rein to each of the feelings. In the early scenes (visually and in the performances), we perceive the idealism. These scenes are funny and charming. As the narrative shifts rather abruptly to paranoia, dark actions and dark visuals replace the earlier sunny tone. Performances are modulated differently so as to be appropriate to this layer of the Middle Eastern male personality. Each phase of the film requires a different tone. When we pull together all the different tones, we have the layered experience of the Middle Eastern male persona. Of course, in this world the women and children are the greatest victims, and their various presentations throughout the film help flesh out a fuller sense of the male personality. The experience of "Time of the Gypsies" is quite unlike almost any other film experience. It is exhilarating and exasperating and exhausting. And, in its richness, we find a layered sense of life in someone else's skin—the Middle Eastern male.

Each of these filmmakers has a different director's idea, but each has used narrative devices to transform their stories into a new view of men and women (Almodovar), of spiritual values in a material world (Arcand), and of life and death in a particular culture (Kusturica). Now, let's turn to the specifics of those tools that directors use to realize their director's idea.

Chapter 6

Text Interpretation

The first step toward developing a director's idea is reading or interpreting the script. Every script, every story can be interpreted in many ways. A writer has fashioned the story using a mix of narrative tools: a premise, a generally goal-oriented main character who is faced with having to choose between two opposing alternatives, and two groups of secondary characters, one of which helps the main character and one that stands in opposition. In terms of structure, the narrative is organized from a critical moment to its resolution along a course of rising action—barriers, people, or events that make it increasingly more difficult for the main character to achieve his goal. The structure includes a plot layer and a character layer and is contained within a genre that implies its own dramatic arc. Finally, the voice of the writer is embedded in the tone of the narrative.

This is the narrative organization to which the director adds his interests, his character, and his specific interpretation. The goal of this chapter is to suggest that the director's interpretation is the critical first step of the decision-making process. It is during this phase that the director's idea is born.

Before discussing strategies that aid development of the director's interpretation, we need to understand that in every story there exist many interpretations. I have already referred to various interpretations of the same story—the adaptations of "Lolita" (1962), of "Une Femme Infidele" (1967), and of "The Manchurian Candidate" (1962). It would be useful to hold onto these examples while reading this chapter. A useful place for us to begin our discussion is those cases in the popular literature for which numerous interpretations already exist, such as Shakespeare's play "Hamlet."

"Hamlet" is the story of the young adult son of a king. His father has died, and his mother has married his uncle, who becomes the king. Hamlet, motivated by an encounter with his father's troubled ghost, learns that his father was poisoned. Driven by a desire for revenge, he puts on a play that reenacts the murder. Seeing his uncle's troubled response, he plots revenge. Hamlet sidesteps a personal relationship with the young Ophelia, avoids his uncle's attempt to get rid of him (Rosencrantz and Gildenstern), and fights Ophelia's brother, Laertes, who is armed with a poisoned sword and wounds Hamlet. Hamlet kills Laertes and his uncle, Claudius, and then he himself dies. This story can be interpreted as either a revenge story or as a palace tale of power politics.

Turning to the various readings or interpretations of "Hamlet," a famous interpretation by Lawrence Olivier views the narrative as a psychological portrait of Hamlet. Here, the neurotic Hamlet is front and center. He has an oedipal relationship with his mother, he is totally out of sync in his relationship with Ophelia (that is, he is incapable of a healthy love relationship), and he seems to have trouble with men. The ghost could represent a rekindling of his negativity or his hatred of men projected outward. Indeed, the ghost of his father is imagined. Hamlet is a troubled teenager working out growing up, but he fails (echoes of Columbine).

A more straightforward interpretation is the Zeffirelli version with Mel Gibson. Here, the injustice of regicide leads a loving son to seek revenge for his father's death. The character of Hamlet is more stable, a worthy king-in-the-making if he survives to become king. In this version, psychology takes a back seat to the plot; Hamlet must revenge his father's death. Plot becomes more important than character, the opposite of the case in the Olivier version.

A third version is Kenneth Branagh's treatment (the longest of the three). In the Branagh version, the trappings of power, the court, the castle, and the kingdom of Denmark are far more important. In this reading what is at stake for Hamlet (the crown and the kingdom) is far more central. The externalities distance the reading even further from the internal issues of the Olivier version.

The issue here is not to suggest the supremacy of one version over another, but rather to suggest that one story, "Hamlet," has yielded three very different interpretations. We could add the nostalgic Kozintsev version in which something grand was lost in the passing of the kingdom from one king, Hamlet's father, to another, Hamlet's uncle. Kozintsev is romanticizing the past and provides yet another interpretation.

Whether the director takes an internal or psychological reading, an intergenerational reading, an interfamilial reading, or a more externalized political reading, the critical point is that every good story is subject to numerous interpretations. If we shift from "Hamlet" to "Romeo and Juliet," we can further explore these perspectives in this tragic love story.

Baz Luhrmann, the latest director to retell the "Romeo and Juliet" story, moved the location and time from 16th-century Italy to 20th-century Mexico. Leonard Bernstein and company set "Romeo and Juliet" to music in modern New York in "West Side Story." In that version, the rival families of the Capulets and the Montagues become rival ethnic gangs, the Sharks and the Jets. The basics of the tragic story, two young lovers from two opposing sides, remain intact.

Other Shakespearean plays have been reimagined for modern times. Jane Smiley's *A Thousand Acres*, set in the modern Midwest, is a retelling of *King Lear*. *The Merchant of Venice* has been shifted from 16th-century Italy to Fascist Italy in the 1930s. *Julius Caesar* has also been imagined in Fascist Italy. Modern versions of *Othello* have been set in South Africa and in the West Indies. Each of these versions is making a Shakespearean plot or character relevant to today and today's audiences. What is critical is that stories about power and the quest for power, such as *Macbeth*, can be set in the Middles Ages in Scotland, for example, but they have just as much relevance to today. The themes of racism (*Othello*, *The Merchant of Venice*), aging (*King Lear*), revenge, love, hate, and envy are as vivid today as they were 400 years ago. This is one of the reasons why Shakespeare's stories lend themselves so well to varying interpretations.

Turning to other authors, the work of Jane Austen has been reconsidered for modern treatment. *Emma* became the basis for Amy Heckerling's "Clueless." Victor Hugo's *Les Misérables* was the basis for the television series "The Fugitive" and later for the Andrew Davis feature film of the same name. Dickens' *Great Expectations* received a modern treatment from Alfonso Cuaron in a film of the same name.

The story of a popular historical character of the West, Wyatt Earp, sheriff of Tombstone and Dodge City, has been given at least five different screen treatments. Perhaps the most literal was John Sturges' "Hour of the Gun" (1969). That version focused on the gunfight at the OK Corral and its aftermath. In Sturges' version, Earp was not mythologized, and the focus on his relationship with Doc Holliday was not deep. This version had a documentary-like feeling that differs powerfully from John Ford's version, "My Darling Clementine" (1947). This version depicts Earp as a Western hero fighting for justice and a way of life different from the evil family, the Clantons, who killed his young brother and stole the family cattle. Here, events have a ritualistic feeling that is both romantic and elegiac with regard to the West and its values. A third version,

Lawrence Kasdan's "Wyatt Earp" (1995), is revisionist and modern. In this iteration of the story, Earp is too human and flawed to be worthy of any mythical stature. Earp, the myth, is attacked and replaced by Earp, the man. A fourth version, George Cosmatos' "Tombstone" (1993), focuses on the power struggle between the Earps, who represent businessmen trying to get ahead, and the cowboys, under Curly Bill and Johnny Ringo, an outlaw group who rob, intimidate, and kill for power. This struggle is not ritualized; it is brutal, and it is about killing—nothing redemptive or romantic here. Finally, a fifth version, again by John Sturges, "The Gunfight at the OK Corral" (1955), focuses on friendship, in this case the relationship of Wyatt Earp and Doc Holliday. The Clantons and Curly Bill become mere backdrops, although the film culminates with the famous gunfight. Each of these versions views the main character, Wyatt Earp, differently, and each interprets the core struggle differently. One might say that each of these readings approaches the historical narrative with a different text interpretation.

The Case of Steinbeck's *East of Eden*

Good stories emanate from strong characterization and compelling plots. They also resonate with the ambitions of the writer. John Steinbeck, the author of *East of Eden*, earlier in his career wrote *The Grapes of Wrath*. In both of these novels, Steinbeck told family sagas set at particular points in U.S. history. He was also trying to say something about America. In *The Grapes of Wrath*, he linked the land and its future to the fate of its farmers, in this case the Joad family. Because of the Midwest drought and the Great Depression, the Joads were forced to abandon their family home in Oklahoma and head to California to begin a new life. Are the Joads victims of history or simply lumpen proletariats to be used up by capitalism's endless appetite for cheap labor? This question is core to *The Grapes of Wrath*, as is the centrality of the Joads as the salt of the earth, America's real strength.

East of Eden is equally vested in an east–west family saga and a religion *versus* materialism struggle. This time, the family migration is voluntary rather than a necessity. Adam Trask leaves the family farm in Connecticut, while his brother, Charles, whom he has never gotten along with, stays east. Charles has achieved material success, but in terms of personal happiness he remains unfulfilled. Adam takes his wife with him to California, but she deserts him and their twin infant sons. He raises them on a farm and becomes more interested in religious than material values. His sons, Cal and Aron, are opposites. Cal is pragmatic, and Aron, the father's favorite, is idealistic, trying to echo his father's values. Cal discovers that his mother is not dead but lives in Salinas, just over the mountain ridge. She is the leading madam in the town. In an attempt to hurt his brother, Cal introduces their mother to his saintly brother. The story ends with the disillusioned Aron being killed in Europe during World War I and Cal taking care of his father, now felled by a stroke. The goal of this three-generation family narrative was to capture the post-Civil War eagerness for material recovery as well as the deep conflict between material and spiritual values in the American character. The biblical overlay of Cain and Abel echoes through two generations—Charles and Adam, Cal and Aron. This pitting of two brothers against one another is the central conflict. The fact that in each case one brother is materialistic and the other taken with religious or spiritual values gives that conflict a deeper layer and allows the novel to explore the national, irreconcilable paradox. The story takes place near Eden (paradise), but remains outside of it, thus the title of the novel.

The film version of this story was written by playwright Paul Osborne for director Elia Kazan. That version focused on the second generation, Cal and Aron, and the events of the last 100 pages of the book. In this version, Cal is the main character and the antagonist is his father rather than Aron. The story begins when Cal finds Kate, his mother, in Salinas. The dramatic arc is Cal's struggle to secure his father's affection. To do so, he earns money in bean futures to pay for losses his father incurred when experimenting with various refrigeration processes. Cal also tries to hurt his brother by taking him to learn the truth about their mother.

By focusing on a single generation, Kazan interpreted the story as a search for the acceptance of one generation by the previous generation. This interpretation frames the story as a clash of values, not between brothers but between generations. The message is that just because Cal is different from others (Aron, Adam) does not mean he is evil. He is just different. The antagonist, Adam, equates being different with bad. Just as he had never understood his wife, Kate, he cannot seem to understand his son Cal. This is the tragedy of this version of *East of Eden*. Viewing those who are different as evil is narrow minded, and Adam's lack of openness leads to tragic consequences for him and his son Aron.

The second version of *East of Eden* was a four-hour TV movie directed by Harvey Hart. In this version, the details of the generational family saga have become the plot. The subtext of *East of Eden* as a struggle of values was set aside, and the story of Charles and Adam, Cal and Aron, and the linchpin that joins these two stories, Kate, becomes central. In fact, Kate's story is the strongest element. Biblical references are made, but the movie gives no sense that the struggle of good (Adam) *versus* evil (Kate) is effectively embedded in the Cal–Aron story. These brothers have become the victims of their narcissistic mother, Kate, and confused father, Adam. Their respective fates do not seem to be the result of any unresolved familial issues.

Recently, production of a third version of *East of Eden* was announced, with Ron Howard as its director. Will Howard go back to the Steinbeck notion of biblical archetypes, Cain and Abel, representing the two sides of the American character? Will the story be an intergenerational struggle? Will it be a female–male (Kate–Adam) struggle? Whether it represents east–west, intergenerational, or female–male conflict, what is clear is that the *East of Eden* novel lends itself to varied interpretations. To understand how to access a variety of interpretations, we must take a look at what directors consider when making their text interpretations.

Interior/Exterior

The first decision directors must make is whether to approach a story as an interior, psychological story or as an exterior story relying on a series of events out in the world. Interior stories are preoccupied by psychological aspects of their characters, such as their inner life, spiritual values, or search for deeper values or meaning. When Somerset Maugham wrote *The Razor's Edge* in 1935, he really wanted to explore the loss of meaning resulting from World War I. The main character, Larry Darrell, has survived the war but finds that he is not able to settle down, get married, and lead the good life in Chicago. He is eager to regain a sense of purpose in his life. This state leads him to Europe and then to India and back to Europe. In Paris, he encounters some of his Chicago friends, including his fiancée, now married, who has never stopped loving him. His friends do not understand him, but he now has a better understanding of himself and his friends. Without bitterness, he tries to help them. Larry survives as a deeper person and moves on in life. His friends, each in different ways, become casualties of a material life. His spiritual depth and strength help Larry to go on. *The Razor's Edge* exemplifies what I would call an internal story. Other writers whose books or plays lend themselves to interior treatments include Flaubert's *Madame Bovary*, Tolstoy's *Anna Karenina*, Nabokov's *Lolita*, Marber's "Closer," and Shepard's "Fool for Love." Directors who like to deal more with the inner life include Roberto Rossellini ("Voyage to Italy"), Luchino Visconti ("The Leopard"), and Darren Aronofsky ("Requiem for a Dream").

An alternative approach to a text reading is to focus on the exterior, the outside of things, and imply the interior. When one thinks of the exterior of things, Frederick Forsythe's *The Day of the Jackal* and Mario Puzo's *The Godfather* come to mind. Exterior readings or interpretations do not make every film look like "Jaws" or "Lawrence of Arabia," but this approach does put a premium on action with regard to characterizations and story arcs. A good example of this kind of novel is Yann Martell's *The Life of Pi*, the story of a shipwreck that leaves a boy, the main character, and a Bengal tiger together in a lifeboat. Will the boy survive, given that he is a potential source of food for the tiger? Another novel that spills over with external events is Phillip Roth's *The Human Stain*, about a black man pretending to be a Jew who is fired from a college for a racist remark to a black student.

Other works that focus on external events include Shakespeare's *Henry V*, Tolstoy's *War and Peace*, and Mel Brooks' "The Producers." Each of these works, from "The Godfather" to "The Producers," could focus primarily on the psychology of the characters or on the actions that shape the characters' behavior, or the focus could be on both. Directors who seem to have a strong sense of external events and a sense that those events push, pull, bend, and break character include Michael Mann's "The Insider," Robert Aldrich's "Attack," David Lean's "The Bridge Over the River Kwai," and Henry Hathaway's "The Lives of a Bengal Lancer." Some directors are able to emphasize external action without sacrificing interior action. John Boorman's "Point Blank" is an example of a powerful external–interior nexus. The film was remade by Brian Helgeland as "Payback," a version that strictly opts for a more exterior reading of the story and suffers accordingly when compared to the original.

Young/Old

Age has often been used to set a tone for a reading. Conventionally, youth implies enthusiasm or optimism, and old age represents regret or reflection. This is the expected reading, but using the expected in unexpected ways has long yielded fresh results. Su Friedrich uses an adolescent narrator to communicate how arrested her character is in the autobiographical film "Sink or Swim." This experimental narrative examination of a daughter/father relationship challenges the convention of expecting optimism from a "young" reading of the narrative. Similarly, numerous films, such as Martin Brest's "Going in Style," challenge the conventions of old age. This film focuses on senior citizens taking action to recapture youthful adventures and ambitions rather than being depressed about their age.

Where the issue of text reading becomes interesting is when the story is told from a different perspective. Jane Smiley's A Thousand Acres, based on King Lear but set in the modern Midwest, tells the story from the point of view of the daughter rather than the aging father, the point of view of the original. One can imagine Harper Lee's To Kill a Mockingbird told from the point of view of the father, Atticus, rather than that of his preteen daughter. Or, consider Günter Grass' novel, The Tin Drum, told from the points of view of both of Oscar's fathers rather than from the point of view of Oscar.

Whether one changes the perspective from young to old or from old to young, there is clear opportunity to make a melancholic narrative more dynamic or a youthfully exuberant narrative more contained and reflective. In either case, the opportunity to surprise the audience makes a clear case for exploring this option.

Male/Female

I have already mentioned Jane Smiley–Jocelyn Moorhouse's "A Thousand Acres" as an example of a shift in perspective; in this case, the daughters of the Lear character are the point of view rather than the father, as in the original presentation of *King Lear*. Because the male/female struggle for power is one of the most sig- nificant social/psychological/ political issues of the day (at least since the sexual revolution of the 1960s), the issue of a male or female reading of a text has taken on a far greater weight.

Although the screwball comedy (comedy of male/female role reversal) is no longer a staple of contemporary genre films, the examination of male/female roles is central to important films from all over the world. In the British film "The Full Monty," unemployed men adopt the long-standing female economic strategy of stripping to make a living. In the Japanese "Shall We Dance" (remade in the United States under the same title), an unsatisfied man takes dance lessons to awaken himself; such a strategy in the Japanese male-dominated macho culture is downright feminine. In France's "French Twist," a beautiful woman takes a lesbian lover to punish her serially unfaithful husband, who eventually returns to her. Coline Serreau, famous for her gender-bending film "Three Men and a Baby," rejoined the gender war with renewed passion in France's "Chaos." All of these films are situation comedies. "Mrs. Doubtfire" and "Tootsie" are two Hollywood examples of films that explore the gender wars.

Because power is a core issue for society and because it is fluid and impermanent, at least in terms of gender, the notion of applying a gender interpretation to a text is simply smart. Men and women do not see events and character the same way, but all want to be on the side of the angels and believe they are empathetic to the other sex. Consequently, telling a male story from a woman's point of view or a female story from a male point of view or, better yet, revealing the male and female dimensions of a main character is compelling.

Contemporary examples abound, including the Wachowski brothers' film noir "Bound," where the classic film noir, a woman's betrayal of the main character, is altered to considered whether a female character will be betrayed by her lesbian lover. The answer of course is "no"; women do not betray other women. Oliver Stone's "Alexander" examines the male and female dimensions of the great warrior king, and "Crouching Tiger, Hidden Dragon," Ang Lee's exploration of the male-dominated action–adventure genre, is utterly altered by focusing on two female main characters, one traditional and the other modern. These characters alter our experience of the superhero narrative. They also make Lee's exploration the core of the narrative (*i.e.*, modern *versus* traditional) and depict a more universal struggle; consequently, the text speaks to a wider and older audience whereas the traditional action–adventure film tends to appeal to (young) males.

Political/Sociological/Psychological

Every story has political, sociological, and psychological overtones, but the filter the director uses determines whether the audience views the narrative as an international, national, local, or personal story. It all depends on the director's choice of emphasis. We have already discussed the various ways in which "Hamlet" has been interpreted. The same choices face each storyteller. Few storytellers have been able to incorporate all three of the political, sociological, and psychological elements. Stanley Kubrick, in "Paths of Glory" and "Full Metal Jacket," comes to mind as one who has done so. More often the director must choose to focus on only one or two of the elements. Costa-Gavras chose a political perspective in "Z" and "State of Siege." Nicholas Ray chose a sociological perspective in "Rebel Without a Cause," as did Todd Haynes in "Far From Heaven." Alfred Hitchcock, on the other hand, is far more interested in a psychological perspective in "Vertigo" and "Marnie."

To illustrate the degree of change possible by adopting a different filter we need only consider how different our experience of three films would be if the director had chosen an alternative interpretation. The first example we turn to is Fernando Meirelles' "City of God" (2002). "City of God" is a classic gangster film, but the gangsters are all 10 to 16 years old. Because the story arc follows the tradition of the gangster film, we watch the rise and fall of a gangster to his death. I suggest that "City of God" is an utterly political reading of the narrative. The fact that a child has to become a gangster to survive in his poverty-drenched environment implies a damning critique of the society the child has grown up within. To change the prism for "City of God" we would need a broader community perspective that would include members of the adult population, parents as well as policemen. In order to interpret "City of God" from a psychological perspective we would need to delve deeper into the fears of the main character, the boy who becomes a photographer. We would also have to delve deeper into the psyche of the leader of the gang, the gangster who is finally killed to make room for the next boy gangster. This might mean exploring their relationships in far greater depth.

A second example is Peter Weir's "Master and Commander" (2002), which has a powerful sociological dimension. In this narrative we explore the culture of a British man o' war at sea, focusing on the roles of the officers and their men. The primary focus of the story is on Captain Jack Aubrey and the ship doctor, Stephen Maturin. Their friendship and their differences—the doctor, a reflective man of science, and the captain, a man of action and war—underpin the larger study of the community of the ship. The experience of the Weir narrative is that the film is a study of the importance of leadership in ensuring that the community, the ship, can effectively carry out its responsibility, to execute the war against the French navy. One can easily introduce the political by fleshing out what the French enemy represents; the British values are well represented. A psychological perspective, on the other hand, would require a more specific examination of the issues of death, sexuality, and relationships than is present in Weir's version. Because Aubrey and Maturin are already the prominent characters, they would be the focus of deeper development.

Finally, Wolfgang Becker's "Goodbye Lenin" (2002) deals principally with a boy's love for his mother. What is he willing to do to demonstrate that love and preserve her life? The answer is to pretend that the Berlin Wall of 1988 still exists. The film takes place in 1990, and the Berlin Wall has fallen; however, stricken by a heart attack, the boy's mother has been in a coma during the regime change. Although there is a political patina here, Becker has chosen to focus on the personal, psychological son–mother story. To make the political layer more prominent, a greater east–west perspective could be added, such as in Billy Wilder's "One Two Three" and Margarethe Von Trotta's "The Promise." To add more of a community or sociological perspective, a wider character population could be explored by factoring in elements of age, gender, and class. In "Goodbye Lenin," Becker comically blends all the characters into a similar level of adjustment after the fall of the Wall. This overall acceptance of change could be replaced by a broader scope of reactions to the changes going on in the community.

The political, sociological, and psychological perspectives are powerful interpretive filters, and each yields a different experience of the narrative.

Tone

Although tone tends to be genre specific, it is possible to reinterpret the tone for a particular purpose. What I mean by this is that Eugene O'Neill's work may be classic tragic melodrama, but that has not prevented particular directors from expanding the humor in Act I to give the tragedy of the last act more impact. Writers and directors can and do use humor and irony to shift or intensify our experience. A useful example here is the work of the Coen brothers. In most cases, the Coens use a straightforward genre approach with the expected tone. "Miller's Crossing" is as emotionally realistic as we can expect a gangster film to be. "The Man Who Wasn't There" is as expressionistic and stylized as we expect film noir to be. "Fargo" and "Raising Arizona," on the other hand, present interesting examples where humor and irony alter the genre expectation. In "Raising Arizona," a serial convict falls in love with a policewoman. All they need is a child. Failing natural means, they decide to kidnap a baby, and they do so from a business tycoon who has quintuplets. The romance, the theft, and the efforts of the tycoon to retake the baby are often cartoonish, more action–adventure than crime story. The consequences of the absurdist humor make the commoditization of the child all the more horrifying. The result is an unsettling experience as opposed to a realistic experience.

The same is true for "Fargo," which focuses on a kidnapping plot generated by a son-in-law in order to get money out of his father-in-law. His wife and son are the kidnap victims. Everything goes wrong, and the kidnap victims and the father-in-law are killed. None of this sounds very humorous as I write it, but it is. The Coen brothers approach this film as a police crime story and an investigation of family values. The police chief (a pregnant woman), her deputies, and one of the kidnappers are treated with humor. The son-in-law, the father-in-law, and one of the kidnappers are treated in a more serious, realistic manner. The dissonance between humor and seriousness, intention and outcome, is shocking and makes the experience of "Fargo" a powerful indictment of those who seem to espouse family values but whose actions undermine, indeed shred, those values operating in their lives. Altering the tone through the use of humor and irony reinterprets the narrative experience of "Raising Arizona" and "Fargo," making the films far more powerful experiences than they would have been as straight crime or police stories.

The Coen brothers used a mixed-genre approach to change the audience's experience and strengthen their voice with regard to the narrative. Directors can also use other genres that enhance, or allow writers and directors to alter, the voice. Those other genres include satire, moral fables, docudramas, experimental narratives, and non-linear films. Each of these story forms provides the director with a larger palette to strengthen their telling of the story or expand the tonal possibilities of the story. Now we will turn to the visual options available to the director.

Chapter 7

The Camera

I have titled this chapter "The Camera" rather than "Production" because the camera conjures up visual images, which are what most of this chapter is about. A more accurate description might be production, because in this chapter we discuss camera shot selection, but we also address other elements that affect the nature of a shot—light and art direction. We also briefly discuss sound, another production variable. Late in the chapter we also address the edit, as many production decisions made are intended to maintain flexibility for the edit. After the text interpretation, two production decisions are critical with regard to the material to be edited—shot selection and direction of actors. We have saved the direction of actors for the next chapter. In both production and the direction of actors, the choices made are principally driven by the director's interpretation of the text.

The Shot

The first decision a director needs to make is whether to use a long shot or a close-up, although the possible range of shots is even broader; for example, the director could use an extreme long shot. Think of the desert shots in David Lean's "Lawrence of Arabia" or the battle between the Romans and their slaves in Stanley Kubrick's "Spartacus." The extreme long shot is used to locate action and tends to be primarily informational. The long shot can include one person or many. The opening extreme long shots of Robert Wise's "West Side Story" locate the action in Manhattan, and long shots are used to introduce the Jets following the opening. These shots provide information and identify characters within the location. The long shot is used to move into and out of a scene.

The three-quarter shot, or American shot, is essentially a shot where we see three-quarters of the character. The shot was used primarily in the studio as opposed to location filming. The shot is used to follow action within the limits of the studio set built for the scene. Three-quarter shots are used less now than they were in the heyday of studio production.

The mid shot is a waist-up shot. It is often used when filming a conversation between two or more characters—in a car or in a bar, for example. The mid shot remains informational but it is more intimate than the long shot and consequently yields more emotion than longer shots do. We can think of this shot as a mix of information and emotion. Great conversation scenes include Joseph Mankiewicz's "All About Eve" and Howard Hawks' "His Girl Friday."

The next option, the close-up, is principally emotional (think of the human face). The primary use of the close-up is for dramatic emphasis. The moment Romeo sees Juliet it is time for a close-up. Close-ups were also utilized for the moment of violent death in Sam Peckinpah's "The Wild Bunch." A variation on the close-up is the extreme close-up—the missing index finger of the villain in Alfred Hitchcock's "The Thirty-Nine Steps" or the key in Cary Grant's hand in "Notorious." This shot is extremely emotional and can be used to add a great deal of dramatic emphasis.

The next variable when it comes to the shot is lens selection. A fish-eye lens distorts the faces and objects closest to it and makes people and objects in the background seem even farther away. John Frankenheimer used this distorting quality to great effect in the opening of "Seconds."

Use of a wide-angle shot requires being aware of and working with the foreground, the midground, and the background. Anthony Mann in "El Cid" and John Frankenheimer in "The Manchurian Candidate" were particularly effective at manipulating wide-angle shots. The wide-angle shot is contextual in that the background and midground provide context for the foreground. Aside from the considerable amount of visual information in such a shot, the wide-angle shot offers an opportunity to visualize conflict, or its opposite, in a single shot. Generally, characters presented the same distance from the camera are working together, while characters positioned at different distances are in effect pitted against one another.

The normal shot provides some degree of visual context but not as much as the wide-angle shot. In the normal shot, the director is working with the foreground and midground. The normal shot is the workhorse of shots and is the one most often used. It is not as elegant or interesting as the wide-angle or telephoto shot.

Finally, the telephoto shot has a single depth; the midground and background are out of focus. The telephoto shot collapses the depth of field so distances become difficult to discern. The shot of Benjamin running to the church from his failed car in Mike Nichols' "The Graduate" is an example of a telephoto shot. As there is no context in this dead-on shot it looks as if Benjamin is running but not getting anywhere. Because he does not have much time to get to the church before his former girlfriend's wedding (so he can prevent it), the sense of running yet standing still exaggerates the tension we feel for Benjamin and his goal.

Camera Placement

Another choice the director must make is where to put the camera. The options are broad, but each has a specific impact. The large questions are:

1. How close should I place the camera to the action?
2. Do I want a subjective or an objective placement?
3. How high or low should I place the camera?

Proximity

Placing the camera at a distance from the action of the characters distances us from those characters and their actions. Doing so puts the audience in the position of observers. Placing the camera very close to the action promotes intensity, intimacy, and even a some-what claustrophobic relationship with the characters and action. In the films of Steven Spielberg and Alfred Hitchcock, the camera is placed close to the action so the audience can identify with the characters. Roman Polanski, in "Tess" and in "Repulsion," crowds the characters with the camera. The camera is all but on top of the characters. Such placement generates intensity, anxiety, and iden-tification. Placing the camera somewhere between at a distance from the action and up close to it puts the camera in a neutral posi-tion where it can be used to record action but does not particularly create intensity. There is no question about who the story is focused on. The more neutral position is where most directors place the camera.

Objectivity

An objective camera position places the audience in a position to watch the action. There is no clear choice of sides being made, no single point of view presented. The objective camera placement consequently distances the audience from the action and at least initially neutralizes the potential for intensity. A director chooses the objective camera position to provide information about what is going on without choosing a distinct point of view or taking sides.

Subjective Camera Placement

More often directors choose sides and vest our emotions in one character over another. This means using a subjective camera placement. As already mentioned, Spielberg, Hitchcock, and Polanski have used the subjective camera placement to establish identification and, in the case of Polanski, a sense of the inner feelings of the character, which are vital to building the audience's relationship with the story. Other examples where subjective placement of the camera is crucial to how we experience the sequence would be the sniper sequence in Stanley Kubrick's "Full Metal Jacket," Reuben Mamoulian's "Dr. Jekyll and Mr. Hyde," and Robert Montgomery's "Lady in the Lake." In the latter two films, the directors positioned the camera as if it were a main character; in fact, this strategy was followed throughout "Lady in the Lake."

Camera Height

There are essentially three camera positions that represent the extreme options in terms of height. Of course, directors can and do choose options somewhere in between the extremes. The first extreme is a low camera position. Using such a camera position, the viewer looks up at the actors and the action in the shot. This "heroic" placement is a favorite in action–adventure, science fiction, and Western films. The second option is high placement. Extremely high-angle shots might be from the top of a spire or palace. Shekhar Kapur in his film "Elizabeth" used high camera placement to provide an omniscient view of the action. This type of shot can be used to chart the quest for power of those who covet power, or it can simply put mere mortals in their place. More often a high-angle shot looking down on a character is used to signify the loss of power, or enslavement. Stanley Kubrick used low-angle as well as high-angle placements to characterize the power relationships in "Spartacus," an epic about a slave revolt against Rome. Stories that require a sense of enclosure or entrapment (*e.g.*, film noir such as Billy Wilder's "Double Indemnity") will use high camera placements as often as possible. The third option is the eye-line camera placement. This is the most natural and democratic of camera placements. It is also the camera placement most often used by directors. Power implications are not the only rationale for camera placements. Many times a camera will be placed in a particular position to allow a longer take while following the action. Although there is a lesser dramatic benefit to such placements, the economic benefit of shooting the film within budget expectations can more than compensate for the dramatic limitations of the shot.

Camera Movement

Generally speaking, camera movement is one of the most exciting choices available to the director. Movement is dynamic and energizing, but the choices the director makes can make the resulting energy more purposeful, or at least they should. The most significant choice the director faces is whether the movement should be stabilized by putting the camera on a tripod or whether the obvious movement of a handheld camera is preferable. If a sense of stability is needed, a tripod-mounted camera is preferable. If a sense of immediacy, of being there is crucial, then the handheld camera can be used to provide a sensation of watching news footage by virtue of its slight to moderate tremor. For example, footage of a bomb going off shot with a handheld camera will capture the photographer's sudden jerk in response to the bomb and will serve to place the audience closer to the action.

A variation of the handheld shot is the use of a steadicam (a gyroscopic offset to smooth out the jiggle) to record the shot. The steadicam glide made famous in walking shots in Brian De Palma's "The Bonfire of the Vanities" and Martin Scorsese's "Goodfellas" seem elegant and artificial, and they move us away from the immediacy of the handheld shot, providing elegance and style over dramatic gravitas.

One additional point should be made about the handheld shot. Certain film movements, such as Cinéma Vérité, New Wave, and

Dogme 95, have maintained the handheld shot as a central tenet of their cinematic goals; for example, Thomas Vinterberg's "The Celebration" was shot entirely using handheld cameras. On the other hand, most feature films around the world are photographed using cameras mounted on tripods.

Movement from a Fixed Point

Camera movement from a fixed point takes three forms: tilt, pan, or zoom. The tilt shot is a vertical movement, up–down or down–up. Generally, the tilt shot is used to follow action or to transition from one location to another. The tilt shot can also simulate the eye movement of a character as that character looks up or down. The tilt shot is rarely used for dramatic emphasis.

The pan, or panning, shot follows movement along a horizontal axis, left to right or right to left. As in the case of the tilt, the pan follows action or simulates eye movement. In both the tilt and the pan, the camera is on a tripod, which remains stationary. The camera pivots are guided by the hand of the skilled camera operator; consequently, the movement tends to be smooth. More rapid movement can be used, but the visual information in the shot tends to blur. The more rapid the movement, the lower the actual visual information and the greater the blur. The illusion of movement is all that results when the cameraman uses a swish pan, a very rapid movement. This shot has been used as a transition from one location to another. It has also been used to simulate the excitement within a scene. Richard Lester used numerous swish pans in the performance sequence that concludes his "A Hard Day's Night." The excitement of the audience for The Beatles is emphasized by the use of swish pans.

The zoom shot relies on a lens that can be moved from a wide-angle shot to telephoto or the reverse. In both cases, the zoom is used to avoid cutting from a long shot to a close-up. Aside from the economic benefit of one setup instead of two, numerous directors from Visconti to Altman, from Kubrick to Peckinpah have used the zoom shot to lengthen a shot. Each had an aesthetic goal. In Kubrick's case (for example, in "Barry Lyndon"), he wanted to slow down our sense of time. "Barry Lyndon" is a film about an 18th-century character made by a 20th-century filmmaker aware that slowing down the film by using zooms will slow down the experience of the film. It may even transport the audience into a sense of the 18th century, at least in terms of time.

Movement from Movement

To move the camera physically, thereby capturing movement while the camera is moving, often requires that a track be built so the movement is smooth. The mounted camera is then moved along the track. Such tracks can be quite elaborate, such as the one used to film an attack on a train in David Lean's "Lawrence of Arabia." Another means of recording movement is to put the camera on a truck or car. A truck with a hoist will give the camera lateral as well as vertical mobility. Orson Welles used just such a trucking setup for the famous three-minute shot that opens "Touch of Evil." Other devices can be as simple as a car, or even a wheelchair. In each case, the technical operation of the car or truck or trestle smooths the camera movement.

Numerous directors have made the moving shot their signature shot. Alfred Hitchcock, Fred Murnau, Max Ophuls, Stanley Kubrick, Luchino Visconti, and Steven Spielberg each has helped define the aesthetic parameters of the moving shot. There are two camps in the use of the moving shot: those who use the shot objectively (e.g., as a means to avoid later editing) and those who use the shot subjectively to enhance identification. One of the most famous objective camera motion shots is the car accident sequence in Jean-Luc Godard's "Weekend." The camera simply records the traffic jam caused by the accident and finally after about five minutes of traffic the camera comes upon the victims. There are no close-ups here, only the objectively rendered traffic jam and accident. Objective movement is also often used to give an overview of a scene. The Omaha Beach D-Day battle scene in Spielberg's "Saving Private Ryan" is an example of this type of movement.

Subjective motion shots, on the other hand, lend a scene intensity and dramatic tension. Whether the movement simulates the point of view of Dr. Jekyll in Reuben Mamoulian's "Dr. Jekyll and Mr. Hyde" or whether it precedes a running Cary Grant as a biplane in the background tries to kill him in Alfred Hitchcock's "North by Northwest," the goal of each shot is to put the audience in the position of the character. Subjective camera movement is perhaps the most powerful tool a director can use to link screen characters and the audience. Motion promotes energy, identification, and excitement. It is no wonder that subjective camera movement is the core shot of thrillers and horror films, two genres where victimization of a character is the core narrative goal.

Lighting

Of the various components of a shot that add to the overall character of the shot, the most critical is lighting. What does a director have to know about lighting? The best cinematographers are well acquainted with lighting issues. In fact, the director should have both "macro" and "micro" ideas about the mood he is looking for in his film.

At the macro level, the decision is essentially natural *versus* dramatic. Film stock, lab instructions, and lighting design decisions can all emanate from this directorial notion about the film. With the dramatic approach, it is important to decide on a romantic tone in the narrative when characters move toward successful achievement of their goal or on an expressionistic tone when outcomes are in question or are darker. An example will illustrate the point. Although Pedro Almodovar's "Talk to Her" is a dark tale about difficult male–female relationships (the women in the two relationships are both in a coma), the filmmaker is really interested in how characters can help each other overcome difficulty, even tragedy, in relationships. Consequently, Almodovar used a bright light to lighten the heaviness of the narrative and to foreshadow a positive outcome. Mike Leigh used a similar lighting strategy to warm up "Vera Drake," a 1950s abortion story; one can imagine how much more uptight a naturalistic or cooler lighting design might have made the experience of this film. On the other hand, the option of natural lighting can yield a documentary realism to a film, such as Joshua Marston's "Maria Full of Grace." This story about a Colombian woman who becomes a "mule" (someone who smuggles heroin into the United States) benefits from the realism of the lighting.

On a micro level lighting can characterize and can foreshadow intention; it can be used to soften or toughen the audience's response to a character or situation. Anthony Mann, a director who worked with the cinematographer John Alton in the late 1940s, liked to use high key light in films such as "T-Men." These stories about gangsters and the police who pursued them benefited from a highly dramatic lighting design.

Lighting can be used to focus on victims and victimizers long before the narrative acknowledges the fate of these characters. Mann is, in fact, part of a tradition of directors who are interested in the psychological complexity light can lend to their characters. Joseph Von Sternberg was interested in using lighting to create a sexual aura around his characters. Michael Mann, on the other hand, used lighting to either question or confirm the honesty of his characters in "Thief" and "Collateral." William Wyler used lighting to reflect the power or powerlessness of his characters in "The Little Foxes." Directors who are interested in using lighting for a particular purpose need to be as specific as they can be when setting guidelines for interpretation of characters and the narrative. In this sense, lighting can be a very important tool for executing the director's idea.

Art Direction

After lighting, art direction is the most critical area that supports the director's idea as it plays out shot after shot. Art direction refers to the nature and organization of all the physical content of the shot. This includes the artifacts in the shot, their organization, and the look of the room that holds the contents, down to the color of the walls. Art direction also refers to the costumes of the actors. All of these elements contribute not only to the veracity of a shot but also to the mood conjured up in the shot.

Yann Samuell's "Love Me If You Dare" is a bold interpretation of a male–female relationship over the 30 years of their relationship. The two characters, who meet as preadolescents, see life and their relationship as a game between only the two of them; consequently, there is a constant sense of provocation, desire, and exclusivity. The film is almost operatic in the mood swings it portrays. The art direction had to reflect all of these moods, which it did through the use of bold colors that are extreme and unnatural.

Jean-Pierre Jeunet's work in "Delicatessen" and "City of Lost Children" is a tribute to the power of art direction. These post-apocalyptic fables are frightening and exciting as they capture an imaginative world where humans have either come to their end or in the darkness have found a new beginning.

Samuell and Jeunet represent one extreme in the use of art direction. At the opposite end of the spectrum is the realist option. Lynne Ramsay's "Ratcatcher," a portrait of hellish poverty in 1970s Glasgow, emphasizes the harshness of poverty and the entrapment it represents, particularly for the young main character. Life is a drab gray-blue, except for accidental color or the color of a new suburban home that is too elusive for the main character and his family; otherwise, flatness, grays, and blues pervade the objects, the rooms, and the life of the main character.

Of course, most directors choose an art direction strategy somewhere in between Jeunet and Ramsay, but the more defined and specific the art direction strategy, the more powerful the nonverbal impact of the director's film. Consider the ennobling sense of the land and the people in Walter Salles' "The Motorcycle Diaries" or the flat television sitcom look of Los Angeles in David Russell's "I Heart Huckabees," a perfect metaphor for the existentially despairing main character. The key here is that the director must have an idea of his narrative goal. From that point, the look of the environments and the appearance of the characters contribute to the nonverbal expression of the character's idea. When directors ignore art direction, they deny the audience the richly layered narrative experience they deserve.

Sound

Sound is a production and post-production consideration. Although many of the creative sound decisions are generated in post-production, it is nevertheless important for the director to be aware of how sound can further the director's idea. As in the case of light and art direction, it is useful to think of sound on a natural *versus* dramatic continuum. Sound in the first case is used to support the recognizability and veracity of the characters and settings. At the dramatic end of the spectrum, sound is used to deepen the emotions surrounding a narrative event or character.

To elaborate what sound is, consider the three broad categories of voice, sound effects, and music. Pitch, amplitude, and the juxta-position of sounds will all impact the feelings of the audience. Also, consider that sound works with the visual images to affect how the audience processes their experience; consequently, sound is critical to the audience's interpretation of the events in the film. Sound can define or alter meaning but above all leads us to meaning when compared to the visual.

The greatest proponent of the importance of sound over the last 30 years has been Walter Murch. His sound work with Francis Ford Coppola on "The Conversation" and "Apocalypse Now" is classic in its focus on the complex, creative deployment of sound. More recently, Murch was the editor on Anthony Minghella's "The English Patient" and "Cold Mountain" (2003), and the sound in each of these films is as impressive as his earlier work with Francis Ford Coppola. Other directors who have employed sound to great effect include Christopher Nolan in "Memento" and "Insomnia," Krystof Kieslowski in "Red," and Danny Boyle in "Trainspotting." Sound, whether deployed naturalistically or dramatically, can pow-erfully highlight the director's idea.

The Edit

Directors must keep in mind that the shots they orchestrate in production must give the editor the material necessary to execute the director's idea. That means producing adequate coverage to make sure the film can be edited, in addition to shots that provide the performances and elements additional to the performances that contribute to the director's idea. Key to achieving that idea are ten important editing ideas, which are addressed in the following discussion.

Continuity
The issue of editing for continuity can be addressed by having several ideas operational during the production. Whenever a new location is introduced, a location shot (generally a long or extreme

long shot) should be taken. This master shot will provide general coverage for anything more specific that happens within the scene. Within the scene, the director should film mid shots and close-ups of the actors and dialogue that are important in the scene. Reaction shots should be filmed as separate shots even if they have already been recorded in a mid shot of two or more characters. This variety of shots will ensure match cutting of the long shots with mid shots or close-ups is achievable. Continuity also requires a respect for the use of screen direction within shots. When the director is filming a chase scene where one character is moving from left to right, then shots of the character who is chasing this character must also be filmed using a left-to-right movement. Screen direction has to be consistent, whether filming long shots or close-ups. Alternatively, when two characters will meet each other in a scene, the first character could be filmed moving from left to right, for example, and the second character could be filmed moving from right to left, implying that these two characters are eventually going to meet.

Clarity

Stories can be confusing. It is the director's job to provide those crucial shots that keep the story progression clear. Think of complex narratives such as Fred Zinnemann's "The Day of the Jackal" and Robert Zemeckis' "Back to the Future." Two principles can help maintain the clarity of a narrative, the first of which is point of view. When a director provides a clear point of view throughout a scene, the audience will know how to interpret that scene. Think of all of those gunfights in Serge Leoni's Westerns! In "Once Upon a Time in the West," we are constantly put in the position of Charles Bronson's character, who is facing Jack Elam and friends. From Bronson's foreground point of view, we see Elam and colleagues in the background of the deep-focus shot. In the next shot, the point of view is Elam's, or his holster, and in the background Bronson's character awaits his fate. A clear point of view helps the audience move through a scene without confusion. A second principle that promotes clarity is the use of specific shots that tell us the true nature of a scene. The clock close-up in Zinnemann's "High Noon" tells us that time is critical to the fate of our main character. The close-up of the missing index finger tells us we are in the presence of the antagonist in Alfred Hitchcock's "The Thirty-Nine Steps."

The shot of what the James Stewart character sees when he looks down from great heights (an unstable sense of the ground—it seems to move) is all we need to understand the character's fear of heights, a state central to the plot of Hitchcock's "Vertigo." The key here is planning specific shots that help keep the motivation, plot, and character clear.

Dramatic Emphasis

Dramatic emphasis can be achieved in a number of ways. The most obvious is to use a close-up rather than a mid or long shot. The close-up has the greatest emotional impact, a core notion for dramatic impact. A second strategy to suggest dramatic emphasis is to move the camera closer to the action of the scene—the closer to the action, the more intense our response to the content of the scene. An alternative strategy here is to consider the shift from objective to subjective placement or the reverse. Such a change will get the audience's attention. A fourth strategy, if shots have been static, is to shift to moving shots or *vice versa*; in this way, the audience will be alerted to changes in the scene. Finally, dramatic emphasis can be achieved by changing the pace of a scene. When the pace has been slow and deliberate, a shift to a faster pace can cue in the audience that what they are now seeing is more important to the narrative than the shots that preceded it.

New Ideas

New ideas are introduced in a scene by the use of cutaways. Cutaways can be used to foreshadow what is to come, to introduce a new character into the story, or to introduce a new possibility into a character's life. Think of the shot of a hatted Andie McDowell in "Four Weddings and a Funeral" or the first murderous dream of the Annette Bening character in Neil Jordan's "In Dreams." In both cases, a new person or new reality is being introduced in the narrative. The cutaway is a classic shot that introduces new ideas into the narrative.

Parallel Action

The use of parallel action has been around as an editing idea since Porter and Griffith—over a hundred years. The best way to explain it is to suggest that separate strands of a narrative will eventually come together. Think of Yuri and Lara in David Lean's "Doctor Zhivago" and the outlaw gang known as the Wild Bunch and the vigilantes who are hunting them down in Sam Peckinpah's "The Wild Bunch." To provide some hint that these disparate characters will come together, some directors use screen direction and others use specific actions. Whatever the strategy adopted, the director must have specific ideas regarding how the audience should feel about the two parties' eventually meeting. Clearly, we want Yuri and Lara to meet, as they are soul mates who represent a romantic ideal in a time and place that had no tolerance for love; however, the feelings evoked with regard to the Wild Bunch and their pursuers are different. Tension and the potential violence that will ensue are the directorial motifs for the Wild Bunch and the vigilantes. Peckinpah nevertheless imbued the Wild Bunch with a sense of friendship absent from the vigilantes. In this sense, he created nobles among the savages, relegating the law-supported vigilantes to savages, an ethos appropriate to the deadly romanticism that roams through "The Wild Bunch."

Emotional Guidelines

The edit of a film is the emotional guideline of a film. A director forgets this at his peril. The director must encourage modulated performances and provide the juxtapositions and compositions necessary to create the context for how the audience should feel. Ridley Scott in "Gladiator" particularly understood this requirement. Maximus may be the general of all the Roman legions but he is also a husband and a father, roles critical to his identity. Those roles motivate his actions throughout the film, even his actions to kill Commodus, his emperor.

Tone

The tone of a film is critical to the emotional character and credibility just mentioned. Tone can be genre specific or it can challenge the genre. Whichever stance, tone is all about specific images. The baptism in the Coen brothers' "O Brother, Where Art Thou" and the shattering of glass in Volker Schlondorff's "The Tin Drum" both go the heart of the narrative—the religiosity of the American character in the Coen brothers' film and the arch response of Oscar, the main character, to the rise of Nazism in Schlondorff's film (his response is, in fact, a primal scream). Tone is all about the specific images that create the romanticism or terror so central to the narrative. As is so often the case in literature, metaphor can make a point more powerfully than can more obvious shots. This is why directors such as the Coen brothers and Schlondorff so often utilize it.

The Main Character

It is important for the director to realize that the audience experiences the narrative through a main character. That means the director must decide how he wants us to feel about that character. It may be ambivalence—such as for George Clooney's character in "O Brother, Where Art Thou"—or it may be understanding and compassion—such as for the two main characters in Alexander Payne's "Sideways." In both cases, the characters are mischievous, manipulative, mopey, even dopey, but in each case the director has moved us toward a very different relationship with the main character. What if a choice is not made? Films for which this is the case include Michael Winner's "Lawman" or Michael Anderson's "Force 10 to Navarone." In neither film is the audience able to establish an emotional relationship with the main character, and the result is indifference to the screen story. For an audience to be fully engaged in a director's film, understanding or even loving the main character is key.

Conflict

Drama is conflict; without conflict, an audience is put in the detached position of observing rather than becoming involved; consequently, a director must be mindful of providing sources of conflict in the story. This sense of conflict can be generated between characters or between characters and the environment. Conflict goes to the heart of the dramatization of the director's story.

Story Form

Finally, shooting with a distinct sense of genre is important to the final edit. Every story form has a particular character who serves as a signpost for the audience. The stylized quality of film noir, the romanticism of the Western, the dark expressionism that chokes off hope in the horror film—all of these characteristics identify and breathe life into a film. By understanding story forms, the director can provide signposts of the chosen genre for the audience. I am not suggesting that these signposts are the be all and end all of story form. Directors such as the Coen brothers and Stanley Kubrick elaborate, push, and pull the story form. These directors work with the baselines but are not constrained by them. When the director understands and works with these baselines, the director's idea can be fully realized during the edit of the film.

Now, on to working with the actors.

Chapter 8

The Actor

This chapter is all about the relationship of the director with the actor. Because the actor is the most direct expression of the director's idea, it is critical that the director understand the actor as well as the critical synergistic relationship of the director and the actor. An analogy that is appropriate here is the therapist–patient relationship. I do not mean this in the sense of a confessional relationship but rather a creative one. When it works, the therapist and the patient together create a pathway to a "new" person who is more actualized and more present in the world. In this sense, a good director and his actor create a pathway (*i.e.*, performance) to a new person—the character in the film. That character will bring alive the narrative and create yet another relationship—with the audience. These creative, compelling relationships are what audiences seek. It is the reason why good actors are so well paid, and it is the reason why directors who do not use actors to their fullest potential are less well paid. I would like to add that actors are the frontline in a production. They take the greatest personal risk, and their courage deserves the audience's respect and, dare I say it, love. They are an important partner in the creation of a film and in deployment of the director's idea.

Casting

Many directors believe that "cast right and half of your job as a director is accomplished." The statement at best is a half-truth. In this era of star-making projects, the politics of finance as often as a director's vision dictate casting. The rise of powerful agents and casting directors have moved the pendulum in the direction of political rather than creative casting. My comments that follow are only relevant to creative casting (let me just say that directors must continue to fight to maintain their vision of the characters in their films).

Casting is the first expression of the director's idea before production begins—all the more reason why the director at this pre-production stage must have a clear director's idea, which, at this stage, is based on an interpretation of the script. The casting process is first and foremost about the look of an actor. Whether or not the actor physically conforms to the director's vision of the character is less important than a checklist about the qualities, both physical and behavioral, the actor projects. I would suggest that at this first meeting between the director and an actor and the reading that will follow that the director keep a list of criteria by which to assess the actor, such as:

1. Professionalism
2. Level of tension the actor brings to the situation
3. Energy
4. Charisma
5. Sexuality

Hold onto the notion that the director should apply these same criteria to the actor's subsequent reading and to the actor's readings with other actors.

First, we will address the issue of professionalism. By professionalism, I mean showing up on time and responding to the interview in a professional manner. The actor is there to be hired for a role, and the director is there to hire an actor. When the meeting strays in any fashion from achieving these two goals, then the director and the actor are in unprofessional territory.

The second issue is the level of tension the actor brings to the situation. When personality, desire, and opportunity mix, tension should result. How much tension is the actor able to produce? How is the actor managing and expressing that tension? Tension can become energy. As a director, I would be concerned if the actor is not able to produce the necessary tension. I would also be concerned if the actor's coping strategy exceeded my expectations, given the circumstances (*i.e.*, auditioning). Key here is that tension is expected and can be useful to the actor.

The third issue is energy. Good actors know that no matter the type of film the essential result is energy. Happiness, sadness, anger, wit, and charm are all part of an energy field. Does the actor generate that energy field or do they instead absorb the energy around them? Perhaps the reader is beginning to think that directors must have a psychology degree to cast. It is not necessary, but having a feel for people, understanding them and what makes them tick as human beings, helps.

The fourth issue is charisma, which is a form of energy, but it links to something more specific—belief, intense, aggressively held, and operational belief. It seems as if the actor wants the audience to join in his or her belief. This belief is so strong that it is inspirational, energetic . . . charismatic. Charismatic actors have extraordinary attraction, or pull. Does your actor have it?

Finally, sexuality. Every good actor knows that his or her film performance is on one level a seduction; in order to draw in the audience, the actor has to be seductive. Does this particular actor have that kind of magnetism? Is this actor attracting you, the director?

This checklist allows the director to determine whether a particular actor conforms to the director's vision of the character. Often actors do not quite look the part but may bring something else to a role.

The second phase of the casting session—the reading by the actor—also should be filtered through the five points discussed above, although the reading itself has additional facets. The "through line" becomes the measure. What interpretation of the character is the actor aiming for? Does the interpretation conform to that of the director, or is it different? How is it different? How has the interpretation been built? Has the actor made a conscious effort to construct the through line? Is there charm? Is there energy? Is there belief? Does the actor want to please or displease? These are all issues that arise during an interpretation. Whether the character is stupid or brilliant, aware or unaware, the director must be able to see how the actor is building the interpretation and evoking feelings for the character such that the director knows that a connection has been made and the performance is developing.

If the interpretation differs from that of the director, then the question becomes one of how interesting the actor's interpretation is. If it has captured the director's attention, then there is obviously something there worth pursuing. The actor may be the right age and have the right look but undermine everything in the reading. For the director, the reading essentially reveals whether the actor has an empathy for the character and whether the actor's interpretation has created something new. Finally, every actor wants a role, so desire and energy are going to be givens in the audition. The director's job is to decide, using the five criteria, whether or not the actor has been seductive enough in his or her reading and interpretation of the character.

A second-level skill test in the reading is to pose the challenge of giving a different reading. Some directors will suggest an extreme situation—your mother has just died, you have just received a diagnosis of pancreatic cancer—and ask the actor to read the scene again. The goal here is to test the flexibility of the actor. Can the actor give more than one reading? This exercise gives the director a sense of the actor's range. Good actors will be able to give a wide range of interpretations—funny, sad, tragic. Such a challenge serves as a warm-up for the role. The actor's flexibility is reflected in his or her interpretation of the character, which might differ from the director's interpretation of the character. How interesting is the difference, and how stimulating is the person's range as an actor?

The third layer of the casting process, which may or may not be a separate session, is to have the actor read the part with another actor, another character. The same five criteria can be used to assess this reading. Is there a chemistry between the characters? If so, what is the nature of that chemistry? Do the actors connect or compete with each other? Competition is not necessarily bad; often it can be quite useful. This reading and subsequent readings with multiple actors can reveal whether or not the actor can sustain a connection with an audience. Does the actor command the audience's attention? Energy, charisma, and sexuality all work together to keep the audience—and the director—engaged.

The Character Arc

Characters all have particular physical and behavioral qualities. Beyond these qualities, deeper into a character's psyche, is what can best be described as the character's core. This core affects the narrative goal through its mix of desires and inhibitions. This "character lava" is what makes the character pulsate with life and above all credibility. It is important for the director and the actor to create a character arc and maintain it throughout the film. A main character must have the capacity to transform and indeed must undergo an actual transformation during the film. (More on this in a moment.) Secondary characters will have significant interactions with the main character that may help or harm the main character. What is critical is that these secondary characters are passionate enough in their goals that they bring about change in the main character. This is their arc in the narrative. Let's look at this process more specifically.

Let's start with the capacity to transform. In most films, we are presented with a situation that forces the main character to adapt. When a daughter is kidnapped by Indians in Ron Howard's "The Missing," what will the main character, the mother, do? A second example is "Spiderman 2." Spiderman is so busy keeping the peace that the love of his life leaves him for someone else. What will Spiderman do? The audience must believe that the mother in "The Missing" and Spiderman in "Spiderman 2" are capable of change. Something about each character has to be in sufficient flux that we believe each will act.

The next question is how does a character transform? Or, to put it another way, what propels a character along the character arc? From a narrative point of view, one of two story elements moves the main character to change. The first element is relationships. Think of Juliette Lewis' character, who was the catalyst for change in Johnny Depp's character in Lasse Hallström's "What's Eating Gilbert Grape?" The second element is plot. Plot applies pressure to the goal of the main character. Think of the decision made by Michael (played by Dustin Hoffman) to pretend he is a female actress in Sydney Pollack's "Tootsie." Michael, a failed actor, becomes an overnight star in a television soap, but as his career soars his impersonation of a woman modifies his male tendencies to lie and manipulate. As he puts it at the end, being a woman was the best part of the person Michael has become.

Main characters are always transformed, and their character arc forms the emotional spine of the film. Secondary characters can also change, but their transformations are in the service of the main character. Think of the confession made by Charlie (Rod Steiger) to his brother in the car ride in Elia Kazan's "On the Waterfront." Throughout the narrative, to satisfy his mob boss, Charlie has continually manipulated his brother Terry (Marlon Brando). Now trying to manipulate Terry one last time, Charlie realizes how much he has harmed his brother. He decides against the ultimate intimidation, Terry's murder, and opts to let his brother live, although it will mean death for Charlie. This sacrifice is Charlie's transformation, his single act of brotherly love. Because Charlie's death will prompt Terry to testify against the mob, Charlie's action (and relationship) has transformed Terry as much as his other significant relationship with Edie (Eva Marie Saint). The character arc of secondary characters has to be in the service of the main character.

Actors have to understand the emotional spine that is the character arc in order to build their performance. Directors need to understand the character arc because for them the character arc is the road map for a performance.

An Aside about Actors as Directors

Understanding the character arc is one of the reasons why actors have made good directors. Although undervalued, there is a tradition of actors becoming directors. The tradition goes all the way back to Charlie Chaplin and Buster Keaton, who in a sense became great directors who were as well known as directors as they were actors. Although Jerry Lewis and Woody Allen are the most obvious directors whose character persona on screen was reflected by their work as directors, many actors have chosen different genres in which to develop their directorial skills. Charles Laughton, for example, chose to direct a nightmarish fable, "The Night of the Hunter." Marlon Brando chose to direct a Western, "One-Eyed Jacks." Both films are powerful, evocative experiences.

More often, however, actors tend to work closer to familiar territory. Dick Powell opted for terse thrillers and war films, such as "The Enemy Below." Lawrence Olivier favored Shakespeare and directed "Henry V" and "Hamlet." Powell and Olivier proved audacious within their familiar territory. Veering away from familiar territory can result in underappreciation and underfunding. Both Ida Lupino ("The Burglar") and John Cassavetes ("Shadows") developed underground reputations as directors, but their projects proved difficult to finance and neither actor could sustain a career as a director.

This situation has changed considerably in the past 25 years. The biggest stars have become important directors. Warren Beatty made "Heaven Can't Wait" and "Reds." Robert Redford made "Ordinary People." Clint Eastwood directed "Unforgiven" and "Mystic River." Mel Gibson directed "Braveheart" and "The Passion of the Christ." Actors Robert De Niro, Ben Stiller, Diane Keaton, Jack Nicholson,

Sean Penn, and Angelica Huston have all directed films, and the trend will only continue to grow. It must not be forgotten that Elia Kazan and Mike Nichols began their careers as performers and both went on to exceptional careers as directors. Understanding that characters change, how they change, and who they become (in essence, the character arc) is an advantage for actors who become directors. The philosophies of acting they use might differ, but the end result is the same—a living, lively, engaging portrayal of a character that grips the audience. We turn now to those philosophies of acting that actors use and directors should understand.

Philosophies of Acting

Philosophies of acting have generally arisen from theater performance rather than film or the media. Ideas about acting revolutionized by a Russian, Konstantin Stanislavsky, have been adapted in, for example, Great Britain, France, Germany, and the United States. Before discussing these ideas, however, it must be noted that their underpinnings are the 19th- and 20th-century advances made in our understanding of human behavior, principally cognitive psychology and psychoanalysis, fields that are concerned with the skin and subcutaneous layers of human behavior. These ideas quickly made their way into literature, the visual arts, design, and theater. It is not surprising that the contradictions and conflicts inherent to the outer and inner lives of a character became the focus of first playwrights, then directors and acting coaches. For each, the instrument that illustrated the conflict was the actor. How to bring the actor into a state of immediacy became the focus of ideas about acting for the next hundred years. It remains the focus today.

In order to understand the philosophies of acting that prevail today it is important to go to the source, Konstantin Stanislavsky, the Russian director and theoretician of acting. His work on the interpretation of the Russian playwright Anton Chekhov crystallized his ideas about acting. Today's ideas about acting differ only in their emphasis. (A good elaboration of these ideas is David Richard Jones' *Great Directors at Work*, University of California Press, 1986.) Stanislavsky felt that acting should be directed toward uncovering or revealing certain universals: the human spirit, or nature, and above all truth. Stanislavsky's examination of acting attempted to method-ize the finding of truth. For Stanislavsky, truth was three things (see *Great Directors at Work*, p. 32):

1. Verisimilitude, which corresponds to what is observable in the world (the outer world)
2. Coherence, an assessment device that is in essence one's sys-tem of belief (equivalent to a character's subjectivity, or the inner world)
3. The spiritual meaning of life, referring to the notion that spir-ituality coexists with material values in a dimension where reality and spirituality complement one another

Together, these three dimensions are symbiotic and help the actor create a truthful character on stage. According to Stanislavsky,

> "What does it mean to be truthful on stage? Does it mean that you conduct yourself as you do in ordinary life? Not at all. Truthfulness in those terms would be sheer triviality. There is the same difference between artistic and inartistic truth as exists between a painting and a photograph; the latter reproduces everything, the former only what is essen-tial" (K. Stanislavsky, *Stanislavsky's Legacy*, edited by E.R. Hapgood, Theater Arts Books, 1968, p. 20).

All of the acting philosophies of the past hundred years have arisen out of these three ideas about acting. Let's get specific.

Outside In

There is an informal school of acting that coalesces around actors such as Lawrence Olivier. Proponents believe that technique begins with the outside, what Stanislavsky called verisimilitude. If the actor wears the clothes of his character, adopts his manner of walking, and has his hair cut as that character would, then that actor can begin to work with that exterior to become the character. Other British actors such as Michael Caine and Anthony Hopkins have found this approach meaningful.

Inside Out

Here, observation is the key to preparing to develop a character. The approach of acting from the inside out (what Stanislavsky called coherence) has become the *modus operandi* for most schools of acting. Strategies that connect an actor to his inner life, including possible emotional memories associated with particular experiences, provide the material necessary to understand and develop the character. Improvisation, sense memory, and articulating inner experiences and feelings with physical outward expressiveness are the mechanical means of bringing out the inner "cohesiveness" to create a character.

113

The American School

The American School of acting arose out of the Group Theater in the 1930s and was very much influenced by Stanislavsky. American School acting teachers created the famous "method" style of acting, but within the school some acting teachers focused on memory — specifically, to readers of this book, the recall of feelings associated with specific events in their lives. These memories were the basis for creating an actor's character, both behaviorally and physically. As in the work of Stanislavsky, the character should have a goal but it need not be searching for the truth, although authenticity in the creation of the character would be a form of truth.

Stella Adler emphasized imagination. Adler promoted the use of memories, feelings, impulses, and observations to create something else — a character. Improvisation is an important tool for directly accessing unconscious material that can be used to create a character.

Sanford Meisner focused on repetition to create an immediate "in the moment" experience. Putting an emphasis on what is going on here and now and focusing on the people, places, and total environment can help create an immediacy by virtue of the audience's reaction to the people and places. The surprise this behavior ellicits invites spontaneous reaction. Energy, surprise, and a particular reality are created before our eyes. This acting style is perhaps the most active because it eschews reflection, while the styles of Adler and Lee Strasberg focus on a character who is in relative terms more developmental.

The European School

The European school of acting was not really a reaction to the American acting style; rather, it was fueled by a passion for new experiences that are more startling, even shocking. The kind of experimentation associated with Antonin Artaud and Jerzy Grotowski and most powerfully with Peter Brook is most aligned to the third Stanislavsky requisite in performance—the spiritual one. The work is focused on visceral expressions and reactions to the material world (realism). Indeed, directors such as Brook are totally disinterested in realism. Madness, religiosity, uninhibited cruelty, the craving for power, transcendence—all of these states were of great interest to Brook. Here is where an actor's performance should be pitched. A character's inner life and the outer world may exist but they are unimportant with regard to creating that character. Greater forces in the world require a style of performance (behavior) that is less individual and more tribal, less psychological and more anthropological. Understanding these larger forces should drive the reading of the play and the performances that articulate that reading. In a sense, the result is a communal, social style of performance as compared to the individualistic, psychological style of performance that has dominated the American theater and film.

In a sense, we can view the Brook style of acting as highly theatrical, searching out the primitive, the historical connections to past generations. This style of performance is best captured by the work of Julie Taymor. In the theater, she is represented by "The Lion King," and on film she directed "Titus" and "Frida." Reflected in her work is Taymor's interest in ancient cultures—their archetypes for the range of human experience, from fertility to healing to celebration to death. For Taymor, life is ritual that connects past and future, and her approach to acting seeks out these same values. Her work connects her to Brook and to Stanislavsky's third rail to truth, the spiritual. This style of acting is best described as theatrical. Put another way, Taymor's work can be viewed as antimaterialistic and acting styles that emphasize the physical or outer world can be considered as materialistic or modern. Here the work of playwrights such as Neil LaBute, Craig Lucas, and Patrick Marber focus and their directors and their actors to approach performance from a perspective different from Taymor.

To further clarify this approach to acting, I turn to acting coach Judith Weston (*Directing Actors*, Michael Wiese Productions, 1999) and director David Mamet (*On Directing Film*, Penguin, 1992), who have best articulated the "how" of it. Weston has adapted a combination of the Adler and Meisner approaches to acting. Her focus is on the imaginative creation of a character and she has devised a series of suggested strategies to help the actor "be in the moment" and create a living character who can reach out and engage the audience. First, actors need to work with a set of resources of their own. These resources include their memories or personal experiences, their observations of others, their imagination accessed by improvisation, and their immediate experience. Immediate experience and observation refer to the outer world, the world around the actor. The actor's memories and imagination refer to the actor's inner life. Critical here is the issue of access. Lee Strasberg developed the strategy of sense memory, complete with exercises to access those memories and the attendant feelings, Stella Adler developed exercises to access imagination, and Sanford Meisner created a repetition exercise to access and elaborate upon immediate experience (and to deliver the actor into the moment). Think of each of these exercises as accessing a well of feeling that the actor can funnel energetically into the creation of a character. Using that energy, the actor creates a character. To develop that character, though, a number of choices must be made. Those choices should be based on a deep understanding of the character and should be directed toward developing a character who is authentic, moving toward a true understanding and articulation of the self in the sense of truth Stanislavsky intended, not just verisimilitude but rather a character who has an inner life, an outer reality, and a spiritual layer.

To move into the mechanics of character creation, the actor needs to determine what the spine of that character will be. In a sense this means coming to an understanding of the subtext of the screen story. When defining the character, it is useful to consider what obstacles the character will face. What is the spine? By spine I mean the underlying goal of the character. Whether the goal is an existential one or Weltanschauung (the reason for being), the actor needs to understand the spine in practical terms. Weston uses the example of Michael in "The Godfather" (see Weston's *Directing Actors*, p. 100). She feels (and I agree) that Michael's underlying goal, beyond being an individual and his own person, is to please his father, Don Corleone. This perception is critical because on a deep level it motivates Michael's character. The spine can and should underlie the character's actions in every scene.

Taking this into the social realm, we see Michael's goal as part of a story subtext in "The Godfather." Whenever Michael, his father (the Don), and other members of the family are gathered, whether the scene addresses professional or personal issues, the subtext is the same—the threat to the family is ongoing, and everything should be done to preserve the family. The outside world must remain outside, and efforts to preserve the family must be constant. The actor should be aware of this subtext if he is to build his character. The third component underlying performance is the presence of obstacles. The actor must constantly be aware of obstacles. In one scene, the obstacle might be simple and easily overcome, but over a sequence of scenes the obstacles should grow larger and more varied. Obstacles are useful to the actor. They are signposts bringing the spine of the character into sharper relief. Spine, subtext, and obstacles form the general outlines of the character, and specific mechanical devices can aid the actor in the actual moment-to-moment creation of the character.

Objective, intention, image, fact, sense of belief, physical life, specifics, and listening all contribute to the creation of a character. By objective, Weston really means two elements. The first element is a conscious short-term objective in a scene; this can be as simple as walking to a window or pouring a cup of coffee. The second objective is unconscious and emotional. By pouring a cup of coffee for his wife, a character can illustrate how service even in its simplest form can be used to gain the approval of another (in this case, the wife). Such a scene can serve to illustrate that the character has an unconscious objective to seek approval. One can imagine how this objective manifests itself in the workplace, in circumstances where the character himself seeks service. Does this character feel uncomfortable, for example, when others provide service to him? This is how the unconscious objective works and when it is operating it implies a living, thinking, feeling person.

Intention involves the actor's reaching for an objective and the means required to make the objective more attainable. What would the character do to achieve an objective? Would he verbalize?

Would he act? Or would he be more subtle? Intention illustrates the character's thought process, intelligence, and chosen pathway for achieving his objective.

Image refers to the surround of the character, what the character would notice in the world—the things and the people and how they transport a character to the sensual world of seeing, hearing, smelling, tasting, and touching. The more specific the images the actor considers, the more complex will be their interactions with the world. Image is not necessarily specific to the script. It can be whatever the actor experiences in order to give his character dimension within the world of the script. Image also tells us something nonverbal about the character and can be used to make the character's world and the characterization richer in imagination (surprise).

Facts are used to create a reality for a character. The more the actor knows about the character or develops through improvisation, the greater the sense of reality for that character. Facts give a character a past and may imply that the character believes in or is moving toward a future. One element of fact is belief. Belief animates a character's movement through the story. Belief is a function of the goals, hopes, and needs of a character. In this sense, belief supplies the energy and movement of the character. This energy is critical to the audience. It helps them identify with the character better. When we see a sense of belief in a performance, we are drawn to the character.

Physical life is an important complement to the sense of belief. The actor must physicalize his performance, which requires turning intention into a physical manifestation. It also requires the actor to physicalize his interactions with the setting as well as with other characters. Costumes and makeup, together with posture and carriage, help the actor create the physical parameters of a character. In order to animate the physical and the sense of belief, actors need to find specific gestures and actions that delineate the character. Generality moves us away from the character; specifics move us into the character. An effort to be as specific as possible is critical in the creation of a performance.

Finally, it is critical that a character listen to the other characters. Active listening will convey the impression that the actor is part of the scene, but an actor who is perceived as not listening will disengage the audience. An actor who is obviously listening will appear to be immersed in the action as it unfolds, and the audience will be more likely to be immersed along with the actor.

Objective, intention, image, fact, sense of belief, physical life, specifics, and listening will all mechanically contribute to the actor's creation of a character. Judith Weston has suggested what the director should understand about the actor from the actor's point of view. We now turn to David Mamet, who speaks to the issue from the director's point of view.

A playwright and a man of the theater, Mamet came late to film work. He was the screenwriter for Sidney Lumet's "The Verdict" and Brian De Palma's "The Untouchables," both lauded screenplays. Mamet turned to directing with "Things Change" and "Homicide" and has directed a film every two years, with each one becoming increasingly plot oriented, such as "Heist" and "Spartan."

In a sense Mamet offers a position on directing intentionally opposite that of an acting coach such as Judith Weston. Even an actor's director such as Elia Kazan overinvests directing in the actor's performance, according to Mamet (*On Directing Film*). Mamet takes the position championed by Sergei Eisenstein and V. Pudovkin: Eisenstein's "method has nothing to do with following the protagonist around but rather is a succession of images juxtaposed so that the contrast between these images moves the story forward in the mind of the audience" (*On Directing Film*, p. 2). The emphasis then is on shot selection and organization. Mamet equates the conversation with the cinematographer regarding where to place the camera (technical) with the conversation with the actor about what the actor should do (technical). Mamet downplays or outright dismisses conversations about motivation. Mamet elaborates this idea later in his book. Using a Stanislavsky anecdote about navigation on the challenging Volga River, Mamet suggests:

"How is it that given the many, many ways one might direct a movie, one might always be able with economy, and perhaps a certain amount of grace, to tell the story? The answer is: 'Stick to the channel; it's marked' (sailing reference). The channel is the super objective of the hero and the marker buoys are the small objectives of each scene and the smaller objectives of each beat, and the smallest unit of all, which is the shot" (*On Directing Film*, pp. 103–104).

Above all, Mamet keeps going back to three ideas for the director: There is a super objective that should guide the directing of a performance. The super objective is akin to the spine in Weston's terminology. Mamet also emphasizes the physicality of the performance; actions must be physical as opposed to verbal (Mamet's ideal for dialogue is a silent scene, an irony for such a fine writer of dialogue). Finally, Mamet emphasizes specific actions within a shot, the more concrete the better. After these guiding principles Mamet is happy to rely on casting and the intelligence and charisma of an actor to flesh out the screen character. For this director, however, less is more.

Having presented the Mamet position, a position that is quite the opposite from the Weston position, I suggest that you, as a director, will have to choose your own approach to acting, one in line with your own experience and character. Directors have ranged from the minimalist (Alfred Hitchcock) to the reverential (Mike Leigh) in their approach to actors and performance. Within that spectrum, directors have adopted particular strategies ranging from the seductive (Elia Kazan) to the sadistic (Otto Preminger). The full spectrum of human behaviors associated with trying to achieve a goal comes into full play with directors, no less than with any other profession. What is not typical, however, when compared to other professional relationships, is that the actor is the most direct expression of the director's idea; consequently, the director's relationship with the actor and the approach to character creation are fundamental building blocks in filmmaking. As a result, the director must know how to work with an actor to create the characters that will animate the director's idea.

Part II

Case Studies
of Directing

Chapter 9

Sergei Eisenstein:
The Historical Dialectic

Introduction

Sergei Eisenstein, together with his colleagues Vassili Pudovkin, Dziga Vertov, and Alexander Dovshenko, revolutionized film directing. Building on the work of D.W. Griffith, each set out on a different path for creating films, but each did so out of a conviction that the power of film should be harnessed for a public purpose—to change society. Each of these directors had a different aesthetic. Pudovkin embraced the theatrical, Vertov embraced the documentary in its most orthodox form, and Dovshenko embraced the poetic. To say that Eisenstein saw film as architecture or as graphic design or as a new malleable medium arising out of literature is too limiting. Eisenstein, like Griffith before him, explored the medium of film and contributed new ideas about film. In addition to Griffith, Eisenstein's ideas about film made him a key explorer of the medium. His ideas about editing remain important (see S. Eisenstein, *Film Form*, Harcourt Brace Jovanovich, 1977; *The Film Sense*, Harcourt Brace Jovanovich, 1975). And his influence on directors such as Sam Peckinpah and Oliver Stone confirms his continued relevance to directing. For Eisenstein, editing is the core creative strategy, and his director's idea is articulated in those ideas about editing. For Eisenstein, history is conflict, the inevitable dialectic of one force fighting another. The clash of images has to be articulated and given a human face.

Text Interpretation

Eisenstein directed fewer than ten films from 1925 to 1945. When he fell out of favor, he would teach and write. At the invitation of Charlie Chaplin, he tried Hollywood in the early 1930s and developed a script for Theodore Dreiser's novel *An American Tragedy* at Paramount. He also directed a film for Sinclair Lewis in Mexico, but his North American interlude was not successful. Eisenstein is best known for his films "Potemkin" (1925), "Alexander Nevsky" (1938), and "Ivan the Terrible" (Part I, 1943; Part II, 1946).

Turning more specifically to Eisenstein's director's idea, although Eisenstein considered editing ideas to be the most powerful manifestation of that idea, he believed that text interpretation as well as style of acting also contributed to the director's idea. With regard to text interpretation, Eisenstein approached his screen stories in a particular fashion. "Strike" (1924) examines the consequences of labor rebelling against management, with the government not mediating but rather aligning with capital against labor. The historical struggle is specific, conflicted, and framed as exploitation *versus* moral or human values. The struggle becomes tangible as well as metaphorical as it devolves into evil *versus* good.

A similar interpretive pattern follows in "Potemkin" (1925), which tells the story of a naval mutiny in 1905 in the seaport of Odessa. Here, again, the mutiny is framed in terms of exploitation — the sailors are the victims, and their officers enrich themselves by providing bad food rather than decent provisions. One sailor, Vakulinchuk, assumes a leadership role and is the catalyst for the mutiny. His death in the struggle makes him a martyr for his fellow sailors and the sympathetic population of Odessa. Sailors and the townspeople become the decent, moral social element while the officers of the ship and businessmen of Odessa and the Czarist troops become the exploiters, the parasites, the evil embodiment of their leaders, as the military attacks the civilians and sailors. The conflict between good and evil is underway.

In "Alexander Nevsky" (1937), a 13th-century narrative, the main character is Alexander Nevsky, a prince of the Russian hinterland. In the east, Russia is under attack by the Mongols; in the west, the Germans have invaded the Ukraine. Nevsky, having already defeated the Swedes, is a natural leader. He chooses to defend the city Novgorod against the advancing Germans. Nevsky is good and strong; his people are simple, virtuous, and dogged, both men and women. The Germans, aided by Russian opportunists, are authoritarian, cruel, and evil. Once again the interpretation is a struggle between good and evil, and the characters are archetypal rather than realistic.

Perhaps the most complex narrative Eisenstein undertook was "Ivan the Terrible." Originally intended as a three-part film, in fact only the first two were completed. Part I of "Ivan the Terrible" (1943) is the 16th-century narrative of the czar who united Russia. Based in Moscow, the film begins when Ivan is crowned czar. The film ends with the funeral of his wife, poisoned (as he will learn in Part II) by his own aunt. Although Ivan faces enemies in the east and the west, his larger enemies are his own noblemen, the Boyars. They want power over the future course of Russia. They represent duplicity, deceit, and exploitation. To fight them, Ivan creates a personal guard, the Oprichnicki, who will be the instrument of his will. Ivan will be betrayed by both his closest friends—Kurbsky, who goes over to the Poles in the west, and Phillip, who chooses to retreat to the east and enter into the priesthood. Both friends ally themselves with the cause of the Boyars. Ivan becomes czar by virtue of his will but must resort to the cruel exercise of power to retain his position. Betrayal is all around him, in his court as well as the country at large. Part I of "Ivan the Terrible" depicts the abandonment of Ivan by his friends; because of the death of his wife, at the end he is alone except for the Oprichnicki.

Part II of "Ivan the Terrible" charts the psychological transformation of Ivan from monarch to murderer. Abandoned by everyone from his childhood, including his friend Phillip, Ivan turns to eliminating his betrayers, particularly his aunt Efrosinia and her son Vladamir. Boyars are executed, Efrosinia loses her son and her power, and Ivan is victorious, but his world seems to have gone mad. Victory is at best empty, for Ivan remains very much alone.

In each of these films, the conflict is elevated to momentous proportions with considerable historical implications. It seems as though Eisenstein wanted to point out that history is created out of such struggles. At no point does Eisenstein suggest a more benign view of the historical process. It is all about conflict.

Directing the Actor

In terms of directing actors, Eisenstein relied heavily on casting. In "Potemkin," beyond Vakulinchuk there is no single character whose screen time requires a performance. Even in the case of Vakulinchuk, only frustration, anger, and indignation are required, and then he is killed. Instead of seeking out actors with a range of skills, Eisenstein was casting for a particular look—in fact, a stereotypical look, such as the intellectual, the obedient child, the adventurous child, the elegant grandmother, the middle-class mother, the peasant mother, the aggressive Cossack, the cigar-chomping businessman, the snobbish officer, the peasant sailor. Subsequent to the casting, Eisenstein relied on editing, primarily the juxtaposition of shots, to create feelings about these characters and their fates. In this sense, the performance requirements were limited. Performance expectations, however, changed considerably when it came to "Alexander Nevsky" and "Ivan the Terrible." Eisenstein continued to rely on stereotypical casting for the secondary roles—the sturdy peasant, the aristocratic Teutonic knights, and the Russian traitor as weasel in "Alexander Nevsky"; the Boyar as overstuffed exploiter, scheming aristocrat, or cruel manipulator in "Ivan the Terrible." But, for the major roles, Eisenstein turned to experienced theater actors who looked the part and could enhance their performance with a large inner passion. A specific example illustrates the point. Eisenstein chose Nikolai Cherkassov, the leading Russian theater actor, for the parts of Alexander Nevsky and Ivan the Terrible. The inner qualities of each character differ considerably from one another. First we turn to Alexander Nevsky.

Eisenstein presents Nevsky in a very particular manner. Given the challenges Russia faces in the 13th century (such as invasions from the east and the west), Eisenstein wants to draw a particular quality from Cherkassov—the strength, determination, and self-confidence necessary to save Russia. Nevsky has to be convincing as the savior of Mother Russia, and Cherkassov is very convincing as Nevsky. Beyond the actor's towering presence and bearing, Eisenstein places him in narrative circumstances that illustrate different dimensions of the Nevsky character. In the scene that introduces Nevsky, he is shown fishing at a time of war. He is presented either in the foreground or alone. The other fishermen are clustered or positioned in a seated position. The character's superiority is apparent. Later in the same scene, a group of Mongols attacks his fellow fishermen when they are not sufficiently humble in the presence of the Mongols. Nevsky not only stops the fight but also attracts the attention of the leader of the Mongol party. Taller and insisting on freedom (and dignity) for his fishermen, Nevsky listens to the Mongol leader rattle off Nevsky's accomplishments (*e.g.*, the general who defeated the Swedes) and rejects an offer by the Mongol leader to join their army with rank and privileges commensurate with his achievements. The Mongols leave.

One of the fishermen suggests Nevsky lead his people against the Mongols. Nevsky says not yet, as the risk is greater in the west. They must fight the Germans and prevent them from taking Novgorod, a Russian city that is their next goal. In his declaration, Nevsky assumes the mantle of a Russian leader, but it is only later in battle that we see another dimension of Nevsky—his skills and risk-taking in battle.

Despite advice from his officers to the contrary, Nevsky decides to meet the Teutonic knights and their army before they reach Russian territory—in the middle of frozen Chudskoye Lake. The danger of fighting on frozen ice will be mitigated by the heavier German armor (they are more likely to break through the ice than the Russians). He also organizes a strategy to draw the Germans into battle and then attack their flanks as they are intensely engaged with the defending Russian force. Nevsky is victorious.

From an acting point of view, Cherkassov must convince us of his resolve and superior strategy. Building upon the charisma and strength of character established earlier in the film, Cherkassov presents a realistic portrait of a Russian hero. The style of acting is no different from the portrayal of that other great general, George Patton, in Franklin Schaffner's "Patton." George C. Scott must convince us of Patton's resolve and his brilliance, just as Cherkassov did in his portrayal of Nevsky.

The performance demands on Cherkassov and Eisenstein are far more complex in Part I of "Ivan the Terrible." Ivan, the 16th-century monarch who unifies Russia under his czarship, faces not only external enemies in the east and west but also internal enemies— his nobles, the Boyars. Faced with enemies all around, Ivan as a character must project strength and determination, as well as an inner psychological complexity. In Part I, Ivan has to deal with betrayal by those princes closest to him—Kurbsky and Phillip. He also loses his wife, poisoned by his own aunt. In Part II, we learn that Ivan's mother was poisoned by the Boyars when he was an 11-year-old boy, and Ivan must summon up the will to be as ruthless as his aunt and the other Boyars. This requires a kind of dementia that embraces cruelty as an understandable, even inevitable adaptation. In other words, Ivan adopts a surname, "the Terrible," to help him prevail, but in doing so he becomes a psychotic killer.

As can be imagined, the depth of performance has to be broad and convincing, and Cherkassov created a performance that is large enough to convince. Whereas the Nevsky performance required a credibility that was believable, the Ivan performance required a theatricality usually associated with opera. Extreme and stylized, Cherkassov's Ivan captures a mercurial character that can love or hate, someone who is up to the task of uniting a country, or someone who feels abandoned by everyone in the world. The performance range demands an "anti-realism" that is so stylized that it can encompass enormous swings in behavior and performance style. The character of Ivan requires a larger than life performance, and Cherkassov provides it. Because Eisenstein's director's idea is all about conflict (peace and war; outer appearances and inner feelings), Cherkassov's performance had to reinforce these conflicts.

Directing the Camera

To understand how to harness conflict, we turn now to how Eisenstein used the camera to portray conflict. There are numerous dimensions to Eisenstein's visual skill as a director. To understand his work as a director we must look at the compositional qualities of his films and the editing of his films. Because Eisenstein's contributions to the art of editing are so great, we will discuss how the editing contributed to his director's idea after we look at his visual style.

In order to frame an understanding of Eisenstein's visual style, we must first examine how it contributes to the historical dialectic of opposite forces in conflict. These ideas require an imagery that suggests different dimensions of power and conflict. We begin with the land and how Eisenstein's presentation of the land created a sense of scale that is important and harnessed a beauty worth fighting and dying for.

Eisenstein uses powerful images of the beauty of the sea and the seaport of Odessa in "Potemkin." These images imply a certain tranquility, a welcome quality for sailors and the civilian population. The land is even more powerfully evoked in "Alexander Nevsky," where the rural imagery is of wheat fields, with shipmasts in the foreground and the bountiful sea in the background. In all the rural images, the sky is endless and dominates and dwarfs humans. In "Alexander Nevsky," the earth is bountiful and beautiful, mother to all men. The urban images are different. Bustling and brimming with religious iconography, the city represents physical protection rather than spiritual sustenance for its inhabitants. Cities are power centers important to Russia but also to its enemies. That sense of power and potential protection is how Eisenstein chose to present the city in "Alexander Nevsky." The land is presented differently in "Ivan the Terrible." The rural and urban areas are never entities unto themselves. They exist but only as an extension of Ivan and his vision of Russia. We will defer observations about these visuals until we discuss how the leader is presented visually.

We turn next to the ordinary citizens. In each of these films, they are important because Eisenstein was making films within a society that viewed classlessness as a central goal. Relative to the shot selection for most other characters, Eisenstein chose to portray ordinary people in close-up or mid shots, which allowed him to present the characters in a more emotional manner. In "Potemkin," individual sailors, the mourning townspeople at Vakulinchuk's funeral, and the victims of the Odessa Steppes massacre are all presented in this way. The shot selection allowed Eisenstein to individuate these characters. It was important that they never be simply the classless crowd. For Eisenstein and his narrative, they were the emotional heart of the land. This pattern of presentations is continued in "Alexander Nevsky." Whether fishermen or urban peasants, soldiers for Nevsky or victims of the Teutonic knights, these characters were kind hearted, simple, and morally good—in a word, admirable patriots and martyrs for their country. Again, Eisenstein's use of close-up and mid shots establishes an emotional connection with these characters.

For his antagonists, Eisenstein resorted to a different strategy. Art direction and the use of lightness or darkness defined these characters. Eisenstein also chose to have these characters move less and used mid and long shots rather than close-ups to distance the audience from these characters. When he did use a close-up, as with the Boyars in "Ivan the Terrible," shadows mottled the faces. When he was emphasizing the cruelty of a film's antagonists, Eisenstein would focus on their victims—children thrown alive into a fire and peasant leaders hung for not bending to the Teutonic will in "Alexander Nevsky." When Eisenstein focused on the antagonists, he tried to convey an image of their power and ruthlessness. For the helmeted foot soldiers of the Teutonic Order, the camera was positioned very close to the soldiers, looking up at their lances. The image crowds the viewer and impresses with its sense of invincibility. Eisenstein also emphasized the vain and threatening nature of the helmets in "Alexander Nevsky"—the horns and the talons appeared threatening to the enemy, and the viewers.

Finally, we should discuss Eisenstein's images of a leader, particularly in "Alexander Nevsky" and Parts I and II of "Ivan the Terrible." Eisenstein excelled at supporting the mythology around leadership in all three films. I have already mentioned the presentation of Alexander Nevsky in the foreground fishing and later gazing landward to assess the altercation with the Mongol soldiers. His response about not disturbing the fish is less impressive than his posture and the visual elements behind him—the extended fishing net and the fishermen deep in the background of the frame. The composition creates a heroic image of Nevsky. He literally towers over his people. Because he shares the same frame with them, the image supports the idea that Nevsky is connected to these people. This heroic presentation of Nevsky continues as he rides into Novgorod to invite the residents to join him in battle with the German invaders. This compositional structure is maintained when Nevsky argues battle strategy with his commanders, goes into battle on the frozen lake, and later declares victory over the Germans. The camera looks up at its hero, a leader of the people.

If Alexander Nevsky is the powerful leader, Ivan the Terrible is transformed into the mythical leader. Early in "Ivan the Terrible, Part I," Ivan is in his palace seated at a desk on which sits a globe. The lighting casts a shadow, and behind Ivan his shadow engulfs an entire wall. Eisenstein created a myth, and man and myth share the same image. Eisenstein amplified this idea at the end of "Ivan the Terrible, Part I," when Ivan has retreated to the village of Alexandrov. He will not return to Moscow until the people of Moscow invite him to return to lead them. In the foreground of one image, Ivan looks from the tower that faces in the direction of Moscow. In the background is an endless, winding, weaving line of people (all the way back to Moscow?). There, in the same shot, are the leader and those he will lead. It is a remarkable image. Few shots in film history are as powerful, but the gates of Babylon in D.W. Griffith's "Intolerance" (1917) and the attack on the train in David Lean's "Lawrence of Arabia" (1962) are two that come to mind. In each case, the director is mixing man and myth. Eisenstein's power as a visualist and as a transformative director is best illustrated by this image.

Directing for the Edit

For our discussion of Eisenstein's editing, we will focus on the Odessa Steppes sequence in "Potemkin," on the Pskov massacre sequence in "Alexander Nevsky," and on the coronation sequence in "Ivan the

Terrible, Part I." To highlight his editing ideas, we need to review particular editing ideas and the manner in which they shape or can shape ideas. To create intensity, the director can use the following devices:

1. Close-ups
2. Camera placement closer to the visual action
3. Subjective camera placement
4. Camera movement, particularly subjective movement
5. A more rapid pace in the length of the shots (*i.e.*, shorter shots as compared to the shots in the previous scene)

To create empathy, the director can use:

1. Close-ups
2. Wide-angle shots to provide a visual context for whatever or whoever is in the foreground
3. Slower pace
4. Shots of other characters reacting to the action of the shot

To create a sense of victimization, the director can use:

1. Camera placement above the subject (looking down)
2. Subjective camera placement, looking up at the victimizer
3. Objective establishing shots that show victim and victimizer
4. Objective movement to make the victimization scene appear more fluid (energized)
5. Increase in pace

My point here is that editing can shape how we experience narrative events. Few directors have considered editing to be a source of power in filmmaking, but Eisenstein recognized its power and developed many of the ideas still used today regarding the use of pace, rhythm, and cutting to add emotional impact.

Applying these editing ideas, then, we begin to see Eisenstein's director's idea in action. Both the Odessa Steppes sequence and the Pskov sequence have a single goal—to shock and outrage the audience through his portrayal of the unjust behavior of the czarist forces in "Potemkin" and the German Teutonic forces in "Alexander Nevsky." Eisenstein wanted to illustrate the misuse of power, its inhumanity, and the worthiness of using power to crush such injustice. In both sequences, creating emotional arousal and outrage were his goals. The Odessa Steppes sequence introduces the future victims, the innocents who are enjoying life when the Cossacks attack. The grandmother, the intellectual, the granddaughter, the peasant mother and her son, and later the well-to-do mother with her baby carriage are all introduced via mid shots. Although each of these characters later becomes a victim, Eisenstein particularly focused on the deaths of the mothers and their children. Detailed in close-up are the shooting of the ebullient son, the peasant mother's shock, her raising the boy's body and appealing to the soldiers to stop, her death, the shooting of the other mother, the command, the baby carriage's descent down the steps, the baby, the Cossack raising his sword, and the killing. The two mothers are the ultimate victims, and watching their efforts to save their children is the equivalent of seeing our future (children) being stomped out; these scenes are shocking and overwhelming.

Eisenstein used faceless rows of boots and rifles marching inexorably toward the victims to portray this march to death. There are no humanizing close-ups of the soldiers (except the Cossack who kills the baby). The inhuman stamps out the human. Cutting between victims and victimizers, Eisenstein uses screen direction (left to right for the Cossacks, right to left for the mothers) to illustrate the conflict. Rhythmic montages or other visuals that oppose each other further deepen the sense of conflict and victimization.

The Pskov massacre sequence in "Alexander Nevsky" is far more subtle. Here, screen direction also plays a role—one direction for victimizers, the other for the victims. Eisenstein also used the wide-angle shot more frequently, with victims in the foreground and victimizers in the background. In this sequence, Eisenstein relied less on pace to whip up emotion and more on visual juxtapositions—the forces of good (the victims) *versus* the forces of evil. The camera is placed closer to the Russian victims and hovers farther back from the Teutonic knights. When the victimization reaches its peak—the burning of the children and the hanging of a recalcitrant peasant leader—the shots are long shots and objective. The content did not require additional editing techniques such as pace and close-up.

Turning to the coronation sequence in "Ivan the Terrible, Part I," Eisenstein's goal was again not to repeat himself. There is a good deal of conflict and power, but there is also hope. Ivan is crowned as czar, but we do not see his face until the end of the scene. In this sequence, Eisenstein focused on the symbols of power—the scepter; God's representative, the Bishop, who endorses Ivan's czarship; the individual Boyars who resist his czarship; his wife, who is the only character who will support Ivan; Efrosinia, his aunt, who will be the primary Boyar antagonist; and the two princes, Kurbsky and Phillip, who ostensibly support Ivan but in the end will betray him. The scene offers some sense of hope when these two princes shower Ivan with gold coins to wish him good fortune in his reign. All of these characters and their actions are presented in close-ups. The pace of the scene implies hope, but Eisenstein's juxtaposition of those who are hopeful and those who will stand against Ivan introduces the conflicted character of the rest of the screen story. The scene ends as Ivan turns to the camera and for the first time we see the young czar, his face and his eyes. He is hopeful and innocent, the polar opposite of what he will become.

133

Notable is Eisenstein's use of light to cast shadows on the enemies of Ivan and light upon Ivan and his young wife. The opposing forces are created and positioned in visual opposition to each other. The juxtaposition is emotional—hope *versus* skepticism, good *versus* evil. Eisenstein in this scene has created the oppositional elements of the czar and the Boyars that will dominate the film throughout both Parts I and II.

In this chapter, I have focused on particular scenes that illustrate the director's idea, the historical dialectic, and conflict as historical determinism. Eisenstein uses text interpretation, performance, and the camera to animate his director's idea. What I have not yet noted, but do so now, is that great directing is about transformation of a film experience into something larger, deeper. Eisenstein was able to powerfully shift our experience of "Potemkin," "Alexander Nevsky," and Parts I and II of "Ivan the Terrible" as stories of a naval revolt and its aftermath or Russian leadership in the 13th and 16th centuries into life-and-death struggles between humane and barbaric values. To do so, he unleashed the power of editing, the aesthetic payoff of visual composition, in pursuit of his passion for the medium and for his country. Conflict is at the core of Eisenstein's narratives, but it is hope that Eisenstein embraced—the hope that good can overcome evil, and when it cannot, as in "Ivan the Terrible, Part II," then at least understanding and compassion can be extended to a man who has experienced so much evil in his life that he has become its ultimate victim.

Chapter 10

John Ford: Poetry and Heroism

HOLLYWOOD

PRODUCTION

DIRECTOR

CAMERA

DATE   SCENE   TAK

Introduction

Many directors are referred to as a "man's director," and many directors have a poetic style, but no filmmaker has dealt with men or visual poetry in quite the same way John Ford did. In short, Ford made films about men—famous men such as Abraham Lincoln ("Young Mr. Lincoln") and Wyatt Earp ("My Darling Clementine") and simple men such as Tom Joad ("The Grapes of Wrath"). Other directors have also gravitated to men and male themes. Howard Hawks ("Only Angels Have Wings," "Red River") was interested in a man's rite of passage, that test in life that makes him a man. Raoul Walsh ("Santa Fe Trail") was interested in men as roustabouts ("The Uncontrollable Male"), and Henry Hathaway ("Nevada Smith") was interested in the passions that drive male behavior. John Ford, on the other hand, was interested in all things that made men noble. For Ford, a noble character and behavior made men both big and small, heroic in their extraordinary and ordinary lives.

This idea about heroism was not as individualistic as the Hawks or Hathaway heroes. For Ford's heroes, their family or community (including the military), as well as ethnic background, made them who they were. Ford's characters all came from somewhere, and that somewhere (be it Ireland or Illinois) made them who they were. Ford's visual poetics contextualized the behavior of his heroic characters. It gave their goals and their passions an equivalent visual ground.

Ford's heroes were not humorless, although they were formal and in a sense old fashioned. Their struggles proceeded in ritualistic rather than realistic fashion. Amplifying inner feeling rather than explaining it was Ford's mission as a director. The consequence is a series of films unparalleled in their impact on other filmmakers. Orson Welles was inspired by "Stagecoach" (1939), Lindsay Anderson was inspired by "My Darling Clementine" (1947) and "They Were Expendable" (1946), and the list goes on.

John Ford began his career as a director in 1917 and made his last film in 1966. His important films are dominated by Westerns: "The Iron Horse" (1924), "Stagecoach" (1939), "My Darling Clementine" (1946), "She Wore a Yellow Ribbon" (1949), "The Searchers" (1956), and "The Man Who Shot Liberty Valence" (1962). Commercial and industry recognition, however, came from his non-Westerns:

"The Informer" (1935), "The Grapes of Wrath" (1940), "How Green Was My Valley" (1941), and "The Quiet Man" (1952). Critical attention was also focused on "Young Mr. Lincoln" (1939) and "They Were Expendable" (1945). Ford is the director most honored by his peers in the history of Hollywood.

In order to understand this unusual director and to highlight his director's idea, we need only look at his approach to the Western. This pastoral form was ideal for Ford, a man who wanted to highlight the best in his characters. The Western, representing the past, was a story form best known for its visuality and its action. Various directors have filmed Westerns according to their particular views of the West. Budd Boetticher saw the West as a place where primitivism brought out the worst in its inhabitants. Ford's characters were not the neurotics that inhabited the Anthony Mann Western nor were they the disillusioned romantics of Sam Peckinpah's West. Instead, they were men seeking an ideal. They were skilled and capable but they were also hard men. If they were wronged, they sought justice ("My Darling Clementine") and sometimes revenge ("The Searchers"). But underneath it all, these characters lived by a code of honor. They would have been as at home in King Arthur's Camelot as they were in John Ford's Monument Valley.

These same values—justice, fairness, respect for differences, respect for family and culture—characterize Ford's non-Western characters as well. Tom Joad ("The Grapes of Wrath"), John Brinkley ("They Were Expendable"), and Abraham Lincoln ("Young Mr. Lincoln") represent the Ford hero in other settings. The challenges confronting these characters differ—economic hardship, warfare, poverty—but Ford's heroes all demonstrate a capacity to persevere, not simply to survive, and to stand up and represent positivity in life, whatever the outcome.

I have chosen the following four scenes to highlight Ford's director's ideas:

1. Muley's story from "The Grapes of Wrath"
2. The marshal's lady scene from "My Darling Clementine"
3. The hospital scenes from "They Were Expendable"
4. The search for cattle to the search for killers following the murder raid in "The Searchers"

These scenes highlight the poetry of Ford's work and the passion and nobility of his heroes.

"The Grapes of Wrath" (1940)

"The Grapes of Wrath" tells the story of the Joad family, who had to abandon their share-cropped land in Oklahoma to migrate to California to seek a new life. Muley's story focuses on the displacement of the Joads' neighbor. Tom Joad (Henry Fonda) has returned from prison only to find his parents gone, preparing to leave for California. His neighbor Muley tells him of their eviction by the bank in Tulsa. Foreclosures and displacement have accompanied the drought in the region, a drought that coincides with the Great Depression and its nationwide unemployment. In this scene, the bulldozers level Muley's home, which has been in his family for several generations.

"My Darling Clementine" (1946)

"My Darling Clementine" tells the story of Wyatt Earp (Henry Fonda). When he and his brothers drive a herd of cattle to California, the cattle are stolen and his brother James is killed outside of the town of Tombstone. Earp becomes the town marshal to apprehend the killers of his brother. He is aided by his two brothers, Morgan and Virgil, and by Doc Holliday. He and his brothers meet the rustler/killers at the OK Corral and justice is done. The clip focuses on Wyatt's relationship (or desired relationship) with Clementine (Cathy Downs), Doc Holliday's lady from the East. In this scene, the two attend a Sunday church meeting. When they dance it is a sign to tell all that Clementine may now be the marshal's lady.

"They Were Expendable" (1945)

"They Were Expendable" begins just before the Japanese attack on Pearl Harbor and ends just before the American loss of the Philippines to the Japanese. The focus of the film is on two PT boat commanders, John Brinkley (Robert Montgomery) and Rusty Ryan (John Wayne). They are advocates of the small mobile boats but the Navy and the Army are not. For the military, PT boats and their men are marginal, expendable. The film focuses on these two commanders and their crews, who want to feel that they are contributing to the war effort. The scene I will discuss takes place in the hospital. Rusty has sustained an arm injury, and a nurse named Sandy (Donna Reed) tends to him. They form a relationship, but Rusty is resistant and wants to fight. The hospital staff wants to help him recover.

"The Searchers" (1956)

Ethan Edwards returns to his home in Texas after the Civil War. In short order, Indians massacre his brother, his brother's wife, and their son. They take the two surviving daughters hostage. Ethan is determined to rescue them and spends the next five years looking for the single surviving young niece (the older niece is killed by the Indians). He is aided by the adoptive son of the family, Martin. The sequence I will focus on takes place early in the film. When their cattle are stolen, Ethan, Martin, and a posse pursue them, but the theft has been a ruse to get the men away from the farm. The Comanche Indians murder Ethan's relatives and kidnap his nieces. The clip ends with the burial of his kin and the beginning of his search for his nieces.

Text Interpretation

John Ford's approach to narrative differs considerably from his contemporaries—Howard Hawks and Henry Hathaway, for example. Hathaway, in "The Lives of a Bengal Lancer" (1936), is concerned with the behavior of his characters but far more of his energy is devoted to making the drive of the plot clear. Few filmmakers of the period were as strong on plot progression and impact as Hathaway. In "Scarface" (1932), on the other hand, Hawks had his hand on the pulse on the character and the plot, and he made sure each worked to augment the other. John Ford was different in that he couldn't care less about plot. He always stayed close to character, and his films drifted back to the plot whenever necessary. "My Darling Clementine" provides a good example of this. Although the film opens with the loss of the Earp brothers' cattle and the murder of their brother, the drive for justice or revenge essentially comes to a halt as Wyatt Earp takes on the job of marshal of Tombstone. He periodically encounters the rustler/killers, the Clantons, but the gunfight at the OK Corral is saved until the end of the film. In between, Ford explores Wyatt Earp's relationship with Doc Holliday's former fiancée, Clementine, and his relationship with Doc Holliday.

Ford devotes much of the narrative to characterizing Holliday as a man of culture and education. When a Shakespearean troupe comes to Tombstone and the main actor is undone during a performance by ruffians, it is Holliday who completes the actor's Shakespearean soliloquy. The arrival of Clementine in Tombstone does not particularly advance the narrative, although she does add yet another touch of civilization to the uncivilized Tombstone. In a sense, she provides an outlet for Wyatt Earp's yearning for a more settled life. Although Clementine and Wyatt Earp do not form a love relationship, her presence in the film shows that Earp is not simply a man of justice but one who has hopes and dreams. Ford used Wyatt Earp's relationships with Doc Holliday and Clementine to humanize his character. Although Holliday is a killer, he is capable of deep sentiment. Although Clementine is a refined Eastern woman, she has the strength to stay in Tombstone in spite of being rejected by her fiancée. These three characters and their contradictions give rise to the heart and feeling embedded in "My Darling Clementine." Depicting this reservoir of humanity in the midst of the Wild West was Ford's goal in his interpretation of the story.

I do want to mention one additional quality of Ford's interpretations. In the midst of tragedy and darkness, Ford always sought out humor. Again, the goal was to humanize characters and plot. In "The Searchers," one of the darkest Ford films, Ford has a character named Mose Harper, who was taken by the Indians. He was spared from torture and death by pretending that he was mad, although Mose's presentation throughout suggests that perhaps it was not entirely an act. When Ethan figures out that the Comanche Indians stole the cattle to draw out the men to carry out a murder raid, Mose does an Indian war dance. Mose is also present when Ethan discovers the bodies of his brother and sister-in-law. Ford made him present for most of the hard moments in "The Searchers" to lighten the mood. This combination of tragedy and humor is another characteristic of Ford's approach to text interpretation.

Turning to our excerpts, two make the point about straying from the main story line or plot. In "My Darling Clementine," one of the most famous sequences is a Sunday morning service on the site where a church is to be built (see L. Anderson, *About John Ford*, Plexus, 1981). In this scene, Clementine accompanies Wyatt Earp to the service, which really is not a service. No minister presides, and when a community leader suggests that he has never read anything in the scripture against music the service becomes a square dance. The scene is set on a platform, the foundation of the future church. The water tower and a flag are all that seem established and complete. A shy Wyatt Earp asks Clementine to dance and as they do the townspeople make way for "the marshal and his lady fair."

The scene has two parts: Wyatt Earp and Clementine making their way through the town to the site and the dance on the site itself. The purpose of the scene is to establish some decency in a town full of hooligans whose constant misbehavior requires a sheriff such as Wyatt Earp. There is a good deal of humor in the scene. Besides the remarks and attitude of the community leader (unclerical at best), the opening conversation between Clementine and Wyatt Earp has Clementine commenting on the morning smell of the desert air. Wyatt responds it's not the desert; "it's me, barber." He was wearing a cologne the barber had used as aftershave. Here, the humor lightens up the obvious tension a shy Wyatt Earp feels in the presence of Clementine.

In "They Were Expendable," the plot concerns the response of the American Navy (specifically, the PT boat commanders) to the Japanese invasion of the Philippines. Although the numerous battle scenes are impressive, most of the film focuses on the disappointment of the two commanders in their assignments, which they consider to have minimal impact on the war. Duty in these terms requires respect for the chain of command, regardless of personal feeling. The director also pays a great deal of attention to the competitiveness and camaraderie of the crews, from commander to the most junior member. This camaraderie sustains these men as they endure losses and humiliation. One of the most powerful scenes is when crew members visit one of their own who is dying in the hospital. Although they pretend all is well, the scene ends with a frank acknowledgment between the commander, John Brinkley, and the crew member. They say goodbye without tears. It is a very powerful scene.

The scene where Rusty Ryan is admitted to the hospital for an injury and meets nurse Sandy, who attends Rusty and falls in love with him, is a scene that adds nothing to the plot of the film but is one of the most powerful in the film. The focus is on four characters: Rusty, another injured officer, a doctor, and Sandy.

Rusty's poor behavior as a patient is simply noted. The role of the other injured officer is to illustrate how every patient falls in love with Sandy. The doctor and the nurse are all about the business of tending to the wounded. In this scene, their actions and commitment are elevated above and beyond the call of duty by the conditions. The hospital is a converted aircraft hangar; lighting is poor and made poorer by the frequent air raids. Even if they have to operate with Sandy holding a flashlight over the wound, they will proceed. Just as John Brickley and Rusty Ryan accept and work within the chain of command so too do these medical professionals. They are committed to the preservation of life, although they find themselves in a war zone, with an enemy aggressively advancing toward them.

The scene establishes a sense of commitment to duty and, in the case of Sandy, compassion for those men who lived and died in that hospital. For Ford, these feelings are more important than plot details. For Ford, it is all about character—its nature, values, and human face. This is the narrative choice that engaged him most creatively.

Directing the Actors

John Ford's approach to actors differs considerably from his contemporaries such as Howard Hawks and Henry Hathaway, both of whom were more interested in creating a greater elasticity or character arc in their actors' performances. John Ford had more limited expectations of performance. To understand Ford's approach to directing actors, it is difficult to underestimate his reliance on casting. Essentially, Ford tended to cast for type. For leads, he gravitated to an actor with a particular persona—the strength and decency of Henry Fonda, the determination and passion of John Wayne. It is not surprising that these two actor/stars formed their principal screen persona in their work with John Ford. Notable and not unimportant is the fact that neither of these actors had an especially modern persona, which made them suitable for roles in Ford's films, which so often took place in the past. Other more modern actors such as William Holden, Richard Widmark, and Sal Mineo worked less effectively with Ford. Ford's actors had to have a look that transcended time.

A second quality of Ford's casting was that he always focused on particular types of men—rugged, outdoor types who either had a taste for drink or at least looked as if they did. It is notable that Ford rarely focused on women in his films (although his last film was "Seven Women"). Maureen O'Hara is one of the only actresses to make a recurring appearance in his films. She was also the only actress to have multidimensional characters in his films. Ford's focus on men was inescapable.

Over time Ford developed in effect a stock company that he used repeatedly in his films. Victor McLaughlin, John Carradine, George O'Brian, Andy Devine, Ben Johnson, and Harry Carey, Jr., made multiple appearances in Ford's films. Although each was used in key secondary roles, as often as not they were used to introduce humor into the narrative; for example, in Ford's cavalry trilogy, McLaughlin played the role of a functional alcoholic whose purpose was entirely to add an element of humor.

In addition to his casting, a second notable characteristic of Ford's work with actors is that he was primarily interested in presenting them as feeling or passionate characters—whether working with an artist (Alan Mowbray, as the actor in "My Darling Clementine") or an intellectual (James Stewart in "The Man Who Shot Liberty Valance"). As a result, Ford's characters did not have conventional character arcs. They are not transformed characters so much as they are revealed characters. Although John Brickley (Robert Montgomery) is a commander, a leader who always obeys the chain of command without dissent, Ford made a point of establishing Brickley as a man who also feels deeply. He is the character who gives voice to feelings for the others—for the passionate Rusty who wants to get on with the war, for the deeply feeling nurse Sandy who is clearly in love with the men she tends to, for the crew as fellow humans whose loss is the cost of war. As these moments occur in the film, Brickley is revealed to be a fine commander who cares but suffers the losses silently to hold onto his dignity.

The brevity of the character arc makes Ford's characters less realistic compared to Elia Kazan's characters, who are psychologically realistic. The characters seem to transcend realism to become icons—the decent lawman Wyatt Earp in "My Darling Clementine" and the passionate Ethan Edwards in "The Searchers," who was just the kind of man to tame Texas for future generations.

Performance, then, is based on feelings within a very narrow range. John Wayne's Ringo in "Stagecoach" (1939) is very different from Gregory Peck's portrayal of Ringo in Henry King's "The Gunfighter" (1951). The latter role is psychologically complex and realistic in the range of feelings Ringo expresses. The former version is simply passionate enough to hate and kill and passionate enough to fall in love. Ford's character is impulsive and compelling, while King's character is soulful and utterly recognizable. Ford's Ringo becomes an archetype while King's Ringo becomes a case study, albeit an interesting one.

Directing the Camera

Just as in his work with actors, John Ford's use of the camera was distinctive. Although Ford, Eisenstein, Lean, and Kurosawa can be considered some of the great visualists of the medium, Ford differed from the others. He did not rely as much on pace and editing as Eisenstein, Lean, and Kurosawa did, and he favored a static camera. His long shots are his most memorable images, and he used close-ups sparingly. In spite of this conservative visual approach, Ford was quite experimental with his use of lighting and sets.

To understand the relationship between the director's idea (a poetic conception of the hero) we will examine four different aspects of the visuals in Ford's work and how each contributed to his director's idea. First up is the long shot in our scene from "The Searchers." Ford has long been the master of the long shot—Tom Joad walking down the road at the beginning of "The Grapes of Wrath," the cavalry march through a lightning storm in "She Wore a Yellow Ribbon," the accident at the coal mine and the women waiting for news of survivors in "How Green Was My Valley." In "The Searchers," the majority of the search for the cattle, the discovery of the murder raid, the burial of the Edwards family, and the subsequent search for the two surviving girls is presented in long shot. Filming in Monument Valley, Ford shot the men small at the bottom of the frame and riding forward toward the camera but overwhelmed by rock abutments and sky. The fact that Ford preferred to film these scenes at dawn or dusk gives the frame a magical, otherworldly quality—let's call it poetic. Because Ford does not pace these scenes to imply what is about to happen, the audience is unaware of what might follow. In an extreme long shot, a rider high atop a hill waves at the other riders to join him. Two shots later, Ethan and the five other riders have found the killed cattle and a shot later we learn that a Comanche spear has killed one of the bulls. To register the point of the scene ("It's a murder raid!"), Ford finally moves into a mid shot. Stealing the cattle was only a ruse to draw out the men. After half the men leave for the Jorgenson ranch, Ford moves into reaction mode. Martin, panicked, rides off to his try to save his adoptive parents, while Ethan takes off his saddle to feed and water his horse. As he brushes his horse down, Ford cuts to a close-up of Ethan but masks his eyes as if to shield us from his pain. Because so much of the scene is long shot, the close-up is almost overwhelming. We understand and feel for Ethan.

Let's move from the still, formal long shot in "The Searchers" to a long shot with more movement in "My Darling Clementine." By movement, I mean movement within the frame as well as the movement of the camera. The scene in "My Darling Clementine" proceeds as formally as does the scene in "The Searchers." It begins with the conversation between Wyatt Earp and Clementine. It is early morning, and behind them is the bright desert morning. After Clementine asks if she can join Wyatt for the morning service, they begin to move in the direction of the service. The camera moves in advance of the couple. The feeling of the shot, given the dearth of moving camera shots to that point, is as surprising as if Wyatt and Clementine were marching down the aisle to be married. What follows is a long shot with the service site in the background. As they move into the shot we are aware of how much sky there is. Below the sky are a flag and the foundation for the church to be built. The image is formal and rather ritualistic. Wyatt Earp and Clementine almost march toward the future church.

Ford cuts to the citizen–preacher who leads the service, but as so often happens in Ford films it is music rather than words that makes up the service. As in "Rio Grande," "She Wore a Yellow Ribbon," and "How Green Was My Valley," music gives voice to the feeling Ford is establishing. In "My Darling Clementine," that feeling is the pleasure of being together, the hope that in the future Tombstone will be a community rather than a lawless outpost, a center of society rather than of sin, an ideal rather than its current reality.

Ford utilized a mid shot when Wyatt and Clementine watch the energetic men and women dancing together and he slowly offers himself to Clementine as a dance partner. Ford films the dance itself in long shot, with the camera still and recording the sky, church foundation, and stiff Wyatt Earp dancing with his "lady fair." As in "The Searchers," there is no pace to speak of in this scene from "My Darling Clementine." The movement within the frame is ritualistic, whereas the movement of the camera shot earlier in the sequence was energizing and deeply felt. The contrast moves the scene from feeling to ritual and in doing so alludes to Tombstone's movement from its past into its future. The composition and the steady camera position take the narrative content in the direction of the music. The scene implies a future for the town, as well as for Wyatt Earp and Clementine. The poetic stirring within the scene merges character and place. The low camera angle that characterizes all of the shots at the church service gives this portion of the sequence a heroic quality that creates confidence in the vision of all who are participating in the service.

So far we have focused on the compositional choices Ford used to support his director's idea. Let's now examine how he used light and art direction to support the ideas of poetics and heroism. In "They Were Expendable," the hospital scene is set in an aircraft hangar. The long, round shape of the hospital is revealed by irregularly placed lighting; entire sections of the hangar/hospital do not appear to be lit. In a number of scenes in this excerpt, the majority of characters are underlit. Light falls across their feet and, if they stand in particular locations, across their face. We are always aware of the source of the light. Often, the lights are at the back of a shot and low so the background is awash in light while the foreground is dark. This same principle is applied to source light during an air raid. The lights are shot out, and the source light becomes a flashlight. When necessary, Sandy or the doctor shines the flashlight on a wound. In this scene, as opposed to earlier scenes in the hospital, Ford moves into close-ups to register Sandy's feelings about the life-and-death operations in which she is participating.

Generally, our image of hospitals is of overlit settings where nothing is hidden. Ford presented the hospital as a more abstract place as if to propose that in the absence of light there is an absence of life and in the presence of too much light there is too much feeling or compassion. Working with these contrasting notions, Ford created in the hospital a metaphor for life during wartime; that is, life shines brightly but is surrounded by darkness. The metaphor is powerful and poetic.

This kind of stylized light was also used by Ford in "The Grapes of Wrath." Muley's story begins in the Joad home. Tom Joad has just returned from prison to find his parents have been displaced from their home. The Joad home has no electricity. Only candlelight reflects on Joad, the preacher, and Muley. Each is presented in close-up. The candle sheds a narrow, flickering band of light, and the high contrast adds drama to the faces of these characters and the story we are about to hear.

Muley's story is told in two distinct scenes. In one, Muley and his family are told by a sheriff that they will have to move. He wants to know who he can shoot to stop this process. The sheriff tells him that the bank in Tulsa is responsible to its shareholders and has ordered the house to be torn down. The Tulsa bank is a faceless and soulless antagonist. In the next scene, the mules and tractors come to tear down the house. This time, Muley, shotgun in hand, faces a more tangible enemy. The operator of the tractor is another neighbor. When Muley asks him how he can do this to a neighbor, he says he's doing it for the $3 a day. He has his own family to feed. He bulldozes the house and Muley, in tears, picks up some dirt and mourns how many of his family have died for this piece of land which is now no longer his.

The scene is presented in stylized long shots. Muley and his family are nailed to where they stand. In the early light, the shadows Muley and his family cast are long and dark. There are very few shots in each scene. The morning shoot provides high contrast, bright whites and blacks. The formality of the images is rooted in a higher-than-eye-level camera position. The camera looks downward toward these victims of a faceless antagonist. Ford holds the shots, including the shot of Muley in tears and clutching the dirt of what was his farm. The passion of the character and his determination are heroic, and the tragedy is all the more powerful. It is not a political tragedy, as it was in Steinbeck's novel; rather, it is a human tragedy. By using a poetic visual style Ford elevated these scenes above the political character of the novel.

John Ford was a great poet among directors. His passion for his characters has been matched only by Akira Kurosawa and the Indian director Sajajit Ray. What elevates his work to this level is a profound understanding that the visual medium of film is a narrative medium with the capacity for poetry. In this sense, he joins a very distinctive group of directors that includes Sergei Eisenstein and Alexander Dovshenko. Today, few directors aspire to create the poetry that Ford did. Xhiang Yimou ("Hero") and Peter Weir ("Witness") do, but this type of director is rare.

Chapter 11

George Stevens: The American Character—Desire and Conscience

Introduction

George Stevens, like John Ford, began his career making short films. In 1927, Stevens was making comedies with Laurel and Hardy. Although he began as a cinematographer, he began directing in 1930. He directed his last film, "The Only Game in Town," in 1968. In between, he made important films in the genres of musical ("Swing Time," 1936), situation comedy ("The More the Merrier," 1943), action adventure ("Gunga Din," 1939), Western ("Shane," 1953), and melodrama ("A Place in the Sun," 1951). Whether working on a modest scale ("Alice Adams," 1935) or on a large canvas ("Giant," 1956), Stevens' work had an emotional power that has marked the work of important directors from D.W. Griffith to Istvan Szabo.

To understand his importance, we must examine Stevens' director's idea. George Stevens was interested in what I will call the American character, but he was not engaged with the poetic iconography of John Ford or the romanticized populist view of Frank Capra. Instead, Stevens seemed to be interested in a more complex view of the American character. Two opposing qualities stand out in Stevens' work: the characteristic of desire and at the other extreme the characteristic of conscience. Desire and conscience might be embedded in different characters in a Stevens film, or they might be embedded in the same character. However he presented them, Stevens was able to look at the many aspects of the American character in all its contradictions—idealism *versus* self-interest, class *versus* classlessness, generosity *versus* greed. The result is considerable complexity and emotional credibility. Whatever genre Stevens worked in he was able to create a character arc and a dramatic arc that had an emotional synchronicity. The result was a series of films unique in American film for their mix of artistic and commercial ambition and success. The spirit of those impulses has been kept alive by Stevens' son, George Stevens, Jr., who in 1968 established the American Film Institute. George Stevens, Jr., also made a fine documentary about his father's work, "George Stevens: A Filmmaker's Journey" (1985). A recent compilation of interviews with George Stevens is an invitation to revisit his work (see P. Cronin, Ed., *George Stevens Interviews*, University Press of Mississippi, 2004). In this chapter, we will focus on five excerpts from Stevens' work that illustrate his director's idea.

GEORGE STEVENS: THE AMERICAN CHARACTER—DESIRE AND CONSCIENCE

"Alice Adams" (1935)

"Alice Adams" is based on the Booth Tarkington novel of an ambitious but poor young woman in the Midwest who aspires to be more. The film focuses on Alice's (Katharine Hepburn) chance to move ahead. She meets a rich young man (played by Fred MacMurray) who is bored by his socialite opportunities. Alice and her family have tried unsuccessfully to be what they are not—part of the establishment. The excerpt I use here is the disastrous dinner when Alice introduces the young man to her family. It is the hottest day of the year, the food is heavy, and the behavior of the family members is worse. For Alice, this dinner is a nightmare come true.

"Gunga Din" (1939)

"Gunga Din" is an action–adventure set in 19th-century Northern India, where the British army is combating a Thuggee uprising. The film focuses on three sergeants, McChesney (Victor McLaghlan), Cutter (Cary Grant), and Ballantyne (Douglas Fairbanks, Jr.). The waterboy, Gunga Din (Sam Jaffe), wants to be a soldier. His transformation from waterboy to posthumous military hero gives the film its emotional arc. The excerpt that I will focus on is the Thuggee attack in Tantrapur. The three sergeants have led a patrol to Tantrapur to repair a broken telegraph line and find out what happened to the army contingent that had been located there. Instead, the patrol is attacked by the same force that destroyed the army contingent. The attack is the first time we see the three sergeants in action. They are confident and playful. The scene gives the action an almost comic or tongue-in-cheek tone. The skirmish is exciting and fun, a tone that the film sustains until the final act of the film.

"The More the Merrier" (1943)

"The More the Merrier" (1943) is a situation comedy set in Washington, D.C. during World War II. There is a housing shortage, and, doing her patriotic duty, Connie Mulligan (Jean Arthur) decides to sublet half of her apartment. Her ad draws many people but one of them, Benjamin Dingle (Charles Coburn), pretends to be the apartment's proprietor and tells all the others to leave because the apartment has been rented. When Connie arrives home from work, Dingle presents himself and talks her into the rental. He is forceful and charming. Connie is not comfortable renting to a man, and the resulting clash of personalities only confirms her intuition about the arrangement. Dingle complicates the rental by subletting half of his half to Joe Carter (Joel McCrea). Life gets even more complicated as Joe and Connie fall in love. Dingle plays matchmaker by undermining Connie's fiancé, a man who earns $8500 per year. Being a comedy, everything works out happily. The excerpt that I will focus on is the first morning after Dingle has moved in. Connie is very organized and has prepared a schedule for them to get ready for work. Both must shower, dress, and eat breakfast within 30 minutes. Dingle has trouble complying with the schedule, and the resulting clash of temperaments leads to a scene of classic comic timing and performance. The scene is directed almost as a silent comedy short.

"A Place in the Sun" (1951)

"A Place in the Sun" is a remake of Theodore Dreiser's *An American Tragedy*. Set in upstate New York, the film tells the story of George Eastman (Montgomery Clift), an ambitious young man who travels east to accept the job offer of a rich uncle. He is given a job at the Eastman plant, first in the shipping area and later in a more managerial position. In shipping, he meets Alice (Shelley Winters) and begins a relationship with her, although he has been warned against having any relationships with the staff (which are mostly women). Later he meets the rich and beautiful Angela Vickers (Elizabeth Taylor) and begins a relationship with her. She is the woman of his dreams and represents moving up the social ladder, but there is a complication. Alice is pregnant and wants George to marry her. If he doesn't, she will reveal all to the Eastmans and to Angela. George takes Alice on a trip, intending to drown her (she cannot swim), but he cannot bring himself to do it. Alice stands up in the boat, accidentally falls out, and drowns. The drowning is investigated, and George is charged with her murder. He is tried, and the film ends with his execution. George Eastman found the love of his life but lost it in the end. The excerpt I will focus on here is George's first visit to the Eastman mansion. In this scene, George is offered a job but is barely tolerated by the Eastman family. Angela Vickers is introduced in this scene, but she does not acknowledge his existence. The scene is full of symbols of wealth and social class.

"Giant" (1956)

"Giant" tells the two-generation story of the relationship between Leslie Litton (Elizabeth Taylor) of Maryland and Jordan Benedict (Rock Hudson) of Texas. The story of their marriage, their life in Texas, and their disagreements about race and the role of women in society makes "Giant" more than a regional story. The differences between their two individual sets of values come to a head in the lives of their children. The more liberal Leslie succeeds in changing her husband from a man who sides with the prevailing social views about race into a man who will fight for the dignity of his half-Hispanic grandchild. The excerpt that I will focus on here is the funeral scene for Angel Obregon, a Hispanic Texan who has died in World War II and whose body has been returned to Texas for burial. The scene has special meaning because earlier in the film Leslie was able to get medical attention for the sick baby of one of the Hispanic workers on the Benedict ranch, Reatta. The baby whose life Leslie saved was Angel Obregon.

Text Interpretation

For George Stevens, it was critical that a main character be positioned to optimize the director's idea. This means that desire has to resonate powerfully in his main character. Alice Adams wants to get ahead in a small town that has labeled her a "have not." Whether this makes her a social climber or simply a person who is desperately ambitious (the American character) depends on the point of view. The upper class of the town views her as a social climber, but her parents see her as an unappreciated jewel of a person.

In "A Place in the Sun," desire is embedded in George Eastman's character. He wants a better life, and he wants the love of his life. Again, conscience resides in the upper crust (his own family) of the town. "Slow your advance or don't join us," speaks the actions or wishes of his rich relatives.

Stevens went to considerable lengths to have the audience identify with Alice Adams and George Eastman. Alice is exceedingly thoughtful and supportive of her father, a character with rough edges. Similarly, George Eastman is so rejected by his family that he seeks Alice's company as a lonely man rather than as an opportunist looking for easy sex. Important here is the antagonist role of the rich peers and their families who reject Alice Adams and George Eastman.

In "Giant," desire is very much present in the two main characters—Jordan Benedict and Jett Rink (James Dean). Jordan is rich and firmly entrenched in the power of his position and status. His desire is to maintain possession of that power. When Jordan's sister wills the poor Jett land from the Benedict property, Jett grabs it, works it, and finally discovers oil on it. He becomes rich, very rich. In "Giant," Stevens has presented these two representations of the American character less sympathetically. Theirs is an aggressive desire, an insatiable desire, and in the end a destructive desire. What saves Jordan is his wife, Leslie. Having no wife, Jett is damned by the outcome of his own desire. In "Giant," Jordan's wife represents conscience in the best sense of the word. Leslie stands up to the Texan men with regard to their attitudes about women and their attitudes toward their own Hispanic employees. The Benedicts' marriages, family, and history are a story of desire plus conscience that points to a better future.

Desire takes on a different form in "Gunga Din." Stevens frames desire within the boyish enthusiasm of Sergeant Cutter. Cutter is caught up in the promise of a treasure map. If he finds the treasure, he will be rich and could leave the army and have the life of an English gentleman at last. His colleague, Sergeant McChesney, sees his desire satisfied in the army. For him, the army means camaraderie rather than duty. His desire is to keep his army triumvirate (McChesney, Cutter, and Ballantyne) together. Ballantyne, on the other hand, is engaged and will shortly leave the army. His desire is the woman of his dreams (Joan Fontaine). All three men share a common attitude toward their friendships and their work. They are physical and capable combatants; theirs is the adolescent pursuit of war games. It is not violence; it is energetic fun. So, another desire they are pursuing in this film is the adolescent pleasure of being together.

Conscience is presented in the character of Sergeant Cutter. He is the only character who takes an interest in the waterboy, Gunga Din. Initially, the contact is to imitate soldierly practices such as marching with Gunga Din. Next he enlists Din in his search for the treasure. When they stumble upon the Thuggee temple (which is the source of the diamonds), he sends Din to alert Sergeants McChesney and Ballantyne to come to his rescue. When all four men are captured by the Thuggees, the wounded Cutter enlists Din to warn the approaching army columns about the Thuggee trap that awaits them. Din dies blowing his bugle in warning. Cutter's sense of conscience made him include the low-caste Gunga Din in his army. Notable is that the other two sergeants are indifferent to or dismissive of Din.

In "Gunga Din," Stevens focused on an adolescent presentation of the American character. In "The More the Merrier" he focuses on an older but no less youthful version of that character. Benjamin Dingle represents the American character in all of its enterprising nature. As Dingle puts it often, "Full steam ahead!" Dingle's desire is to get what he wants when he wants it. In "The More the Merrier," the Dingle character lies readily and is constantly manipulating someone in order to get what he wants. He is an energetic transgressor whose age belies his methodology. Instead of being a sage or a wise old man, Dingle could be considered an older version of Sergeant Cutter from "Gunga Din." He is all desire but he lacks Cutter's conscience. In "The More the Merrier," as in "Giant," conscience is represented by a woman. In "The More the Merrier," the woman is Connie Mulligan, but she is too rational and too wrapped up in doing the rational thing. Stevens pokes fun at the conscience for its overdeveloped view. It is as if in this comedy Stevens is saying that transgression can go a long way in bureaucratic wartime Washington, a place in need of Dingle's particular style of organizational skills. Stevens embraced Dingle's enterprising nature, regardless of its rough edges, and suggested that we need the Dingles of the world to help the other characters deal with matters of war and love.

Directing the Actors

In directing actors Stevens relied far less on casting his actors than he did on capitalizing on the strengths of his actors and seeking compensatory strategies to minimize their weaknesses (see comments on his work with Jean Arthur in Cronin's *George Stevens*

Interviews). Coming as he did from a family of actors, Stevens was both comfortable and confident with actors. Stevens had a number of expectations regarding the performances in his films. He expected above all an emotional realism in the performances, and he understood that emotional realism could come from orchestrating the performances around the main character, somewhat akin to developing a better understanding of a person by meeting his family. Looking at Alice Adams, for example, she is energetic but nervous about her station in life, and certainly she deserves better. Looking at her family, we can see that Alice's mother is ambitious to the point of desperation. She badgers her husband constantly to do better. The father, on the other hand, is so beaten down by the pressures of his wife that he is in his pajamas, either sick or in retreat, for half of the film. Alice's brother is her opposite; he accepts and revels in his low class and caste. Alice and her mother, father, and brother create an emotional realism that is readily recognizable. We see the same qualities in George Eastman's surviving mother in "A Place in the Sun" and the families in "Giant."

The second quality Stevens cultivates in his main characters is a depth of desire that is understandable and sympathetic. We do understand George Eastman's desire to advance. He does not want the circumscribed life of his mother and father. He wants more from life. So, too, does Sergeant Cutter in "Gunga Din." As does Alice Adams. As does Connie Mulligan.

Creating further sympathy for these characters are the antagonists. For Alice Adams and George Eastman, their antagonist is the snobbery of society. For Sergeant Cutter, it is the British class system. The desires of the main characters are made more understandable because all of these characters are victims of social values that have protected the power structure in society and penalized the "have nots" (our main characters).

Finally, Stevens has an exceptional sense of the character arc. In his films, his characters are tested by the plot and opposing characters, and they change; they are transformed. George Eastman is penalized by society for his desire in "A Place in the Sun." Jordan Benedict is changed from a racist Texan to a defender of differences in race in "Giant." This transformation is due to the continual pressure of his wife, Leslie, and the birth of a child to Jordie, his son, and his Hispanic wife. Connie Mulligan is transformed from a lonely, rational woman to a loved and loving woman in "The More the Merrier." Here, Benjamin Dingle (and his enterprising sensibility) is the catalyst. In his direction of actors, Stevens makes certain that this transformation is not only credible but also emotionally gratifying for his audience.

Directing the Camera

Filmmakers who are great directors are of two types: (1) the director who favors set pieces, such as Alfred Hitchcock, David Lean, and Steven Spielberg; and (2) directors who focus on the emotional arc of the film. These latter directors include Max Ophuls, Luchino Visconti, and George Stevens. Stevens is particularly impressive with regard to how he created shots for scenes and how those shots were edited. In the end, he was subtle but very effective in his directing of the camera.

To explore his director's idea we begin with an examination of Stevens' work in "A Place in the Sun," where camera placement and art direction operate with considerable force. The set is the Eastman mansion. The camera is placed deep inside the house. In the far background is the door through which George Eastman enters his uncle's home. Doric columns define the middle of the frame and add even greater scale to the house. Charles Eastman and his family are seated and observing George's entry. He walks toward the camera, and it seems to be a very long walk. His uncle offers George a seat. The camera is now positioned not too close to the couch occupied by Charles Eastman's wife and daughter. George sits on a chair in the middle ground. The camera is far from the Eastmans and even farther from George. In this shot, we are not close to any party. The distance between the Eastmans and George is physical but it is also social. The conversation is not an easy one. Again we are very aware of the separation between these family members. The entire sequence to this point has been shot in long and medium shots, again distancing the characters.

Angela Vickers enters as George did earlier. Stevens cuts to a close-up of George as he turns to look at Angela, then a close-up of Angela as she stops near George but speaks to his family. Notable is the fact that she does not even look at George. The attention and energy in the room are now focused on Angela. The young Eastman son, a contemporary of George, rushes over to Angela and offers her date a drink (but nothing for George). Angela leaves quickly, as do some of the Eastmans, all but abandoning George. When George leaves, he assures Charles Eastman that he will be happy to accept the job opportunity offered him. In this scene, the art direction sets up the objects of George Eastman's desire—a home like his uncle's, a life that includes someone like Angela Vickers. The placement of the camera suggests the difference between him and his uncle's family. The camera does not portray George as a victim, but it strongly implies that these people are not going to make it easy for him to fulfill his desires.

To the issue of camera placement Stevens added pace in the Thuggee attack on the village of Tantrapur in "Gunga Din." The focus is on creating suspense that culminates in a 12-minute action sequence. The tone of the sequence is very much in keeping with that of the film—energetic adventure. In order to create suspense, the camera initially follows Sergeant Ballantyne as he searches the seemingly empty village. The camera shifts from long shots that establish the emptiness against the backdrop of mountains towering in the background to a subjective moving mid shot of the sergeant, as if the camera is creeping up on him. Finally it stops in close-up. Ballantyne turns his head. He sees one of his soldiers standing guard atop a building. As he turns back to the mountains, the same cutaway of the guard reveals a Thuggee strangling the guard. Stevens then cuts to a shot with Sergeant Cutter in the foreground. Deep in the background, slightly out of focus, we see another guard being strangled by a Thuggee. The threat is established.

When Sergeant Ballantyne enters a building dark from its sheltered windows he discovers a group of Thuggee pilgrims. He forces them out of the room and a fight ensues. Sergeants McChesney and Cutter come to his rescue, and they handily regain the upper hand. At this point, no guns have been fired; only fisticuffs are necessary. But then the leader of the group invokes Kaali, and from the mountains a flood of Thuggees on horseback launches a full-scale attack.

The attack that will lead to the rooftop escape of the three sergeants is marked by particular details, including the sergeants' retreat to a gated compound and their ascent to its roof to escape the attack. This sequence is fast paced and interspersed with humorous

157

details. In leaping from one roof to another, Sergeant Ballantyne crashes through the roof and one of his feet becomes stuck. Sergeant Cutter's efforts to save Ballantyne include a back and forth toss of a stick of dynamite, first from Cutter, back via the Thuggees landing adjacent to Ballantyne, and then back via Cutter to explode near the Thuggees. The humor assures us that our outnumbered heroes are in no danger. In this sequence Gunga Din reintroduces his desire to be a soldier. He has a weapon and wants to use it, but Sergeant McChesney takes it away. This kind of dramatic detail keeps the longer-term narrative strand at the forefront for the audience.

The sequence is very physical and marked by the confident prowess of the three sergeants. Stevens sustains the energetic tone through the use of detail and a lively pace. The sequence is clear from a narrative point of view and stimulating from a visual point of view. The location shooting of the film yielded considerable visual and narrative benefits. This sequence became the benchmark for later films and filmmakers in this genre, particularly the "Indiana Jones" series made by George Lucas and Steven Spielberg.

Pace and timing with differing intentions characterize the excerpts from "Alice Adams" and "The More the Merrier." Stevens began his directing career working on two reelers with comedians, primarily Stan Laurel and Oliver Hardy. Creating comedy based on farce and comedy based on tragedy (strong emotional responses involving tears and laughter) were goals in this early work. These are the very qualities we see in "Alice Adams" and "The More the Merrier." The key here is to be as specific as possible to make the sequence plausible.

In "Alice Adams," the dinner scene should be the culmination of Alice's hopes and dreams. She is having Arthur—rich, handsome Arthur—over to her house for dinner. It is the first time he will meet her family, and it is her first reality check. Dinner is a disaster, Alice's worst nightmare. Making this long (10-minute) sequence both emotional and funny was the challenge for Stevens.

Let's first address the specifics on which Stevens relied. A meal progresses through its various courses (*e.g.*, appetizer, soup, salad, entrée, dessert). The key here is that each course of Alice's important dinner is inappropriate. The appetizers, caviar on crackers, are untested and a pretense in a household aspiring to present itself as something it is not. The rest of the courses are very spicy and heavy and thoroughly inappropriate for the hottest day of the year. Stevens is also specific in the conflicting roles each participant plays. Mother is thrilled Arthur has come for dinner. For her, it is a triumph and she acts accordingly. Father is uncomfortable in his tuxedo and does not consider dinner to be a social occasion. Alice is nervous that all will fall apart. Arthur remains silent, having heard before attending this dinner that Alice's father is a thief (who stole a manufacturing process from his former employer, Mr. Lamm, another font of wealth in this small town). And the maid who serves the food is indifferent to the competing interests at the table; for her, tonight is just a job.

Specific details beyond the food courses and the emotional state of the participants include Arthur sweating profusely from the food and the temperature, Mr. Adams' failure to present himself as a convincing success (the buttons on his tuxedo shirt pop and his shirt opens to reveal his bare chest), and the maid's failing uniform and her growing impatience with the pretensions of her employers. All these details are presented in close-up. To present the emotional arc of the scene (growing disaster) Stevens relied on Alice to be the barometer. He used Walter, Alice's brother, to bring the sense of disaster to a peak. Near the end of the meal, Walter enters and invites his father into the parlor, where an argument ensues. Alice's mother exits, leaving Alice and Arthur as the last "pretenders" in the dining room. Stevens used food to introduce humor into the scene—Mr. Adams' attempts to eat and enjoy the food and the efforts of the maid to serve the food. The humor contrasts with Alice's rising sense of disaster and humiliation about the meal and the evening and serves to create an intense arc of feeling as well as entertainment for the scene. Stevens paced the scene to follow that arc.

In "The More the Merrier," Stevens played the morning scene more for humor than tragedy. The 10-minute scene follows the efforts of Benjamin Dingle to meet the morning scheduling expectations of his landlady, Connie Mulligan. In 30 minutes, each must get ready for work, including washing, dressing, and eating. Dingle is a total failure in his effort to meet the schedule, and this is the source of humor in the sequence. Connie is the set-up (Oliver Hardy) to Dingle's Stan Laurel.

Again, the sequence is clear and progresses naturally. The first shot is a close-up of an alarm clock—it is 7:00 a.m. Retrieving the milk from outside the door and later the newspaper, making the coffee, showering, dressing, and eating are all specifics of the scene, and each character operates within the specifics of his or her purpose. Connie is the straight man who must keep reminding Dingle of the schedule. Dingle's constant failure to stick with the schedule is increasingly exasperating for him. His failures are also the sources of humor in the scene. When Connie reminds him of the milk, he goes outside to get it and is promptly locked out of the apartment. When she reminds him of the paper, he goes outside and again is locked out. When she reminds him to shower, he goes into the bathroom but forgets he is holding the coffee when he starts to undress. He loses the coffee in the tub. When she asks for coffee, he has very little but pours it into her cup anyway. The sequence ends with her leaving at 7:30, offering him a lift that he cannot accept because he has been unable to get dressed, as he misplaced his pants when she told him to make the bed. The contrast between these two characters could not be greater. The specific details of the scene and the performance and pace of the scene make it an amusing condemnation of efficiency. Dingle, although enterprising, is all too human, as this scene so humorously points out.

The last excerpt we will focus on is Angel Obregon's return home in "Giant." Angel is a Hispanic–American hero who has come home for burial. His father is an employee of Jordan Benedict, and when he was an infant Angel's life was saved by Leslie Benedict, who cared about the well-being of Reatta's Hispanic employees and their families.

The sequence unfolds slowly, formally. A train at dawn leaves its cargo at the station. As the train pulls away, the camera cuts to the flag-draped casket on a trolley. A family stands by its side. Soldiers approach to wheel the casket to its final destination. More of the population of Benedict stands in respect to Angel. Stevens cuts to a small boy playing in the foreground who is bored. He represents a future Angel. Jordan and Leslie bring a Texas flag to commemorate the baby Leslie saved. We cut to the funeral. Here the shots are formal—the casket awaiting being lowered into the ground; the family and friends behind and to the side; the military honor guard, principally Hispanic. The U.S. flag is folded and given to Angel's mother. Father and grandfather stand by proud but crushed by the burden of the loss. Jordan offers the Texas flag to Angel's mother. The coffin is lowered. The young boy continues to play in the foreground—he is the future and is totally disconnected from the burial and the meaning of the loss. The scene unfolds slowly in long and medium shots. The pace is slow and respectful, the light of dawn filled with reflection and possibility. The inclusion of the young boy makes the scene about the past and the future in America. Very little sound is used in the scene, making it all the more soulful.

George Stevens may be the perfect director. Where he puts the camera, his sense of pace, shot selection, and inclusion makes this sequence overwhelming. As I have stated, Stevens' director's idea was a particular take on the American character. He focused on two aspects—desire and conscience. At times these qualities are embedded in the same character, but in films such as "A Place in the Sun," "Alice Adams," and "Giant," these qualities are embedded in different characters. Stevens' ease with actors and with the camera and his willingness to shoot much footage to explore the editing options that could capture his vision allowed him to achieve an unusually effective articulation of his directors' idea. Indeed, he brought together a blend of commercial and artistic acuity never again replicated in American film. Stevens' work represents a high mark for American directing that remains as vivid today as it was in its own time.

Chapter 12

Billy Wilder:
Existence at Stake

Introduction

In Billy Wilder's films, whether situation comedy or film noir, the very existence of his characters is at stake. Wilder, a journalist and then a filmmaker in Germany, migrated to Hollywood in the mid-1930s. There he established a firm reputation as a screenwriter ("Ninotchka," 1939) and then began directing in 1942. Over the next 40 years Wilder specialized in two genres—situation comedies and film noir. Although he is best known for those genres he also directed a classic thriller ("Witness for the Prosecution," 1956) and a classic war film ("Stalag 17," 1952). In the situation comedy category, Wilder is best known for "The Major and the Minor" (1942), "Some Like It Hot" (1958), and "The Apartment" (1960). Wilder put film noir on the map with "Double Indemnity" (1944) but is probably better known for "Sunset Boulevard" (1949).

Although Billy Wilder is a highly regarded director, he is even more highly regarded as a screenwriter. He always partnered with another writer. His partnerships with Charles Brackett, Raymond Chandler, and I.A.L. Diamond are among his most famous, both for the writing and the performances in such films as "Double Indemnity" (1944, with Barbara Stanwyck), "Sunset Boulevard" (1949, with Gloria Swanson), and "Some Like It Hot" (1958, with Marilyn Monroe). Less flamboyant but no less memorable is his work with William Holden ("Stalag 17," 1952), Walter Matthau ("The Fortune Cookie," 1966), Ray Milland ("The Lost Weekend," 1945), and Jack Lemmon ("The Apartment," 1960). His work with screen icons Erich Von Stroheim ("Sunset Boulevard," 1949), Marlene Dietrich and Charles Laughton ("Witness for the Prosecution," 1956) is so well regarded that these performances have risen to the level of legend in an immodest profession.

Although known for their caustic wit, Wilder's films fluctuate between two polarities—the utterly romantic and the utterly cynical. The best of his work—"Avanti" (1972), "The Apartment" (1960), "Sunset Boulevard" (1949)—blends the two. At the extremes, however, we have the romantic "The Private Life of Sherlock Holmes" (1969) and the cynical "Ace in the Hole" (1951) and "Kiss Me Stupid" (1964). But all of Wilder's films share the director's idea that the very existence of his characters is at stake. This existential trap may be external (the hated prisoner of war in "Stalag 17") or internal (the prisoner of alcohol in "The Lost Weekend"). Whatever the cause, the struggle of Wilder's main characters is a struggle for existence. The consequence is a titanic struggle for survival in each of Wilder's films.

To amplify the struggle Wilder uses two elements—the desperation of his main character and the presence of an antagonist. Joe Gillis (William Holden), the failed Hollywood screenwriter in "Sunset Boulevard," is at the end of the road. His car is about to be repossessed, he can expect no more favors from producers, and he is about to return home to Ohio a failure when he meets his antagonist, Norma Desmond (Gloria Swanson), a silent screen star who is lonely and eager to make a comeback. Joe Gillis and Norma Desmond need each other but in the end destroy one another.

In "The Apartment," C.C. Baxter (Jack Lemmon) is so desperate to move up in the insurance business that he does favors for insurance executives who are in a position to help him be promoted. He lends four of them his apartment for sexual trysts even though they endlessly put him out of his own home. Only when he lends his apartment to Mr. Sheldrake (Fred MacMurray), the executive in charge of personnel, does he get his promotion. Sheldrake is C.C. Baxter's antagonist, principally because he controls Baxter's professional horizon and because his mistress is Miss Fran Kubelik (Shirley MacLaine), the woman with whom Baxter hopes to have a relationship. For both Joe Gillis and C.C. Baxter, their existence is wrapped up with their professional identity.

In both "Sunset Boulevard" and "The Apartment," whether the main character can survive is tested. As expected in film noir, Joe Gillis is destroyed. As expected in situation comedy, C.C. Baxter survives, a better man than his corporate antagonist.

In "The Lost Weekend," the main character Don Birnam (Ray Milland) is an alcoholic. His demon is himself and his fear of failure that has made him risk averse in his career as a writer and in his personal life with Helen (Jane Wyman). That fear has made him what he is, an alcoholic. The film focuses on a weekend when has Don promised to try to change but it turns out to be the weekend when he bottoms out, a process that takes him to the brink of suicide. In this case, Don is his own worst enemy, his own antagonist.

THE DIRECTOR'S IDEA: *The Path to Great Directing*

"The Lost Weekend" (1945)

The first excerpt we will explore is the opening of "The Lost Weekend." We see New Yorker Don Birnam hide a bottle outside of his window while he packs to go to Connecticut with his brother (Phillip Terry) for the weekend. In Connecticut, Don will write, and his brother will make sure he does not drink. Helen, Don's fiancée, comes over to wish him well. She is going to a concert that afternoon. Don convinces his brother to accompany her, and suggests that they meet for the later night train. The brother is wary, but Don berates both the brother and his fiancée for not trusting him. When the brother finds the bottle of alcohol, however, an argument ensues, during which it is clear that Don badly wants a drink. His brother empties the bottle. The brother has tried to alcohol proof Don's life in other ways; for example, Don has no money to buy more alcohol, and his brother will not give him any. Clearly, Don is supported almost entirely by his brother. Exasperated by the failure of all of his efforts, the brother goes off to the concert with Helen, while Don can only think of where his next drink is coming from.

165

"Sunset Boulevard" (1950)

The next excerpt we will explore takes place at the end of "Sunset Boulevard." In a fit of jealousy and rage, Norma Desmond has shot and killed Joe Gillis (nobody leaves Norma Desmond). The police attempt to talk to Norma but she is mute. Her manservant (Erich Von Stroheim) is aware of the large gathering of media downstairs, waiting to shoot lurid footage for the evening news. He suggests that Norma will respond to the cameras, and the police agree to take Norma downstairs. When he tells Norma that the cameras are waiting, she is engaged and alert but still in her own reality. She descends the stairs and responds to the cameras as if she were performing. At the bottom of the stairs, she expresses her happiness. She is ready for her close-up. The film ends as she moves toward the cameras, certain she will never again leave her fans.

"The Apartment" (1960)

The third excerpt I will use occurs early in "The Apartment." The scene establishes how much C.C. Baxter is willing to sacrifice for his ambition. The sequence has four parts. The first establishes how

Baxter's apartment is used. Mr. Kirkaby is trying to hurry his mistress home while outside Baxter waits for his apartment to be free. Kirkaby's heightened self-interest knows no bounds, and he suggests that Baxter update his liquor supplies. The second scene focuses on Baxter's loneliness—warming up a TV dinner and drinking Kirkaby's leftover martini. Baxter is misunderstood by his neighbors. Given all the commotion and drinking next door, they think he is an iron man. The third scene introduces another participating executive when Mr. Dobisch calls from a bar. Baxter has already taken a sleeping pill but agrees to Dobisch's unreasonable request. Dobisch arrives with his Marilyn Monroe look-alike and the party begins. The final scene focuses on the neighbors' misperceptions of Baxter, juxtaposed with Baxter waiting in the park, cold, tired, and feeling abused.

"Double Indemnity" (1944)

The last excerpts I will use are the meeting and parting scenes between Walter Neff (Fred MacMurray) and Phyllis Dietrichson (Barbara Stanwyck) in "Double Indemnity." The first meeting of Neff and his love interest proceeds as a seduction. Neff arrives to renew Mr. Dietrichson's auto insurance. Dietrichson is not home but his wife is, and she greets Neff wearing only a towel. After she has dressed she comes back downstairs, and a verbal seduction follows. Neff is more interested in her ankle bracelet than he is in her insurance status. She, on the other hand, is quite interested in insurance. Neff presses on and becomes more forward. She stops him cold but not without some encouragement. She invites him to return the next evening. The final meeting between Neff and Phyllis follows Neff's discovery that she has been two-timing him with her stepdaughter's boyfriend. He comes to see her with the knowledge that claims adjuster Barton Keyes (Edward G. Robinson) believes Phyllis murdered her husband and that the boyfriend was her accomplice. For Neff, the purpose of this meeting is to end his association with Phyllis. Whether he feels the spurned lover or simply the foolish victim of Phyllis' attention and affection, he is here to break with her, but no one breaks with Phyllis. She shoots Neff but is unable to finish him off, realizing that she loves him. Neff kills her and leaves to confess his sins on tape for Keyes. Both scenes drip with desire and danger.

Text Interpretation

Because Billy Wilder began as a writer and continued writing his own screenplays throughout his directing and producing career, the text has always remained clear and forceful. The virtues of Wilder as a dialogue writer and a world-weary critic of capitalism and communism are focal points of books written about Billy Wilder and his work. Because my focus here is on his director's idea, I will examine one particular polarity that for me best illustrates how the existence of characters in Wilder films is continually at stake—the coexistence of extreme romanticism and extreme darkness, or cynicism, in his characters and their stories. Wilder used the clash of these two opposites to raise the stakes for his characters.

Don Birnam, in the opening scene of "The Lost Weekend," is thinking only about the whiskey bottle that is outside of his window. In the scene, he is ostensibly preparing to leave for a weekend with his brother. The arrival of his fiancée, Helen, gives Don the opportunity to appear altruistic when he suggests that his brother go to a concert with Helen; however, we know that his true motivation is to be alone with that whiskey bottle. When Don's motives are uncovered, his brother becomes cynical about Don's intentions but Helen remains the romantic. She is, as she will be throughout the film, optimistic and hopeful that Don can overcome his addiction to alcohol. When Helen and Don's brother leave, Don lies to his cleaning lady in order to keep the $10 his brother left for her. The scene ends cynically, implying that Don's little lie to the cleaning lady will become a bigger lie about the weekend and about all other aspects of his life. What is important in this scene is the existence of both romanticism and cynicism.

Wilder used the same polarity in "Sunset Boulevard." He set up the main character with two women: the cynic, Norma Desmond, and the romantic, Betty (Nancy Olson). Because of Betty and Joe's love for her, he finally decides to leave Norma Desmond. This decision leads to Norma's killing Joe in the scene that precedes Norma's descent into madness. In the madness scene, Wilder created a new polarity—the romantic madness of Norma and the cynicism of the press, who have been absent from her life since her career as a silent star ended. Now that she is a murderess she is newsworthy again, and they are there with their cameras. Norma's madness is strangely romantic as she assumes they are there for Norma Desmond, the star of the silver screen. Only her manservant (and former director) Max understands and loves Norma. The cynical media are there to exploit Norma's new celebrity as a murderess. Again, the clash of the romantic and the cynical raised the stakes for both Joe Gillis and Norma Desmond.

In "The Apartment," this polarity is represented by the romanticism of C.C. Baxter, who is naïve in believing that Kirkaby and Dobisch will advance his interests at work in return for using Baxter's apartment after work, and by the cynicism of the executives, including Sheldrake. Their view that personal favors are the basis for advancement within the insurance company is a corrupt position that is supported by Fran's later observation that there are two kinds of characters in life—those who take and those who are taken. She views the executives as the takers (cynical position) and herself and Baxter among the taken. Baxter as a character will turn against this Darwinian proposition and leave the corporate world (a romantic position) for his love of Fran. In "The Apartment," the polarity between Baxter and the executives raises the stakes for each of his decisions. The environment in which Baxter finds himself is more than an economic or political environment; for Baxter, his moral choice at the end of the film is ultimately both economic and existential.

The choice between the romantic and the cynical is never clearer than in "Double Indemnity." Walter Neff pursues a romantic goal, Phyllis Dietrichson, while Phyllis pursues a cynical goal, the insurance money due her because of her husband's accidental death. In the meeting scene, it is great fun to see Neff and Phyllis pursue their respective goals. He is blinded by desire, and she is blinded by dollar signs. Neither can really see the other. We see what is happening, but Neff doesn't. As a result, we see a man destroy himself. To make this unsavory journey palatable, Wilder and fellow writer Raymond Chandler created a confessional narration. Neff confesses to his mentor, Barton Keyes, and to the audience. When he talks about being humiliated by Phyllis, his confession is a romantic device—"I was fooled by love, a blind man who couldn't see it, but you could, Keyes, because you weren't driven by the same feeling for Phyllis Dietrichson."

Wilder revisits this dichotomy in reverse in the second scene. This time, Neff is the cynic; he is at the Dietrichson house to tell her that she has failed in the insurance scam. She is going to be arrested, and he will be free of her. Phyllis, this time the romantic, shoots Neff but cannot kill him (she is in love, a revelation to her).

Neff embraces and then kills her. Again, the polarity amplifies the idea that everything is at stake.

Directing the Actor

"A director who can crack jokes about suicide attempts ('Sabrina' and 'The Apartment') and thoughtlessly brutalize charming actresses like Jean Arthur ('Foreign Affair') and Audrey Hepburn ('Sabrina') is hardly likely to make a coherent film on the human condition." —Andrew Sarris (*The American Cinema*, University of Chicago Press, 1968)

169

Andrew Sarris is not an admirer of Billy Wilder's directing skills, as he placed him in the fourth rung of his directorial pantheon, "Less Than Meets the Eye." There Wilder is in good company with Elia Kazan, David Lean, Joe Mankiewicz, and William Wyler. This is not the point at which I launch a vigorous defense of Wilder's work. I believe my inclusion of Wilder in this book states my own view of his work. Rather, I use the Sarris position to begin our exploration of Wilder's work in light of performance. What was he seeking in his direction of performances? And how do the performances amplify the director's idea that the very existence of his characters is at stake?

To understand Wilder and his expectations of actors, it is clear that he and his collaborators wrote roles that required confident actors. This explains the very public difficulties he encountered with Jean Arthur and Marilyn Monroe; nevertheless, he secured from Monroe her best screen performance in "Some Like It Hot." The roles often positioned the main character as an outsider in his particular situation—William Holden's opportunistic, unpatriotic prisoner-of-war character in "Stalag 17," Jack Lemmon's small-fish-in-a-pool-of-sharks character in "The Apartment," and Kirk Douglas' aggressive, big-city reporter in the boondocks of New Mexico in "Ace in the Hole." These roles required actors who could work in a marginalized dramatic space and amplify their actions to have an impact beyond their confines, physical and emotional.

Wilder had a penchant for mixing icons from directing as well as acting with the rest of the cast. On the surface, this might seem arrogant but in fact it worked. Examples include a bevy of silent film stars, including Buster Keaton in "Sunset Boulevard," Erich Von Stroheim as Irwin Rommel in "Five Graves to Cairo" (1943), and Otto Preminger as the camp commandant in "Stalag 17."

Although to a certain extent Wilder cast for type (Jack Lemmon, Walter Matthau, and Tony Curtis, for example), he was as likely to challenge type in casting. Consider his use of Fred MacMurray in "Double Indemnity" as the romantic hero and later as the antagonist in "The Apartment." MacMurray's performance in the latter has a coldness to it that makes Sheldrake the exact opposite of Baxter, the main character. Wilder also used Ray Milland in similar fashion. In "The Major and the Minor" (1942), Ray Milland is the romantic lead to Ginger Rogers, who plays an adult pretending to be 14 years old to secure a children's fare train ticket back to the Midwest. In 1945, Wilder cast Milland as the alcoholic lead in "The Lost Weekend." Here, a tortured inner life has replaced the honorable life of a major.

Certain characteristics notable in Wilder characters made many demands on his actors. First, Wilder characters have a self-awareness that expresses itself in irony or self-deprecation and requires a performance capable of evoking this emotional complexity when the character steps out of character and comments on himself. Consider Joe Gillis in "Sunset Boulevard," C.C. Baxter in "The Apartment," and Walter Neff in "Double Indemnity." Neff, in particular, confesses to the audience in the narration—he acted for money and the woman. He reflects: "I didn't get the money and I didn't get the woman."

Another issue is the dialectic that exists between a character's aggressive pursuit of a goal and his vulnerability. This is where we begin to perceive the humanity of the character. Neff's love/desire for Phyllis was sexual and bottomless enough for him to agree to embezzle from his insurance company and kill a man. Here, the relationship is all about sexual desire. In Neff's relationship with Barton Keyes we see another side to the man—his vulnerability. Neff is always lighting Keyes' cigar, and Keyes is always confessing to, confiding in, complementing Neff. He tries to enlist Neff as his assistant, promising that the satisfaction would be greater although the money would be less. The distracted Neff, now involved in the Dietrichson issue, is complimented and touched by Keyes' offer. The scene reveals another side of Neff. When Keyes becomes angry at Neff's turning down the offer, he insults Neff. Neff's response is "I love you too." It is in those scenes with Keyes that Neff reveals his vulnerable self.

A similar pattern emerges around Joe Gillis' character in "Sunset Boulevard." I have already mentioned the romantic/cynical paradox that plays out in Gillis' relationships with Norma Desmond and Betty White. Another layer in these relationships is Gillis' work as a screenwriter. Gillis, a writer of modest success, is losing the battle in Hollywood, but he is holding on for dear life to stay and continue his dream of achieving success as a Hollywood screenwriter. To hold onto that dream, he takes on the job of rewriting Norma Desmond's "Salome" script. He knows the story is childish and not worthy of being produced, but he does the rewrite to stay in Hollywood and hold onto his dream. When he meets Betty, a development person who liked his past work, she encourages him to let go of his cynicism and be vulnerable and committed as a writer. Working with Betty he gets back in touch with the positive dimensions of himself that were important to his past writing. Wilder directed Holden to be less cynical and more vulnerable. The performance of William Holden, in all its modulation, embraced cynicism and conveyed a passion for achieving Gillis' goal, as well as a vulnerability that hinted at the deeper, more positive dimensions of his original goal—to be a writer in Hollywood.

Also critical to performances in Wilder films is that everything is at stake for the character. The actor not only has to pull out all the stops but must also enter a kind of obsessive madness. If the character is too stable, the performance will fail. If the character is either excessively rational or unstable, the performance will fail. This is why it is difficult to imagine Marlon Brando or Clark Gable in a Wilder film. They represent opposite extremes of characters. Instead, Wilder cast for "normality" or at least its appearance—Ray Milland, Fred MacMurray, Jack Lemmon—and then explores what happens to his characters when they enter into an obsessive madness. It is their very ordinariness that enables these performers to transport us to the eerie edge where we understand that their very existence is at stake.

Directing the Camera

The first thing one notices about Wilder's work is how well written it is. Performance and camera are far more subservient to the writing than is the case of the other directors discussed so far. As a result,

Wilder's use of such elements as lighting, art direction, and sound was far more subtle. Pace also is secondary, and edit decisions were made to clarify the story progression. There are nevertheless some notable visual characterizations of Wilder films; for example, environments (sets) in Wilder films are important. Norma Desmond's house in "Sunset Boulevard" is more museum than home, according to Gillis; it is a mausoleum memorializing the grandeur of the silent film period.

The insurance company offices in "The Apartment" are cold and corporate. Wilder emphasized their regimented character, and when he filmed the Christmas party at the office he stressed the claustrophobic quality of the setting. Baxter's apartment is also an important environment in the film. The dominant quality of the apartment is how dark it is. It seems a center for feeling lonely rather than a warm hearth suitable for sexual pleasure. Fran's suicide attempt is a key narrative event very much in harmony with the tone of the apartment, an act enabled by the environment.

Another quality of Wilder's visual style is the use of visual motifs. Usually these motifs are singular and support a character goal. In "The Lost Weekend," the motifs are the whiskey bottle and a shot glass. The film opens on a whiskey bottle dangling out of an apartment window. When Don meets Helen, he is looking for the whiskey in his coat pocket, but the coat check mixed up the check slips and gave Don Helen's coat. In short order the whiskey bottle falls out of Don's coat pocket and shatters. Liquor stores have bottles prominently in the foreground just as bars have bottles lined up in the background. When Don has a drink after sending Helen and his brother off to a concert, the shot glass on the bar is in the foreground. To signify the number of drinks Don has had, Wilder went to a close-up of the condensation rings from a half dozen shot glasses. The condensation clearly marks the growing number of drinks Don has had. He drinks so much that he forgets to meet his brother to catch the late train.

In "Sunset Boulevard," the motif is the car. Losing his car will mean the end of Joe Gillis in Hollywood. When his car is repossessed from the Desmond garage, he becomes totally dependent on Norma. Later, he travels around, a kept man, in Norma Desmond's limousine. The car that takes Norma and Joe to the Paramount studios is the reason why Cecil De Mille invited Norma to visit his set, as he wants to rent the antique as a prop for his next film; however, Norma believed that De Mille was interested in her "Salome" script, now being rewritten by Gillis. Here, the automobile represents status and the desire of Joe and Norma to be stars.

In "The Apartment," the motif is a bowler hat. Wearing such a hat means C.C. Baxter has arrived; he has achieved the promotion he sought. In "Double Indemnity," the motifs are all sexual. Phyllis Dietrichson's ankle bracelet, the towel she wears when first meeting Walter Neff, Barton Keyes' cigars, and Mr. Dietrichson's crutches are all psychosexual elements of a highly sexualized narrative.

A third visual element Wilder uses is to place his camera in such a way that it establishes a power relationship. When Neff first sees Phyllis, he is on the first floor and Phyllis is on the second-floor landing. This position tells us immediately who holds the power in the narrative. When Dobisch calls Baxter to make arrangements for the use of his apartment in "The Apartment," Dobisch is filmed in mid shot but is foregrounded in the shot. When Baxter takes Dobisch's call, Baxter is more in the background of the shot. Again, who has the power and who does not is made clear by the camera placement.

The director's idea for Wilder was to explore the behavior of a character when that character's very existence is at stake. This idea and the films that emanated from it earned Wilder enormous praise and industrial recognition. His films have also given rise to considerable criticism—he was a cynic who trashed his country and its values when he was benefiting from being one of its citizens. These responses suggest that Wilder did what an artist should do—prompt examination of the *status quo*.

I admire Wilder's capacity to engage and enrage us with his characters, and he did so with enormous wit. We should remember that Wilder was displaced by the politics and racial policies of his country of origin. When he came to the United States, he could not speak a word of English yet became one of the great wordsmiths of American film. Because Wilder positions his characters in narratives that raise the stakes to the point of his characters' very existence, he goes to the very heart of great drama. How he set up the text, how he organized performance to articulate the dilemma for his characters, and how he orchestrated the camera in service of the story are clear examples of narrative ambition. He took us further than most directors choose to go, and for that reason his work deserves to be revisited by new generations of directors. His work incites the courage these directors will need.

Chapter 13

Ernst Lubitsch:
The Life Force of
Romance

HOLLYWOOD

PRODUCTION

DIRECTOR

CAMERA

DATE   SCENE   TA

Introduction

Ernst Lubitsch began his career in Germany during the silent era. In Germany, he was known for his historical epics. When he was invited to Hollywood in 1924 by Charlie Chaplin, he established himself there in the sound period as the leading director of romantic comedy. For Lubitsch, romance was complex, and he explored all its layers—idealism, desire, sexuality, pleasure, love. He did not avoid dealing with jealousy and its by-product, rage. In films such as "To Be or Not To Be" (1942), "Ninotchka" (1939), "The Shop Around the Corner" (1940), "Angel" (1937), "Design for Living" (1933), and "Trouble in Paradise" (1932), Lubitsch celebrated the life force of romance—his director's idea. In his work, he felt that all the layers of romance were energetic, creative, and affirming. Although Lubitsch's films were well plotted as well as character driven, he never lost sight of his focus on the personal over the political, pleasure over pain, romance over cynicism. Lubitsch worked with a number of collaborators, including Billy Wilder and Samuel Raphaelson, as writers, but his work was so singular that critics referred to the "Lubitsch touch" when reviewing his films. More on this shortly.

Because Lubitsch was so focused on the romantic comedy, we will look at four of his romantic comedies and how Lubitsch used plot to open up different avenues within the genre. We will focus on "Trouble in Paradise" (1932), "Ninotchka" (1939), "The Shop Around the Corner" (1940), and "To Be or Not To Be" (1942). Because imitation is one form of flattery, I should mention that three of these four have been remade—"Ninotchka" as the musical "Silk Stockings" (1954), "To Be or Not To Be" as Mel Brooks' 1982 remake of the same name, and "The Shop Around the Corner" as Nora Ephron's "You've Got Mail" (1999).

Generally, the romantic comedy follows the course of an unlikely relationship. The comedy arises out of the attraction of two opposites and how who conquers whom in the relationship plays out. A film such as George Stevens' "Woman of the Year" with Spencer Tracy and Katharine Hepburn is a model for the genre. What makes Lubitsch's work in the genre so unique is that not only was he interested in the chase but he was also interested in the complications that become barriers or opportunities in the chase.

Two of the four films discussed here mix politics and romance. "Ninotchka," set in Paris, puts a capitalist, Count Leon d'Algout (Melvyn Douglas), with a communist trade envoy named Ninotchka (Greta Garbo). Will politics or love prevail? The plot of "Ninotchka"—the sale of a famous set of jewels confiscated from the Grand Duchess Swana and now in the possession of the Soviet Government—only serves to complicate the agendas of the two lovers. For the Count, it is a matter of love or money; for Ninotchka, it is a matter of love or duty. Naturally, love prevails.

In "To Be or Not To Be," the politics of nationalism complicates the relationship between two married actors, Joseph (Jack Benny) and Maria Tura (Carole Lombard). They are the leading actors in pre-World War II Poland. Narcissistic Maria encourages a young Polish flyer to develop a relationship with her. When war intervenes, the flyer escapes to England, and the jealous husband remains in Warsaw with his wife. A Nazi spy infiltrates the Polish command in London, takes the names of Poles in London working for the Allies, and returns to Warsaw and the Gestapo, list in hand. The young Polish flyer is enlisted to stop the spy. Returning to Poland, he enlists the help of Joseph and Maria Tura to help him kill the spy and save the flyers. This requires Joseph to pretend to be the spy with the Gestapo and an actor in the troupe to be Hitler. All is well with the jealous Joseph, who retains at least for the moment the devotion of his narcissistic wife.

In "Trouble in Paradise," Lubitsch focuses on the politics of the romantic relationship. Gaston Monescu is a thief. When his pocket is skillfully picked by Lily, also a thief, they fall in love. The politics of the relationship are challenged when Monescu also falls in love with a rich victim, Madame Colet of Paris. Will Gaston survive? Will Gaston and Lily survive, both professionally and personally?

The politics are more complicated in "The Shop Around the Corner." At Matuschek and Company, a high-end retailer in Budapest, Hungary, Alfred Kralik (James Stewart) is a serious and successful employee. Indeed, he is the senior salesman. His main challenge is a needy Mr. Matuschek (Frank Morgan), an older man with a younger wife. Matuschek considers Kralik to be a valued employee but also a serious rival. The story focuses on the relationship between Kralik and Clara Novak (Margaret Sullivan). Clara, a new employee, is a constant irritant to the officious Alfred. The plot of the film is the letter writing between Alfred and Clara. Both are lonely in the big city, and each has begun a correspondence in response to a personal ad in the newspaper. This secret correspondence has led to an idealistic love affair between the two. The correspondents have not arranged a meeting, but they know they have found true love. Each is convinced that when they meet they will become companions for life. In real life, at Matuschek and Company, Alfred and Clara become bitter enemies, routinely calling each other names and insulting each other. What will happen when they finally meet and discover that they are each other's true love? Being a romantic comedy, everything deliciously works out by the end of the film.

Before I go into detail about these four excerpts, it is necessary to point out a number of unique characteristics about Lubitsch's work. The first impression of Lubitsch's work is that words are more important than images; consequently, it is easier to consider Lubitsch a theatrical director for whom performance and setting override the other filmic qualities of a work. Directors such as George Cukor, Stanley Donen, and even Luis Bunuel have taken a similar approach. This first impression, however, can be quite misleading. And here we arrive at the "Lubitsch touch," which refers to the way Lubitsch uses visual detail. For example, in "Ninotchka," Ninotchka considers a hat in the hotel window a sign of capitalist ostentation, but later it becomes an object of desire. When she buys the hat, it is a declaration of her embrace of femininity and of her pursuer, Leon. In "Trouble in Paradise," Madame Colet's necklace becomes the target of theft, a signal of Madame Colet's allure for Gaston, and later it is presented as a gift to Lily to confirm Gaston's love for her. In "The Shop Around the Corner," a letter is private, confessional, and a vehicle for the idealized love of Clara for her "true friend." The cigarette box that plays "Ochi Chornya" is equally multifaceted, moving from retail item to desired object to a gift for someone you hate, and so on. In "To Be or Not To Be," the beard of a spy is as multifunctional as Hitler's moustache. Lubitsch worked in these visual details to reflect something about a character and that character's pursuit of his romantic ideal. What is surprising and delightful for an audience is Lubitsch's capacity to transform something as simple as a hat or a letter or a beard into something far more complex.

A second unique characteristic of Lubitsch's work is that the pursuit of a love relationship seems to occupy the entire universe of his characters. Nothing else seems to matter and all else falls away. What this means for the experience of his films is a kind of unique intensity. His characters have no past and they will have no future if the relationship fails. The result is a focus on the present quite unlike the experience of most films. Although the films are comedies, they have an intensity quite unique in the experience of screen stories.

A third quality of Lubitsch's films is that they are quite sophisticated. The people have lived not in a fishbowl or an idealized state such as Frank Capra's Mr. Smith in "Mr. Smith Goes to Washington" (1934), or Ben Hecht's cynical Walter Burns and Hildy Johnson in Howard Hawks' "His Girl Friday" (1938). The consequence is that his characters have a lived-in quality, a zest for life that is recognizable and attractive. A bonus of this characteristic is that when Lubitsch's characters speak it is a pleasure to listen to them. Often written by Samuel Raphaelson, the dialogue in a Lubitsch film is as pleasurable as in the films of Billy Wilder and Joseph Mankiewicz.

In the excerpts discussed here, I have decided to focus on the first meeting of the opposites whose relationship will carry us through the film.

"Trouble in Paradise" (1932)

"Trouble in Paradise" opens in Venice. At the outset, a robbery occurs in a luxury hotel. The scene we are focusing on occurs after the robbery. An elegant nobleman (Herbert Marshall) awaits a woman whom he has invited to dine with him in his rooms. He is distracted by the preparations and directs the waiter to make sure the champagne is perfect and the food enticing, but he also wants the waiter to disappear as quickly as possible. When the woman (Miriam Hopkins) arrives, the two joust with one another as the waiter reports the robbery down the hall to them. A phone call interrupts, and we learn that the woman is not who she is pretending to be. The nobleman accuses her of picking his pocket, and she in turn accuses him of robbing the man down the hall. Each returns the items stolen from the other—he returns her garter and she returns his watch and wallet. They reveal their identities—he is the famous Gaston Monescu and she the thief Lily—and they declare their love, becoming partners instead of victims.

"Ninotchka" (1939)

In "Ninotchka," the setting is Paris. The plot to sell Countess Swana's jewels is under way, but the three trade commissioners from the U.S.S.R. are already intoxicated by capitalist Paris and have failed in their mission. A new trade representative, Ninotchka, has been sent to take over the negotiations. She is appalled by what she has found (the opulent quarters, the penchant of the trade commissioners for scantily clad cigarette girls). The scene opens with the austere Ninotchka stepping out of the hotel to inspect Paris from an engineering point of view, such as visiting the Eiffel Tower.

Ninotchka makes her way to the island in the middle of the road. As she waits for traffic to clear, Count Leon d'Algout arrives at the island from the opposite direction. Ninotchka asks Leon for directions as well as information about the Eiffel Tower. He cannot answer her questions and resorts to flirting with her. The scientifically minded Ninotchka keeps the conversation technical while Leon tries to keep it romantic. She looks at Leon as if he is a species for study. He finds her surprising and finds himself intrigued.

The scene shifts to the Eiffel Tower. Leon has followed Ninotchka there with romance in mind, but again Ninotchka seeks technical information. The verbal jousting continues as they climb to the top of the Eiffel Tower, the symbol of romance in the most romantic city in the world. There, at the top, their relationship progresses when Ninotchka boasts of the superiority of the communist system and Leon makes his case for capitalists. He points out a particularly charming site, an escape from the politics of the world—his apartment. The scene then shifts to Leon's home.

In Leon's apartment, Ninotchka encourages his manservant not to be exploited by Leon. The manservant replies that, under the communist system, he would have to share his savings and he is appalled by that possibility. Leon dismisses the servant, and he and Ninotchka get down to his agenda of embracing and kissing. The technically minded Ninotchka considers the kissing to be strictly physical, and Leon is growing increasingly exasperated by Ninotchka's rationalizations; however, it is clear that she is melting. The scene ends with Leon and Ninotchka becoming more than acquainted. Political and personal progress has been made.

"The Shop Around the Corner" (1940)

"The Shop Around the Corner" begins with the introduction of the main character, Alfred Kralik, at his workplace, Matuschek and Company, in Budapest. Kralik is a conscientious employee and popular with his boss, Mr. Matuschek, who invited him to dinner at his home the night before. He is the envy of his fellow workers. Matuschek arrives at the store, and it is clear that he is admiring and perhaps envious of Kralik. And here our excerpt begins. Matuschek asks for Kralik's opinion of a cigarette box he is thinking of stocking in the store. The box plays music in addition to holding cigarettes. Kralik is not impressed by the cigarette box and discourages Matuschek from stocking it. Matuschek acts like a scorned lover; clearly, he is immature and not at all confident about his own judgment.

Enter Clara Novak. Clara is looking for a job but does not say so. Kralik clearly mistakes her for a customer and is quite charming until he learns her real intention. At that point, he becomes politely dismissive. Matuschek, still concerned about his cigarette box, mistakes Clara for a customer and seeks her opinion on it. She is impressed. Matuschek is encouraged until he learns that Clara is job hunting. He walks away but Clara is not so easily dismissed. She intends to show Matuschek and Kralik that she can sell anything, even this cigarette box. She approaches an overweight customer and promotes the box as a candy box that will alert her every time she reaches for another piece of candy. She assures the woman that the purchase will help her lose weight. Clara sells the box for double the price and has a job. Kralik has an employee he did not want, but Matuschek is justified in ordering many more of the boxes. The scene ends; the romantic couple has met, and they seem to be antagonists rather than potential lovers.

"To Be or Not To Be" (1942)

The focus of "To Be or Not To Be" is slightly different. The romantic couple is a narcissistic wife and a would-be young lover. The scene opens in the theater where "Hamlet" is being performed. Joseph Tura, who is playing Hamlet, is backstage ordering a sandwich from a nearby delicatessen. His wife, Maria Tura, who is playing Ophelia, exits the stage and solicits opinions about her performance. She also offers support to her obviously insecure husband and assures him that he has never been better. What Joseph is insecure about, however, is his relationship with his wife. The reason why is revealed in the next scene.

Backstage, flowers arrive for Maria. Joseph is jealous, but she is reassuring and tells him she does not know who they might be from. This is the third consecutive evening flowers have arrived. As Joseph leaves to go on stage Maria acknowledges to her dresser that she has a strong suspicion regarding who might be sending the flowers. She writes a note to accept his invitation to introduce himself and tells him that he should leave the audience when Hamlet begins his soliloquy. When Joseph takes the stage and steps toward the audience, ready to utter "to be or not to be," a young flyer (Robert Stack) in the third row stands and exits. Joseph cannot help but see the handsome young lieutenant leaving his seat. In the dressing room, Maria greets the young flyer, who invites her to go flying with him the next afternoon. She suggests they meet at the airport, and he leaves as Joseph's soliloquy will soon end.

A crushed Joseph returns to the dressing room—it is the first time someone has walked out on him. Maria suggests that the flyer might have taken sick; perhaps he had a heart attack. A grateful Joseph embraces Maria. The scene ends with Joseph being consoled by his wife. Jealousy, rivalry, and desire have been important dimensions of this scene. For Joseph, the scene has ended on a note of conciliation. For Maria, the scene has ended on a note of anticipation.

Text Interpretation

Directors tend to emphasize different issues in their interpretations of scripts. For a director such as Ridley Scott, masculinity and its habitual need to prove itself is a presence even in his films about women ("Thelma and Louise" and "GI Jane"). The value that prevails in a Scott film is the positive value of masculinity. What is valued most in a Paul Mazursky film is the struggle for independence. What is valued most in a John Cassavetes film is the tug of war between the life force and the death force in each character. My point here is that directors have core beliefs or issues that they work with in their films. For Ernst Lubitsch, that core issue is romance.

Working with romance, Lubitsch implied that all else in life—politics, money, career, status—is secondary. Such a notion has implications for text interpretation. First, the focus of Lubitsch's work will be on one character's relationship with another, a woman with a man or a man with a woman. As I mentioned earlier, Lubitsch was interested in all dimensions of romance, but in all his explorations the emphasis was always on the emotional aspects of romance and the pursuit of Lubitsch's version of happiness. Bliss is finally securing the desired relationship. In Ninotchka's case, she never knew about men like Leon d'Algout, but when she was sent to Paris, the city of love, she discovers what love can be. Similarly, Madame Colet in "Trouble in Paradise" discovers love when the thief Gaston enters her house with the goal of robbing her.

In order to create this aching sense of the value of romance, Lubitsch works with a number of narrative devices that highlight the importance of romance. First, the principle of opposites operates on the lovers as well as with the rest of the cast. For lovers and would-be lovers, Leon d'Algout and Ninotchka are the most obvious examples, as are Clara and Kralik in "The Shop Around the Corner"—she is emotional, and he is rational; she is kinetic, and he is steady; she is idealistic, and he has a darker outlook.

As we look at the love triangles in the films, the opposites become even more striking. In "Trouble in Paradise," Gaston must choose between Lily and Madame Colet. Lily is a thief who is pragmatic about money. Madame Colet is rich and thoroughly impractical about money. In "To Be or Not To Be," Maria flirts with a young, handsome flyer as her jealous older husband doubts his wife's love. Both men, although opposites, feed Maria's vanity.

Lubitsch also uses the idea of opposites as a source of humor outside the romantic couple. The lovers and would-be lovers are serious when the surround is not serious. Edward Everett Horton and Charles Ruggles portray two rich elderly suitors for Madame Colet, although her preference is for Gaston. In "Ninotchka," the three trade commissioners (Iranoff, Bulganoff, and Kopalski), with their self-deceptive interpretation of Soviet cant and self-indulgent interpretation of Western capitalism, are a source of humor, just as the theatrical company surrounding Joseph and Maria Tura is the source of humor in "To Be or Not To Be." This strategy provides a layered narrative without detracting from the seriousness of the couple seeking romance.

Another element of Lubitsch's text interpretation is how he avoided idealizing a character. It may be that romantic love is idealized but not

182

THE DIRECTOR'S IDEA: *The Path to Great Directing*

its practitioners. All of Lubitsch's lovers are imperfect characters. Gaston Monescu is a thief. Leon d'Algout is a scoundrel. Joseph Tura is vanity personified, and Alfred Kralik is stiff and too serious for his own good. The women fare little better. Clara Novack is hot tempered, as is Lily. Ninotchka is as serious as Kralik, and Maria Tura is far more vain than her famous husband.

The consequence is that Lubitsch is telling stories about realistic characters finding out that in their lives the only important thing, or the most important thing, is to love and be loved. All else—money, position, status—means very little. The pursuit of love is not only crucial; it is essential. When we experience the Lubitsch characters, we join them in the pleasure of the pursuit of love. 183

Directing the Actors

Lubitsch cast for charm, sophistication, and the capacity for comedy. Often this meant hiring theater actors (Herbert Marshall, Miriam Hopkins, Melvyn Douglas) and vaudeville performers (Jack Benny). In casting his female roles, the greater the glamour the better. Star power on the order of Greta Garbo, Marlene Dietrich, and Carole Lombard set the standard for a Lubitsch film. Lubitsch also employed ensemble performers (Edward Everett Horton, Charles Ruggles, Sig Rumann) to flesh out his cast. Another dimension of a Lubitsch cast is its ethnicity. Lubitsch films were often set in Europe, so Lubitsch cast for faces that would look at home in Paris, Venice, Moscow, or Budapest.

Characteristic of Lubitsch performances is the range he asked of his performers. Greta Garbo in "Ninotchka" had to be a Soviet ice queen as well as a romantic heroine who could laugh. James Stewart had to be serious, stiff, pliant, and romantic in "The Shop Around the Corner." Jack Benny had to be a great performer and jealous husband in "To Be or Not To Be." Melvyn Douglas had to be a scoundrel and a lover in short order in "Ninotchka." This meant utilizing actors with the flexibility and emotional range to shift gears in a performance. It also meant hiring actors who had the sense of timing to make these shifts convincing. Lubitsch needed confident actors who trusted their director and his interpretation of the material. He was a director who had a very clear sense of direction for his material. Performance was one of Lubitsch's strengths as a director, but underneath that performance Lubitsch was also able to elicit the joy of performance in the film. This joy, whether it arose from the character or the actor creating a character, was the real key to experiencing the performances in a Lubitsch film. The audience catches onto the pleasure of these performers. They are having a great time creating these characters, and the audience has an equally great time experiencing their creations.

Directing the Camera

Lubitsch was one of those directors who seems on first look to have a very simple approach. There is no urgent editing. The camera is placed before the action and at the requisite moment is moved closer to record a close-up. But, behind this simplicity is a director of enormous sophistication. I have already mentioned Lubitsch's capacity to use a visual for multiple purposes (the Lubitsch touch). Probably more helpful is exchanging the word "simplicity" with "economy." Lubitsch seems to achieve in one or two shots what requires one or two scenes for most directors. Only Luis Bunuel seemed as adept at conveying so much with so little. A few examples will illustrate my point.

In "Trouble in Paradise," François (Edward Everett Horton) characterizes the thief who stole his wallet in Venice as a doctor. Later, the major (Charles Ruggles) mistakes Gaston Monescu for a doctor, and when the François character comes to realize that Gaston and the doctor and the thief are the same person, the end is near for our charming thief. The same pattern emerges in the way the jewels are viewed in "Ninotchka." Initially, the jewels occupy a key role in the plot. The sale of the jewels is the reason why the Russian trade commission has come to Paris. Stopping the sale of the jewels brings Leon into contact with the three Soviet trade commissioners, and eventually those jewels will become a barrier to his relationship with Ninotchka. As they become less of a barrier, their sale becomes an expression of Countess Swana's jealousy toward Ninotchka, and finally their sale becomes the Countess' means of getting Ninotchka back to Moscow and away from Leon.

This sense of economy is not intended to convolute the plot with more twists and turns but rather to exploit each plot device (to its maximum). Lubitsch does the same with the stage of the theater in "To Be or Not To Be." The stage is a stage, but it also serves as Gestapo headquarters to be used to trick a Nazi spy. This elegant sense of economy is no less surprising to the audience than a more elaborate narrative would be, but its benefit is that it keeps us close to Lubitsch's main focus—the chase at the heart of every romantic comedy.

A second characteristic of the Lubitsch approach to the camera is that every aspect of production—camera placement, shot selection, light, art direction—is in support of character and the character arc. That means performance is in the foreground and all else is in the background. The result of this approach is that emotion, hope, desire, and despair are at the forefront while all else falls away.

A third characteristic of Lubitsch's films is that comedy is important and is the highlight of his films. Generally, comedy is generated by the characters. Lily takes a call in Gaston's suite in "Trouble in Paradise." Until that point, she has appeared to be a mysterious, excited woman with too much time and money on her hands. The call punctures this illusion because her roommate is calling her about the unpaid rent. Lily the pretender has replaced Lily the pretentious. In the same film, François' hypochondria and the major's military bearing are offset by their adolescent behavior with one another and with Madame Colet.

Finally, a few words about Lubitsch and his management of the dramatic arc. Romantic comedy is not a fast-paced or plot-driven genre. At its core it is all about the course of a relationship—they meet, they pursue, they date, and they are together. Lubitsch understood that the joy of the pursuit is the core experience for the audience. If the audience is cheering for the couple, all the better. Lubitsch was exceptionally good at charming us into a relationship with his characters and then using a plot to trip them up. The selling of the jewels is the plot in "Ninotchka." Stealing Madame Colet's jewels is the plot in "Trouble in Paradise." Catching a spy and living to act on the stage again is the plot in "To Be or Not To Be." Lubitsch understood that it must all fall apart in Act III if the audience is to feel satisfaction as the lovers come together at the resolution. In "Ninotchka," the lovers are separated in Act III when she is in Moscow and he is in Paris. In "Trouble in Paradise,"

Gaston is unmasked as a thief in Act III. Will he be caught? Will he stay with Madame Colet? What will happen to Lily? In "To Be or Not To Be," the acting troupe was successful at killing the spy but not at escaping from Gestapo headquarters and must reach new heights of performance in Act III. They act out one of their plots, pretending that Hitler is one of Maria's most avid suitors. Hitler himself rescues Joseph from Gestapo headquarters and flies husband, wife, and troupe on to England. This capacity to perceive the genre as a chase and to keep the chase going until the resolution was a trademark of Lubitsch, who fully understood the importance of keeping the dramatic arc taut and effective to the happy end.

Although Lubitsch's camera work seems simple, its intent was to emphasize the characters and the joy in their performances. Because of Lubitsch's choices and the performances of his talented casts, we can better understand and value the life force of romance.

Chapter 14

Elia Kazan:
Drama as Life

Introduction

Individual will struggling powerfully against another person, family, society—this is Elia Kazan's view of the world that infuses his films. Kazan in his time was the most celebrated director of theater and film in the United States. Working with Arthur Miller and Tennessee Williams on stage or with playwrights and novelists such as Moss Hart, John Steinbeck, Paul Osborne, Budd Schulberg, and William Inge, Kazan created a unique group of films. Although his reputation was tarnished and career ruined by his testimony before the House Un-American Activities Committee in the 1950s, his work as a director is unique in American film. His director's idea, that drama is life, infuses his work with a rawness that makes his films stand apart.

What do I mean by drama is life? What I mean is that there are no quiet moments in a Kazan character or film. The character is conflicted in an extreme fashion. Torn between personal desires and pleasing others, Kazan's characters see the world as an emotionally violent place. Secondary characters are equally volcanic. The result is an emotional quest that never ends. Kazan was a serious filmmaker attracted to serious subject matter, but at the core his films and the characters that inhabit them are combustible characters who can explode or implode. This is why I suggest that Kazan's director's idea is that drama is life. I could add that it is a struggle to the spiritual or physical death, an interpretation that would move Kazan's work toward that of John Cassavetes, the film-maker to whom his director's idea is closest. Kazan's work, however, takes place more in the outer world than Cassavetes' films.

In "Splendor in the Grass" (1961), Bud (Warren Beatty) and Deanie (Natalie Wood) are adolescents at a turning point. Will they do their parents' bidding, or will they give in to their desire for each other? In this struggle, the parents prevail, and although Bud and Deanie move on in life, they do so diminished by the lost love.

In "Viva Zapata" (1952), Emiliano Zapata (Marlon Brando) is a peasant with a sense of injustice about his life and society. Zapata, however, is not political in a political world, and he suffers for being a principled idealist. Indeed, he is killed by the politicians who considered his existence to be a threat.

In "A Face in the Crowd" (1957), Lonesome Rhodes (Andy Griffith) is a vagrant musician who becomes a populist radio commentator and later an influential television star. This trajectory is due partially to Lonesome's talent but more often to his lying, cheating, and manipulating those who have helped him the most. Whether in matters of labor or love, Lonesome Rhodes becomes a monster made by the media. Where a performance begins and real life leaves off is blurred. His agent, Marcia Jeffries (Patricia Neal), is blinded by Lonesome's charismatic personality. He marries another woman a day after promising to marry Marcia simply to let her know he is the master of his life and career, and she begins to awaken to the true Lonesome Rhodes. When she switches on a microphone during his television show to let his audience know what he really thinks of them, she is trying to destroy the myth and the man she herself helped create.

In each film, the life situation and the characters—Bud and Deannie, Emiliano Zapata, Lonesome Rhodes—are extreme in their nature, their goals, and their character arcs. It is as if larger forces are at work propelling the characters to the highs and lows of mythic characters. Protagonists and antagonists all take on equivalent proportions in a Kazan film. The battle of will *versus* will allowed Kazan to bring his director's idea into play.

Kazan's film career spanned 30 years, from "A Tree Grows in Brooklyn" in 1946 to "The Last Tycoon" in 1975. In between he went through recognizable phases. The social/political films are represented by "Gentleman's Agreement" (1947) and "On the Waterfront" (1954), both Academy Award winning films. His prestige projects include "A Streetcar Named Desire" (1952) and "East of Eden" (1954). His personal films include "America, America" (1963) and "The Arrangement" (1969). After growing disillusioned with commercial theater and film, Kazan increasingly moved toward more personal work, primarily writing novels. In the mid-1980s, he wrote his personal memoir, A *Life* (Doubleday, 1988). That book is a compelling read. Kazan, the writer, working with his director's idea, transports us vividly into the drama that was his own life.

Before we move into the films we will focus on in this chapter, it is useful to discuss a number of qualities that stand out in Elia Kazan's work. Above all, Kazan was a director of great performances. No other actor was more fused with Kazan than Marlon Brando.

Brando's performances in "A Streetcar Named Desire" and "On the Waterfront" are transcendent in their importance to film performance. Anthony Quinn as Zapata's brother in "Viva Zapata," Zero Mostel as Raymond Fitch in "Panic in the Streets" (1950), James Dean as Cal Trask in "East of Eden," and Andy Griffith as Lonesome Rhodes in "A Face in the Crowd" are no less accomplished. Also, Natalie Wood, Kim Hunter, Julie Harris, Patricia Neal, Barbara Bel Geddes, and Lee Remick were all compelling in their performances for Kazan. Rod Steiger, Lee J. Cobb, Eli Wallach, and Karl Malden became stars because of their work in secondary roles in Kazan films. James Dean, Warren Beatty, and Marlon Brando became superstars because of their work in Kazan films.

A second characteristic of Kazan's work is how he embraced a style to evoke his director's idea. Often this meant a combination of two extremes—an almost documentary-like approach combined with a highly theatrical or expressionist style. "Panic in the Streets," "A Face in the Crowd," and "On the Waterfront" exhibit these extremes of style. "A Streetcar Named Desire" on the other hand is strictly theatrical, with no reference to realism. Perhaps the most fully realized execution of this mixed style is "America, America." The interesting question is why Kazan utilized two such opposite styles in the same film—which brings us back to the director's idea. An explanation of why Kazan merged two very different approaches is that life is inescapably real, but drama requires a more expressionistic, visual presentation. Occasionally, this technique derailed into stylization and stiffness, such as in "Viva Zapata," but when it worked, as in "A Face in the Crowd," the fusion of the two styles raises the work to a powerful level. Other directors such as John Frankenheimer and Sydney Lumet have also worked with this stylistic mix to good result.

A third characteristic of Kazan's work is his use of an inner demon/outer devil approach to the main character and his antagonistic relationships. Although somewhat psychoanalytic, this notion helps us look at the restless energy of all of his characters and their explosive emotional clashes. First, let us look at Kazan's main characters. Whether we consider Terry Malloy (Marlon Brando) in "On the Waterfront," Cal Trask (James Dean) in "East of Eden," or Stavros Topouzoglou (Stathis Giallelis) in "America, America," these are men who outwardly maintain a veneer of sociability but inwardly burn to the point of torment. For Terry Malloy, his inner conscience keeps telling him that his life could be better than it is. Cal Trask's demon is his family's past. If he can own up to the fact that he was deserted by his mother and convince his brother and father to do the same, then his life within the family and how they see him will change. For Stavros Topouzoglou, his inner demon was his dream of going to America, where he believes that at last he will be free. Their inner demons certainly drive each of these characters, but without opposition they would be no more than conflicted or ambivalent characters. The antagonists—indeed, all who oppose them—elevate their struggles to something far greater.

In "On the Waterfront," Johnny Friendly (Lee J. Cobb) is the ostensible antagonist. He is joined by numerous associates, the most important being Terry's brother, Charlie the Gent (Rod Steiger). While Charlie puts gentle pressure on Terry, from the outset we see Johnny physically beating an associate. Johnny spars with Terry, implicitly telling Terry that he can and will fight anyone who gets in his way. Johnny is as physical in expression as is Terry. His explosiveness is the source of his power, and his associates are willing to kill for him. This is Terry's opposition.

In "East of Eden," Cal Trask's antagonist is his father, Adam (Raymond Massey). Although early on Cal's hatred was aimed at his mother, the character whose approval he seeks now is his father. Adam, religious and judgmental, is as rejecting of Cal as he is accepting of Cal's brother, Aron (Richard Davalos). Adam attacks Cal's pragmatic business suggestions as being immoral. Even though he was simply trying to help his father, Cal feels as though his father is accusing him of being immoral.

In "America, America," Stavros Topouzoglou wants to go to America. Everyone—family and strangers—seems to be standing in his way and want him to do their bidding. In the first act, his father and the Turks want Stavros to remain as they perceive him—filial son and loyal subject. In the second act, a fellow traveler steals from Stavros everything of value he is carrying to Constantinople. In Constantinople, his cousin sees Stavros as a meal ticket out of an impoverished business, and Mr. Sinnikoglou (Paul Mann) sees Stavros as a dutiful husband for his daughter, Thomna. In the third act, the rich Mr. Kebabian tries to have Stavros deported from his America-bound ship back to Turkey. Each of these men stands as a barrier to Stavros' dream of going to America to create his own destiny. Collectively, they represent an adult power structure that wants Stavros to remain powerless. Together, they intensify the character and constancy of opposition to Stavros' inner goal of being a free man.

The final characteristic that distinguishes Kazan's work is that he was a director of great scenes—not visual set pieces such as the battle on the ice in Eisenstein's "Alexander Nevsky" or the burial scene in David Lean's "Doctor Zhivago," but dramatic scenes emanating out of the director's work with his actors. Consider the taxi scene in "On the Waterfront," one of the most famous scenes in filmmaking. Kazan is very modest about the evolution of the scene (see E. Kazan, *My Life*, Doubleday, 1988, pp. 524–525). Essentially, Terry is being taken for a ride, in more ways than one, by his brother, Charlie. Charlie's task is to convince Terry not to talk to the crime commission; if he cannot talk Terry out of it he, Terry, will be killed. When Terry accuses Charlie of a lifetime of betrayal ("I could have been a contender but instead . . ."), he lets Terry go free, knowing it will mean his own death. Brotherly love, personal confession, moment of truth—the scene is all of these and more because the performances breathe a level of humanity into a scene that is magical.

Other key scenes created in Kazan films include the nightclub anti-Semitic confrontation scene with Dave (John Garfield) and Skylar Green (Gregory Peck) in "Gentleman's Agreement," the collapse of Lonesome Rhodes' career in "A Face in the Crowd," and the next scene that I will detail from "Panic in the Streets," which is a police story with an unusual twist. The murder victim, Kochak, died of two bullets but would have died anyway—he was carrying a pneumonic plague and could have spread the disease. The killers must be found because they have been exposed to the plague. The killer, Blackie (Jack Palance), and his associate, Raymond Fitch (Zero Mostel), are convinced that the victim was bringing something valuable into the country. Their other associate, Vince Poldi (Tommy Cook), is the victim's cousin. In one scene, Blackie is trying to get the secret out of Poldi. The problem is that Poldi is now bedridden; in fact, he is dying of the plague. The scene plays out, as did the taxi scene, almost in a single shot. Blackie climbs into bed with Poldi. His hands are all over Poldi. He is verbally intimidating, but the scene is a seduction. Blackie takes Poldi's face in his hands, his lips pressed up close to Poldi's lips. The crux of the scene is this narrative paradox. Blackie is looking for a confession to a secret but he is getting something else—the plague. The tension in the scene visually and narrative-wise is excruciating.

To examine more closely the realization of Kazan's director's idea in his work, we will look at the opening of "Panic in the Streets" (Blackie's crime) and the final scene when Blackie is captured; the hiring scene in "On the Waterfront," when Cal follows his mother; the opening scene of "East of Eden"; and the negotiation–betrayal scene in "America, America."

"Panic in the Streets" (1950)

The murder scene from "Panic in the Streets," set near the port of New Orleans at night, introduces the victim as a sick man who has left a card game when he was winning. Blackie, a petty hoodlum, and his two associates, Raymond and Poldi, follow the victim outside. Blackie wants the sick man's money. The victim pulls a knife but is killed by Blackie. He takes the money and orders his associates to get rid of the body. This scene proceeds in an expressionistic fashion with highly dramatic lighting.

The second scene, the capture of Blackie, proceeds in a documentary fashion. The police arrive as Blackie and Raymond transport Poldi to their disreputable doctor's private clinic. They carry him on a mattress down a flight of stairs. As the public health official, Dr. Reed (Richard Widmark), calls for Blackie to turn over the sick man, Blackie dumps Poldi over the side of the walkdown (the external stairs leading to the street). Poldi falls to his death as Blackie and Raymond run for their lives. With the police in pursuit, Blackie and Raymond flee to the port area. They enter a large warehouse housing coffee. The security guard recognizes Blackie and they exchange greetings. It is clear that Blackie used to work here as a stevedore. The guard asks if Blackie is coming back for a job. Blackie states he wants to ship out and asks if any ships are leaving port. As the police and Dr. Reed arrive, Blackie kills the security guard. He and Raymond escape through a hatch in the warehouse floor with Dr. Reed in pursuit. They climb down and make their way toward a ship. The police are everywhere. Blackie assaults Dr. Reed and kills Raymond. He finds the ship but cannot climb all the way up and falls into the water, where he is picked up by the police.

"On the Waterfront" (1954)

The hiring scene in "On the Waterfront" is also filmed documentary style and brings together various narrative strands. Earlier, Terry Malloy has betrayed a friend, Joey Doyle. Prompted by his brother Charlie, Terry tells Joey that he found one of his pigeons. Joey reluctantly agrees to meet Terry on the roof, where gangsters are waiting for him. They push him off the roof and he falls to his death. Terry feels bad but is rewarded by the head of the union, Johnny Friendly. Joey's family, particularly his father, feel that he would be alive if he was deaf and dumb and unwilling to report the corruption he has discovered. Joey's sister, Edie (Eva Marie Saint), is outraged. Her brother was the nicest kid on the block, and she wants justice. The priest (Karl Malden) tries to comfort her but she accuses him and his religion of making empty promises. He feels impotent in the situation.

The purpose of the hiring scene is ostensibly to illustrate the corruption of union hiring practices. The men line up awaiting the call for the union steward. Favors and bribes yield work assignments. Terry is the first one assigned a reward for helping the union with its problem, Joey Doyle. Mr. Doyle passes Joey's jacket (the mantle) to Dugan, a loose-lipped longshoreman who will become the next one courageous enough to go up against the mob's union control. Two investigators approach Terry to talk to them. Terry aggressively rejects the invitation; he won't be a pigeon, d and d (deaf and dumb). When the shop steward throws the job tickets for the day to the ground, a stampede for the right to work ensues. Terry meets Edie when they fight for the same ticket. When he finds out who she is he gives her the ticket. The priest is also present; this is his parish, and he declares that he will take a more active role. This scene presents the corruption and brings together Terry, Edie, Doyle, Dugan, and the priest, setting up the narrative events and relationships to follow. Kazan uses a documentary style to emphasize the realism of corruption and the characters involved.

"East of Eden" (1954)

Turning to "East of Eden," we focus on the opening. The time is 1907; the place is Monterey, California. Cal Trask is following a woman, Kate (Jo Van Fleet) to her bank. Kate is a madam and is making a substantial deposit. He follows her to her home, where she looks out her window and tries to figure out who he is. He is too well dressed and young to be one of her customers. Kate asks the girl cleaning the floor about him. She says she saw the boy there last night, asking about Kate. Cal pitches a stone and shatters the front window. Kate summons a man who is more handyman than bodyguard. He rushes out and tries to reason with Cal. Cal's response is to send a message back to Kate, "Tell her I hate her." He then rushes to catch the train back to Salinas. We will soon learn that Kate is Cal's mother and that she deserted him and his brother when they were infants. She also shot their father when he tried to stop her. Kate is settled in Monterey while her husband Adam has become a farmer in Salinas and raised their two sons.

"America, America" (1963)

The last excerpt is the engagement scene from "America, America." To this point, Stavros has endured robbery, the loss of all his family's worldly possessions entrusted to him, the effort to earn the £110 fee for passage from Constantinople to New York, the theft of his earnings, and almost dying in a police raid on a political meeting he was attending. Stavros, not a man to be discouraged, allows his cousin to introduce him to a rich businessman with four unmarried, rather plain daughters. The scene begins in the midst of a dowry negotiation. The prospective father-in-law, surrounded by his brothers and Stavros' cousin, suggests a £500 dowry. Stavros refuses. The man, angry then conciliatory, asks what Stavros wants. Stavros asks for £110, the exact price of one fare to America. Mr. Sinnikoglou is perplexed but agrees, to the chagrin of Stavros' cousin.

The scene shifts to a celebratory lunch. Thomna flutters about, as do all the women. She worries about pleasing Stavros. Mr. Sinnikoglou says he will not be able to eat until the next day, but his wife thinks he will be hungry again in a few hours. Clearly a rich man attached to his lifestyle and his family, he wants to speak to his future son-in-law. We can see that Thomna is his favorite and he wants to keep her near him. Mr. Sinnikoglou imagines how life will proceed with Stavros as part of his family. He talks of the birth of a child, then another—two sons, that's all he wants. Any more than that is up to Stavros and Thomna to decide (as if anyone could). Here, in Constantinople and at their summer home, these two men will grow old together, cared for by their women. Stavros only smiles as Mr. Sinnikoglou talks about births and deaths here within this place and this family. The audience understands that Mr. Sinnikoglou's imagined future is exactly the opposite of the one Stavros sees; nevertheless, he does not challenge the head of this household. The scene concludes with a present. The entire family marches down the street to a new apartment that Mr. Sinnikoglou gives to his future son-in-law. The marriage that represents such a barrier to Stavros' goal is becoming more of a complication by the minute. The last shot shows the daughter sitting in her father's lap, as if a child, wondering what it will be like to leave her father for another man. The image suggests it will be more than complex. Thomna wants Stavros' opinion on the offers of a life for Stavros—a wife, the apartment, her family—and the father ushers the family away to allow the couple a few moments alone.

Text Interpretation

Drama is life is the director's idea. In order to work with this idea, Kazan had to convince us of the credibility of his characters and the situations in which they found themselves. He also had to infuse the character and the situation with enough conflict to raise the material beyond realism, bringing it much closer to the hyperdramatic form of theater or even opera. Our interpretations should focus on the factors that complicate the apparent narrative purpose of the scene.

We begin with the simplest scene, the opening of "East of Eden." The straightforward narrative purpose is to show Cal looking for and finding his mother. Conflict begins with the mother in that she does not want to be found. In addition to asking the girl about Cal, she sends her man out after him. An additional complication here is that, although Kate is a madam, she does not see Cal sexually, but the young girl and the neighboring black madam do. This sexuality complicates the search issue and the mother–son issue. Anger is the only thing Cal shares with the mother. She is angry at an overly inquisitive bank teller, and she is angry at Cal.

The most complex scene is the "On the Waterfront" scene. Ostensibly, it is a scene about corrupt hiring practices, but it is full of conflict. Terry gets the job all the other longshoremen want. Doyle needs work to pay for a funeral for his murdered son and is forced to accept money from the union loan shark. The crime commission investigators want Terry to work with them, but he refuses. The gangsters are there to keep order, Edie is there to get her father a ticket to work, and the priest is there to take a stance against the gangsters on behalf of the longshoremen in his parish. The scene is brimming with opposing views, in fact crowded with them.

Somewhere in the middle of these two extremes is the scene from "America, America" about how Stavros could improve his bleak situation by marrying into a wealthy family; however, Stavros is really trying to secure the money he needs for passage to America. His cousin hopes that if Stavros does well it might save his own impoverished carpet business. Thomna is torn between the past (life with her father) and a new life with another man (Stavros), and the prospective father-in-law wants grandsons to preserve his name. Everyone in the scene wants something different; consequently, the scene is rife with drama.

Directing the Actor

Directing the actor is the key to the success of Elia Kazan's director's idea. As a former actor and a devotee of the Group Theatre, Kazan developed a powerful understanding of the director's vision and actors as the instruments of that vision. As a result, Kazan always imagined casting the best (*e.g.*, Brando), but when that was not possible he worked with the next best choice. In "The Arrangement" (1969), that proved to be Kirk Douglas. In "America, America," he settled for the unknown Stathis Giallelis. Kazan tells it this way:

"I believe that if I'd found a De Niro, a Hoffman, or a Pacino, the film might have been more and certainly more successful commercially, but this boy had one merit superior actors do not have: He was the real thing. "America, America" is my favorite film both despite the performance in its central role and because of it." (A *Life*, p. 629)

When Kazan worked with Marlon Brando, Anthony Quinn, Richard Widmark, or James Dean, the results are without comparison, the very best imaginable. Beyond the casting, it comes down to the creative malleability of the actor and the vividness of Kazan's director's idea. First, the look of the performance has to be real. Second, the subtext keys the emotions surrounding that look. Finally, the performance must have a certain level of energy, direct as well as sexual.

Terry Malloy is a boxer. As we would expect, he moves swiftly on his feet. He wrestles with Edie when she tries to retrieve a ticket for her father from Terry. His body motion looks like he is in a clinch in the ring. Brando's performance is driven by this reality about Terry. Raymond Fitch in "Panic in the Streets" is a petty criminal who is always being pushed around by someone—his wife, Blackie, the police. Raymond is pliant to all these demanding characters. His nervousness is a physical presence throughout. Mr. Sinnikoglou, on the other hand, is not at all pliant in "America, America." He is a successful man who, unlike Stavros, carries himself with the pride of success. His physical presence reflects the forcefulness of his personality. When we look at his brothers, who are more pliant, we understand he is the reason the business is a success. He is in all matters forceful and successful.

The next layer to these performances is the subtext or inner goal. Terry is a man looking for a second chance, for redemption from the loser image gained by going along with his brother's request that he throw fights to enrich Johnny Friendly. Terry sees Edie, a girl brought up by nuns, as a new beginning for a person like him. Raymond's inner goal is to please people. He will do anything to satisfy those he cares for. When faced with two strong and opposing forces (*e.g.*, his wife and Blackie), the man simply comes undone; this quality is very much at the heart of Mostel's performance. Mr. Sinnikoglou is a worried man beneath all the forcefulness. He has four daughters, and all are plain looking. His concern is whether or not he will be able to marry them off. If he cannot, he

199

will have no male to carry on his name; consequently, he is eager to buy a son-in-law. This is why he offers a generous dowry. This is why he buys Stavros and Thomna an apartment nearby. He is forceful but he is also almost desperate to secure a marriage.

Another quality that is critical to the performance is the energy. In the case of Terry, beyond the physicality and beyond the inner goal is Brando's sexual energy. The famous scene where Terry is playing with Edie's glove as they sit on playground swings getting to know one another is brimming with what is unsaid. Terry's handling of the glove illustrates a desire that runs through the entire performance. Even the scene with Charlie in the cab has a physical dimension and an intimacy that has little to do with the narrative content and everything to do with Brando's energetic and authentic flow of desire in the scene.

Raymond, like Blackie, has his own physical moments, particularly when it comes to dealing with a sick person such as Poldi. Like Blackie, he is animated, enthusiastic, and physical with Poldi. The consequence is a charm that could be misleading. If we did not know Raymond's agenda, to get Poldi's secret for Blackie, we could easily mistake the two men for lovers. Mr. Sinnikoglou and his daughter are not lovers; they are father and daughter, but just as the daughter embraces the father seeking protection against the unknown (marriage to a stranger), the father embraces the daughter possessively. He does not want to lose her. As he physically possesses her he hopes to hold onto his favorite by buying her a husband and binding him to the inner circle of his family. Paul Mann is shamelessly sexual in this scene with his daughter. Does he cross a boundary with her? Yes, but this is one of those dangerous areas where Kazan wants to take the audience in each of his films.

Directing the Camera

As I mentioned earlier in the chapter, Kazan articulates his director's idea by using alternatively a highly theatrical style and a documentary style. The model for "Panic in the Streets" seems to be Fritz Lang's "M" (1931), in which a child molester is the danger and unorthodox means are required to bring him to justice. In "Panic in the Streets," a pneumonic plague is the danger, and again unorthodox means are necessary to find a killer who is carrying the disease. When Kazan was trying to capture the danger of the disease he utilized a theatrical style; when the narrative devolves into a police story, as in the last scene, Kazan adopted a documentary approach. Within the theatrical opening scene, the light is expressionistic, the shots formal and stylized. Here, Kazan favored long and mid shots, except for Kochak, the sick man who is carrying the disease. Kochak gets the close-ups.

We see the same principle operating in "On the Waterfront." The killing of Joey Doyle, the opening scene, is highly dramatic. Cantered (*i.e.*, tilted camera angle, off centered) camera positions, high key light, and very low angles alternating with high angles give the sequence a theatrical dynamic feeling. The hiring scene that follows shortly, however, is given a documentary feeling to lend a veracity to the multiple characters and narrative threads introduced in the scene.

Turning to the excerpt from "East of Eden," we have a very formal scene. Not as theatrical as the opening of "On the Waterfront," this opening gives us a mystery. A well-dressed young man follows a madam to the bank early in the day; the bank has just opened. He follows her home as well. All these shots are long shots. The close-ups focus on the gloved hands, the bankbook, and the hat and shaded face of Kate. The audience is given the impression that Kate is hiding from something. Whatever it is, a clandestine quality to Kate is created by the camera position. It is watching Kate but it does not show us her eyes. All else proceeds more directly. The girl cleaning Kate's floors, the handyman just out of sight until called upon—their presentations illustrate not only who is the boss but also their dependent position. They rely on Kate for their livelihood. They are not friends or equals; they are employees, and the visuals convey as much.

Cal stands up to the handyman although the man would seem to be more imposing. Kazan organized the shot to show that the man is not as powerful as he appears and the boy is more forceful than he appears. The sequence is simple, yet Kazan succeeded in creating impressions about both Kate (she has something to hide) and Cal (he is more than just a kid; he is an angry young man). Kazan's use of the camera keeps the narrative clear and captures the conflictual nature of this relationship between Cal and Kate. The theatrical opening throws the audience into the key conflict in the film in the very first scene.

Drama and life—for Kazan in his work the two fused and informed one another. Kazan was serious and ambitious in his director's idea. His characters are unusually present, alive, and brimming with inner conflict. His films at their best suggest conflict that is not easily resolved, and lives that are energetic, sexualized, committed. His characters do not always work things out fully, but they do leave us with a feeling that they will keep trying, as Kazan did in each of his films. He kept trying through a dramatic enterprise (a play, a film, a novel) to work out the life issues that all of us struggle with. This is the importance of Kazan's work and of his director's idea.

Chapter 15

François Truffaut:
Celebrate the Child

HOLLYWOOD

PRODUCTION

DIRECTOR

CAMERA

DATE   SCENE   TA

Introduction

François Truffaut was unique among directors. He had many film heroes—Hitchcock, Hawks, and Renoir—but the one that he chose to emulate made few films. That hero was Jean Vigo, the man who made "Zero de Conduite" (1932). Vigo celebrated the spirit of children, and this is François Truffaut's director's idea. Truffaut did not consider childhood to be an ideal state; rather, he saw it more fully. Perhaps the best way to capture his view is to consider the world as either uncorrupted or corrupted. For Truffaut, childhood was an uncorrupted state, a state where the real person uncluttered by agendas resides. The child is good but also mischievous. The child is sexual as well as loving. The child is happy as well as sad. The child is not idealized or perfect, but rather authentic, a true self. Truffaut in his best work explored this state in children as well as adults. When Truffaut's director's idea was realized, we see a playfulness in his films that is special among directors. Only Fellini has been able to employ this playfulness in creative ways similar to Truffaut.

Truffaut, like Hitchcock, became a character in his films, although he took it a step further. Truffaut played the director in "Day for Night" (1972) and the doctor in "The Wild Child" (1970). Steven Spielberg, who often chooses the child's point of view in his more personal work, cast Truffaut in his inner-space/outer-space epic, "Close Encounters of the Third Kind" (1977). In this sense, Truffaut became both a director and a star identified for a particular approach to his work. That approach, simply put, was his celebration of and empathy for the child.

Truffaut's work can be grouped into three categories: (1) films about children and the child in the adult, (2) homages, and (3) women's films. In the category of homages, I would include "Shoot the Piano Player" (1961), "The Bride Wore Black" (1968), "Fahrenheit 451" (1966), and "The Last Metro" (1980). Among the women's films I would include "Jules et Jim" (1961), "The Soft Skin" (1964), "Confidentially Yours" (1983), "The Story of Adele H" (1975), and "The Woman Next Door" (1981). Children's films that we will focus on include the Antoine Doinel films—"The 400 Blows" (1966), "Stolen Kisses" (1968), "Bed and Board" (1972), "Love on the Run" (1978), and "Antoine and Colette" ("Love at Twenty") (1962)—as well as "The Wild Child" (1968) and "The Man Who Loved Women" (1977). Each category seems to have its own stylistic approach, with the child films being the most playful and unfettered in their stylistic choices. This latter group is the focus of this chapter.

In this chapter we will discuss excerpts from "The 400 Blows," "Stolen Kisses," "Love on the Run," and "Day for Night."

"The 400 Blows" (1966)

"The 400 Blows," Truffaut's first feature film, was the first film in the Antoine Doinel series, which starred the same actor, Jean-Pierre Léaud, over a 20-year period. Through four films and a short, Truffaut followed Antoine from troubled adolescent to confused adult. Through parenthood and sundry relations, the boy in the man defeats adult concerns and Antoine remains difficult and eccentric and boyish to the last. In "The 400 Blows," we meet the adolescent Antoine. The film chronicles his difficulties at home and at school. Because of a petty theft he is sent to a juvenile evaluation center. The film ends with his running away from the center. The sequences we will discuss are the opening and the closing of the film. The film opens in the classroom. The strict teacher is irate when he discovers Antoine is focused on a pinup picture rather than the class work. He forces Antoine to stand behind the blackboard while the other students go out for recess. When the students return, the teacher returns to the assignment. Antoine's assignment will be punitive (he is asked to write multiple times a declaration of what he will not do in the future), and the recitation assignment for the rest of the students is a poem the teacher puts up on the blackboard. While the teacher is writing on the blackboard, Antoine silently makes fun of him. Many of the other students also begin to misbehave and rebel against the strictness of their teacher. In this excerpt, Antoine is playful and rather angelic, not particularly angry. The last scene of the film begins at a soccer match at the juvenile detention center. Antoine knows he is to be sent to a more severe juvenile facility, and he runs away. He is pursued by the soccer coach but eludes him. He runs down to the sea, and by the edge of the water he slows down and turns toward the camera. A freeze frame of Antoine ends the film. This sequence is open and filled with movement, while the opening school sequence was static and closed.

"Stolen Kisses" (1968)

"Stolen Kisses," the second feature film, opens with Antoine being dishonorably discharged from the army. The narrative then follows Antoine's early work history and his love life. The film ends with the growing seriousness of his relationship with his girlfriend, Christine. The first scene we will discuss begins with his first work experience as a night clerk in a small hotel. He is naïve when two men lie to him to gain access to a woman's hotel room. Antoine believes their story and upon opening the door discovers the woman in bed with a man. One of the two men he has let into the room is the woman's husband, and the other is a private detective. Antoine's mistake leads to his being fired, but the private detective offers Antoine a new career opportunity as a private detective. In the next scene, Antoine practices detective work by following an attractive woman. She sees him and complains to a policeman. Antoine is not a very promising detective.

"Love on the Run" (1978)

The third Antoine Doinel film, "Bed and Board," chronicled Antoine's marriage to Christine, the birth of their child, and the result of Antoine's infidelity on their marriage (it dissolves). "Love on the Run" begins with Antoine's divorce from Christine. His son is now 10 years old. Antoine has published an autobiographical novel. His first girlfriend, Colette, a character Truffaut highlighted in his short "Antoine and Colette," reappears. Colette is now a lawyer and also having trouble in a relationship, and her story is interwoven with Antoine's story. There appears for a short time the possibility that they will get together again but it does not happen. In the end, Colette returns to her love, Sabine's brother, Xavier. Sabine is Antoine's current girlfriend.

In this excerpt, we begin with Antoine delivering his son to the train station where he will depart for summer camp. Colette is also at the train station, to take a train for Aix-en-Provence; however, at first they do not see each other. Antoine calls Sabine to tell her he cannot see her tonight, and she berates him for not thinking to invite her to go with him to the station so she could meet his son. Antoine is defensive and compartmentalized. It is all too complex for Alphonse, his son, and in fact it is all too complicated for Antoine, too. Piqued, he rushes off the phone. He exhorts Alphonse, who is not responsive to practice the violin so he can become a great musician. If he does not practice he will fail and become a music critic.

From the opposite train Colette, holding Antoine's book, *Love and Other Troubles*, tries to get his attention but succeeds only in catching Alphonse's attentions. He alerts his father that a woman on the other train is a spy. Antoine does not pay much attention to what his son has said and says goodbye to his son. As he turns to leave, he finally sees Colette, whose train has started to pull out of the station. As she sees him notice her, she holds up the book. That does it for Antoine, and he dashes onto the departing train, although Colette does not see him do that.

In her sleeper cabin she reads the book, and the film cuts to clips from "Love at Twenty," which focused on their relationship 16 years earlier. The clips include Antoine's first sighting of Colette at a concert, his anxieties about approaching her, and meeting the parents for dinner. It also includes an excerpt of Antoine becoming a neighbor of Colette's family. The clips then move through Antoine's relationship, courtship, and failed marriage to Christine. All are included in Antoine's book. Finally, the porter brings Colette a note. Someone is waiting for her in the dining car. She is certain it is Xavier; instead, she finds her old boyfriend, Antoine. And here our excerpt ends.

"Day for Night" (1972)

The last excerpt is from "Day for Night," Truffaut's film about filmmaking. The film chronicles the production of a film, which is the plot of the film, although it focuses on the relationships of the actors and crew. Old stars and new actors mix with the crew in what can only be described as a soap opera. The handsome older Alexandre (Jean-Pierre Aumont) decides after many marriages that he is gay. The great Italian actress Severine (Valentine Cortese) cannot remember her lines. The young actor Alphonse (Jean-Pierre Léaud) is so needy and childish that he is unpredictable and unreliable. The foreign star Julie (Jacqueline Bisset) is fragile, hardworking, and generous to the point of getting herself into emotional trouble. The director (François Truffaut) has nightmares about the work of a director against whose work he measures his own. The joke here is that he compares himself to, who else, François Truffaut. And the crew acts according to stereotype—the stuntman is a stud, and the script supervisor is pragmatic ("I'd leave a guy for a film, but never a film for a guy"). The prop man is anal retentive and the producer is smooth as glycerin. Truffaut used the making of the film to celebrate filmmaking and to humanize the creative people who have chosen filmmaking as their work.

The scene that we will focus on is the death of the character Pamela in a car accident. It begins with Alphonse's girlfriend, Liliane, saying goodbye to him before leaving for work. He thinks she will only be gone for a few hours but he is wrong. When the script supervisor (Natalie Baye) is headed for that day's location, her car breaks down. The prop man, Bernard, stops to help her change the tire. She cleans up in a nearby pond, and the two decide to have sex. She barely arrives in time at the location where an accident scene is to be shot. The stuntman prepares for the shoot, and the scene is shot from several angles. It is a success. The scene ends back at the main location as the stuntman is leaving, but he is leaving with Liliane, Alphonse's girlfriend. Julie, the foreign star, tells Liliane this will hurt Alphonse, and she should tell him what is going on right away. Liliane casually says she is leaving Alphonse because she was only hired on the film to please Alphonse, and since Alphonse was becoming impossible she does not want to hang around. Besides, she is in love. She and the stuntman leave.

Text Interpretation

Although Truffaut focuses on the celebration of the child, he does not present the child as being the victim of an adult but rather as a state of life where the spirit within is irrepressible. That spirit may take on a certain nobility, such as in "The Wild Child." More often, however, the child is more of a rascal than a symbol of nobility. Although the child is dependent on adults as parents or teachers, there is independence to Truffaut's child, a center all his or her own. In this sense, Truffaut's child is far from Ken Loach's child in "Wednesday's Child" (1969) or Lyn Ramsey's "Ratcatcher" (2000). These children are victims of the adult world, whereas Truffaut's child is never a victim. The consequence is that we can admire the child in Truffaut's films, but we are not necessarily invited to be sympathetic to the child. We watch his children occupy their own worlds, not caring if they are transgressing adult rules of conduct. As Truffaut's children grows into adults, their view of the world does not change. His characters remain occupants of their own worlds—functional and dysfunctional. This view is carried forward by Antoine in "Stolen Kisses" and "Love on the Run." It is also the prevailing view of the males in "Day for Night."

Women in all of these films present differently. Christine in "Stolen Kisses" and "Love on the Run" and Sabine and Colette in "Love on the Run" are all far more knowing and more honest than Antoine and Xavier. The men are grown-up boys, guarded, secretive, and disingenuous about the issue of commitment. The women seek stable relationships, and the men elude stable relationships.

The men seem equally unsettled in their work life. Antoine, having published a novel, works in a print shop. Xavier owns a bookstore. The actors and the director in "Day for Night" also have chosen a creative field, but both Alphonse and the director have fears and anxieties that threaten to undermine their commitment to their work.

In terms of the text interpretation, it is critical that the view of men and women underscore a particular perception of each. Truffaut's focus on the progress of relationships, or lack of, highlights the respective roles within a relationship. The view that men are really self-absorbed and rather deceptive boys is consistent throughout the four films excerpted here.

In terms of these boy-men, their spirited resistance to embracing adult responsibility is part of their charm. A second strategy of Truffaut's was to reveal their discomfort with honest communication. In "Stolen Kisses" and "Love on the Run," Antoine is constantly calling Christine and Sabine to make excuses for disappointing them. He forgets commitments made, he dissociates himself from accepting responsibility for what he has decided to do (perceived as negative by his girlfriend) and often will become defensive, but he always calls. In other words, Antoine is always trying to do the right thing but falls short. A third strategy Truffaut used to engage us with his boy-men was to draw attention to their artistic aspirations. These characters are too nonconformist to fit into the commercial world; maybe they can fit into the creative world where imagination (including lying) is viewed with greater tolerance. Truffaut also shifted genres to make his frustrating characters more engaging. "The 400 Blows" is unquestionably a serious melodrama, but it is also a film about a child who does not fit in. The genre of melodrama simply would not work once Antoine became an adult; consequently, Truffaut adopted a situation comedy approach to "Stolen Kisses," "Bed and Board," and "Love on the Run." He treated Antoine as a character who simply does not fit into the adult world but keeps trying.

In dramatizing the two worlds—the child's world and the adult world—Truffaut put a positive spin on the child's world and a less appealing spin on the adult world. In "Stolen Kisses," Antoine's youthful view of the world is illustrated by his playfulness with regard to his feelings for Christine. Whenever they go to the wine cellar in her parent's home, he steals a kiss. When he practices for his new profession of detective, he is again playful as he follows a woman down the street. Adult life, however, is filled with unfaithful people: Antoine bumps into Christine's father when he visits a bordello; Antoine's client's wife is more interested in the love-sick Antoine than she is in her own husband. But, the characteristics of adult life do not end with betrayal; for example, Antoine's client came to the detective agency to find out why people do not like him. And, of course, there is death. The detective who first encouraged Antoine to come into the business drops dead as he is interviewing a lead in his case.

"Love on the Run" is also filled with a similar view of adult life. Colette was sexually abused, her young daughter was killed in a car accident, her marriage failed, and she does not trust the man she loves. No less is the case with Antoine. He freely alters facts in his book which he has passed off as autobiographical. He lies to his girlfriend Sabine and is not forthcoming with his soon-to-be ex-wife (the mother of his son). Antoine the adult can only be straightforward with his 10-year-old son. To be an adult is to be a liar, a cheat, or at best disingenuous in all of one's dealings. This is Truffaut's view of adult behavior.

The schism is slightly different in "Day for Night." Here, the filmmaking is viewed as playful, and the behavior of all of the adults involved is characterized as selfish and self-destructive. Filmmaking, the act of making a fantasy manifest, is childlike, playful, and a reconstruction of reality, whereas real life (adult life) is fully a failing enterprise. I must point out that the theme of elevating the child and debunking adults coping with adult life is an utterly romantic one that recurs throughout Truffaut's work. Although Truffaut occasionally explored the dark side of this romantic sensibility, such as in "The Story of Adele H" and "Confidentially Yours," for the most part he embraced romance and its relationship to the child in all of us.

Directing the Actor

Few filmmakers cast so strongly for type—the look of the actor is key to the role and in turn to that actor's performance. Although Truffaut often worked with very talented actors such as Oscar Werner and Jean Moreau, more often he would choose actors for their looks. Françoise Dorleac, Catherine Deneuve, Natalie Baye, and Fannie Ardant were among his favorites. If you read the Truffaut biography by Antoine De Baecque and Serge Toubiana (*Truffaut*, Knopf, 1999), you will discover that Truffaut either had long-lasting affairs or married his leading ladies. Life and filmmaking merged.

And what of his alter ego, Jean-Pierre Léaud, who appeared in at least a half dozen films with Truffaut? Léaud had a particular look of a boy-man and an energetic, agitated style of performance. One has the impression that he always played himself. Nevertheless, Léaud is so identified with the Antoine Doinel character and the Doinel character is so identified with Truffaut that the issue of performance is not an issue. It is as if Truffaut simply asked Léaud to appear. At times, Léaud seems to deliver lines as if he is reading the text or improvising. He would appear to be a natural non-actor, although his petulant performance as Alphonse in "Day for Night" is convincing.

In "Day for Night," we can see how Truffaut cast for type; however, with regard to the actresses in his films the sense of performance is more powerful. Dorothea as Sabine, Dani as Liliane, Claude Jade as Christine—all of these actresses gave a more nuanced performance, energetic and goal directed. When we add the star performances of Dorleac, Deneuve, and Moreau, we have a very different style of performance—more filled with feeling. Each of these women also injected into their performances a sly sensuality utterly absent from the performance of Jean-Pierre Léaud. Perhaps the most we can say is that the male character actors such as Michel Lonsdale as the hated client in "Stolen Kisses" or

Albert Remy as Antoine's father in "The 400 Blows" offer credible performances within the range of believability, whereas actors such as Léaud only had to appear as themselves. The women performers added the sparkle and *raison d'être* to feel romantic. They drive the arc of each of these stories far more than do the men.

Performance tended to fall into a narrow range for Truffaut. Type was important and presence even more so. The charisma of the female performers and their performances suggests an antidote to the men who have taken on the acting style of a poseur. It is as if the male characters are deciding when to rather than whether to change direction. Changing direction from the drive of the narrative seems to be the primary style to the performance of the men in the four films we have been examining.

Directing the Camera

Truffaut, as a "New Wave" filmmaker, had a vested interest in being innovative as a director and differing from the leaders of the French film industry at the time who were considered stodgy and old fashioned. Truffaut proved to be less eccentric than Louis Malle, and not as cerebral as Jean-Luc Godard, nor was he as genre-centric as Claude Chabrol. Instead he found his own way.

Characteristic of Truffaut's visual work was the use of the jump cut rather than conventional pace devices in the editing of his films. Truffaut used jump cuts throughout the discovery of the unfaithful wife scene in "Stolen Kisses." Rather than cutting continually to close-ups of Antoine's reaction to being duped by the private detective, the scene relies instead on jump cuts to put us in the position of Antoine. The jump cuts create confusion and surprise, mimicking how Antoine felt at that moment, and it creates the feeling without resorting to the obvious, which would result from using the editing convention of the close-up.

Truffaut also used a moving camera freely but to different effect. When Antoine practices detective work on a Paris street in "Stolen Kisses," we have the classic subjective movement throughout the scene. Here, Antoine following a person and the inherent suspense are treated ironically, as the woman realizes she has been followed and alerts a policeman.

The more objective camera movement following the adolescent Antoine down to the sea in "The 400 Blows" is quite lyrical because of the length of the shots. Here, the moving shots flow one into the other to create a lengthy sequence. Before running away from the soccer match there was a scene with Antoine's mother on a visitor's day, but the message in that scene was accusatory and harsh. Antoine will be sent to a stricter reformatory, and his stepfather has totally rejected him, as has the mother apparently. It is a scene of profound abandonment. The lyrical moving shots of Antoine running to the sea beautifully illustrate his act of bravado, of rebellion against authority, and the lyricism offsets the pain we associate with the previous scene. Antoine seems to be reclaiming the energy of being free.

In the opening scene of "The 400 Blows," the moving camera is once again used differently. Here, the camera is restless; first it is moving, trying to find out what is happening in the classroom. The restless camera follows the pinup from student to student until it lands on Antoine's desk. At that point he is challenged by the teacher and punished. The camera continues to move about the classroom and later moves outside during recess. Quite what the camera is looking for we do not know, but it continues to move in the classroom as Antoine is ordered to clean the board of the message he scribbled during recess. My association with this probing camera is that it introduces unpredictability and surprise into an otherwise long take. Rather than quick cutting or using cutaways, Truffaut relied on this style of camera movement to create tension in the scene.

Another characteristic of Truffaut's approach to visualization is that he seems to prefer long and mid shots over the close shot. Truffaut uses few close-ups; consequently, his scene construction tends to use fewer shots, longer takes, and a more literary approach to the ordering of scenes. I have already discussed the hotel scene in "Stolen Kisses" where we see Antoine lose his first job. Another example would be the train scene in "Love on the Run." We know Antoine and Colette are both at the train station because a pan from one to the other establishes their presence; we also know that they have not seen each other. In this way, a parallel action sequence follows first Antoine and his son and then Colette. We guess that they will eventually meet, and they do, but Truffaut makes what happens before they do more compelling by relying on cutaways to the past. Those cutaways are connected by the book Colette is reading,

Antoine's *Love and Other Troubles.* In these cutaways, we see Antoine and Colette and the development of their relationship in a very short time. By using clips from his past films, Truffaut was able to intertwine the story of Antoine and Colette, two characters, with the work of François Truffaut, film director. Truffaut is being playful, just as he was playful with his use of the moving camera in "Stolen Kisses" and "The 400 Blows."

Whether we think of Truffaut the director celebrating filmmaking or celebrating the young romantic yearnings of Colette and Antoine or the adult yearnings of Antoine and Colette for romance in their contemporary life, the net effect of a visual narrative strategy such as using parallel action and cutaways becomes so much greater. Truffaut surprised us with his playful attitude toward these techniques and thrilled us with his nostalgic narrative. This is the real purpose of his visual choices—surprise and pleasure.

Clearly Truffaut could use pace when he chose to. In numerous sequences in "Day for Night" he used a quick montage of close-ups to characterize the details of filmmaking—lights, camera, and action. He also used long takes of the film to open and close the film. These shots were accomplished with the use of a dolly and crane, again illustrating the nature of the techniques of filmmaking.

But Truffaut never forgot the apparent narrative purpose of a scene and its real purpose. The excerpt that I described earlier in the chapter focused on a stunt, the death scene of Pamela. The stunt itself, the center of the scene, is the ostensible narrative purpose of the scene; however, the real purpose of the scene is to reveal that Liliane is leaving Alphonse for the stuntman. The scene opens with medium shots of Alphonse in bed and Liliane saying goodbye. He chastises her for wearing someone else's watch. He appears jealous. She tries to be reassuring. He grabs her genital area, an act of possession. The childish Alphonse is content (but he shouldn't be). All this is detailed in a series of mid shots. The Joelle/Bernard encounter follows, and then the stunt itself. The scene ends with Liliane leaving with the stuntman. Julie drives up to thank the stuntman for making her character's death look good. When Liliane tells her she is leaving with the stuntman, Julie becomes upset and speaks on behalf of Alphonse. Liliane says she cannot be lover, mother, sister, and nurse to Alphonse. It is too much. Besides, she is in love. As in the opening scene, a series of mid shots detail the scene, particularly Liliane and Julie. The real purpose—to emotionalize the human cost of filmmaking in broken relationships and broken hearts—is communicated by spending more film time on the relationship between Liliane and Alphonse and its dissolution than on the stunt itself. The message is clear—that we value the people who appear in films more than the film itself, that the act of filmmaking is a means of bringing people together, and that this coming together is short but as meaningful as any other relationships in life.

Although the camera strategies adopted by Truffaut are subtle and sometimes surprising, they do suggest his director's idea and serve to connect us to that idea in creative and surprising ways. Truffaut is playful with these powerful visual devices. This is his celebration.

Chapter 16

Roman Polanski: The Aloneness of Existence

Introduction

In Roman Polanski's work, the main characters are abandoned and the question is whether they can continue to exist. At times the answer is no, as in "The Tenant" (1976). At other times the answer is yes, but the character has suffered a complete emotional collapse, as in "Repulsion" (1965), or has borne the devil's baby, as in "Rosemary's Baby" (1968). At yet other times, the character survives with the wounds less obvious but no less deep, such as in "The Pianist" (2002) and "Chinatown" (1974).

So the question that persists in Polanski's world is the existential paradox that if each of us is alone how can we survive or sustain ourselves? Other filmmakers have concerned themselves with these dark questions—Ingmar Bergman, Andrei Tarkovsky, Krystof Kieslowski—but each of these filmmakers has suggested occasionally in their work a remission from loneliness. The religious component in the work of each of these directors creates a space for solace, for union with another. Not so Polanski. Polanski is unique in his obsession with the nature of aloneness and unique in his capacity to take us, his audience, into this space of aloneness.

In this chapter, we will explore Polanski's work and his director's idea. Distilling that director's idea is somewhat more difficult because Polanski's work has ranged so widely. If we were to look at the two genres that have dominated his work, horror and film noir, we might opt for victimization as a feature of his director's idea. Certainly "Repulsion" (1965), "Rosemary's Baby" (1968), and "The Tenant" qualify as horror, while "Chinatown" (1974), "Cul de Sac" (1966), and "Bitter Moon" (1992) qualify as film noir. If we add the war film "The Pianist" (2002), the melodrama "Tess" (1981), and the thrillers "Knife in the Water" (1962) and "Death and the Maiden" (1994), we begin to flesh out a world view that, on one level, depicts life as disappointing and relationships as betraying, in addition to the historical forces that conspire against the individual. Is this a paranoid view of life, or is it simply a modern as opposed to a romantic acceptance of life as a primal struggle where physical survival is possible but spiritual survival more unlikely? If we accept this view of relationships and community and national struggles, we begin to sense that the outcome for his characters will be that they are and always will be alone. How they cope with this state and the nature of their existence in the condition of being alone comprise Polanski's director's idea.

To depict and emotionalize such a bleak state, Polanski must take us deep into the core of his main characters. To do so he uses a set of strategies that allow the audience to literally be with his character. These strategies include an orthodox almost austere approach to narrative. As with Elia Kazan, he will take an almost documentary approach to the presentation of the world around the character. To depict the inner life of the character, however, he relies on point of view rather than on an expressionist style. He relies on that point of view to the exclusion of objective or alternative views, including his own. The result is an obsessive subjective perspective in a Polanski film. That point of view is that of the main character.

Another characteristic of the Polanski world is that specific details puncture the subjective world view of the character and remind the audience that circumstances have changed, time has passed—a rotting potato in "Repulsion" and a sudden execution in "The Pianist" to illustrate that the circumstances of the Jews in Warsaw have worsened.

Finally, Polanski, like Billy Wilder and Ernst Lubitsch before him, is a genre filmmaker of the classic sort. Although his contemporaries, such as Volker Schlondorff and Krystof Kieslowski, have opted for genres of voice, the moral fable, and the satire, Polanski has been far more classical, preferring to use film noir, horror films, or war films and their traditions of mixing plot and character layers in accord with the particular genre convention. The result is less adaptation of a genre. When Polanski has attempted to modify the genre in tone or plot, as in "Fearless Vampire Killers" (1968) or "The Ninth Gate" (2000), his films have been far less effective. The reverse is also true. When Polanski has made classic horror films ("Repulsion" and "Rosemary's Baby"), classic film noir ("Chinatown"), classic melodrama ("Tess"), and classic war films ("The Pianist"), he has created a number of timeless classics that also carry his director's idea. In this chapter, we will focus on excerpts from the following films: "Rosemary's Baby," "Chinatown," "Tess," and "The Pianist." In each of these films, I have tried to choose the main character's moment of abandonment or absolute aloneness.

"Rosemary's Baby" (1968)

In "Rosemary's Baby," a young couple looks at an apartment near Central Park. They love the apartment and take it. The young woman, Rosemary (Mia Farrow), is keen to have a baby, and her husband, Guy (John Cassavetes), is intent on advancing his career as an actor. Rosemary and Guy meet their eccentric neighbors Minnie and Roman Castevet (Ruth Gordon and Sidney Blackmer). The elderly couple is taking care of a young woman who shortly after meeting Rosemary commits suicide. As the Castevets become a more significant part of their lives, Rosemary and Guy pursue their individual, seemingly mutually exclusive agendas, much to the frustration of Rosemary. However, eventually the increasingly distant Guy agrees to have a baby. Minnie provides Rosemary with an old charm necklace that contains an aromatic tannis root. She is ready to be impregnated (but not by Guy). At a special dinner given by the young couple, Minnie and Roman provide the dessert. The chocolate mousse is drugged, and after Rosemary falls unconscious she is prepared by Guy for the rape that will follow. With his minion present, the Devil rapes Rosemary. Although Guy claims he was the one who did it, he has made a bargain with the Devil. Both the pregnancy and his career advance quickly. The Castevets makes sure one of their doctors cares for Rosemary, and any barriers (*e.g.*, Rosemary's friend Hutch) are eliminated. In the end, alone, Rosemary has the child-devil. She is aware that she has been a victim but motherly instinct prevails—she will care for her child. The sequence we will focus on here is the abandonment of Rosemary by Guy, which highlights her aloneness, Guy's success as an actor (his competitor for a role suddenly goes blind), and the preparations for becoming pregnant. The sequence concludes with the rape and its aftermath, Guy claiming to have had intercourse with his unconscious wife and explaining the scratches on her back by his drunkenness and his being carried away as a result.

"Chinatown" (1974)

The second excerpt is from "Chinatown," which is set in 1930s Los Angeles. A private detective, Jake Gittes (Jack Nicholson), is hired to look into the infidelity of a husband, Hollis Mulwray

(Darrell Zwerling), a city official responsible for the Water Department. His wife, Evelyn Mulwray (Faye Dunaway), did not hire Gittes; instead, it was an actress claiming to be Mrs. Mulwray. Gittes is being set up as is Mulwray. Gittes does find Mulwray keeping company with a very young woman. In short order, he is being sued by the real Mrs. Mulwray, and Mr. Mulwray, after witnessing various Water Department irregularities, is murdered.

Gittes, threatened in every direction, is hired by the real Mrs. Mulwray to find out what happened to her husband. What Gittes discovers is that someone is diverting water from Los Angeles to the Valley and also buying up land in the Valley. The trail leads to Evelyn Mulwray's father, Noah Cross (John Huston). Cross in turn hires Gittes to find Mulwray's young mistress.

At this point, Gittes get emotionally involved with Mrs. Mulwray and quickly discovers that her dead husband's young mistress is Evelyn Mulwray's sister and soon thereafter finds out that she is also her daughter. Siding with Mrs. Mulwray, he tries to help her escape with her daughter/sister. In Chinatown, all the parties come together and Evelyn Mulwray is killed by the police. Although Noah Cross killed Hollis Mulwray, he is wealthy and gets away with the murder and with his young daughter. Gittes is tragically unable to prevent harm to his new love, Evelyn Mulwray. He is led away by colleagues as the film ends.

The sequence we will focus on is the growing intimacy of Jake Gittes and Evelyn Mulwray. Just as he is taken with her, she receives a call. She asks him to trust her and says that she will return soon. He shatters one of her tail lights and follows her. He sees her drug Hollis Mulwray's young mistress. He confronts her in her car, and she confesses that the young girl is her sister. He believes her, but he is set up by the police to bring Evelyn Mulwray in for questioning in the death of Ida Sessions, the actress who initially impersonated Mrs. Mulwray to hire Gittes. She is also suspected of killing her husband. When Gittes confronts her she reluctantly tells him that the young woman is both her sister and her daughter. She then confesses that she willingly had sexual relations with her father; it wasn't rape. She is crushed by the admission. Although Gittes promises to help her, he in fact has initiated a chain of events that will lead to her death.

"Tess" (1981)

The third excerpt is from "Tess," which is the story of a poor girl from an old but noble family in England during the Industrial Revolution. When Tess' father, an alcoholic with a large family, discovers that his name, d'Urberville, is a noble name, he sends his eldest child Tess (Nastassja Kinski) off to find the rich relatives. Perhaps they will buy his title or at least help their family. Reluctantly, Tess seeks out the d'Urbervilles and finds that they are, indeed, rich but are not really d'Urbervilles. The family bought the title and lives on the estate. The son Alec (Leigh Lawson) is a ne'er-do-well and he sees in his "cousin" Tess an easy conquest. After the modest Tess takes a job on the chicken farm of the estate, Alec pursues her and finally, a bit drunk, she gives in. She quickly leaves Alec for home, where she has his child. The sickly child soon dies, however. Tess sees the child's death as punishment for her loveless affair. When the local church will not allow the bastard baby to be buried on church grounds, Tess sees this as further punishment. She leaves home and goes to work on a dairy farm. There, Angel (Peter Firth), a vicar's son, falls in love with her and she with him. He wants to marry her. She is reluctant because of her past. She tries to tell him her shameful history but cannot, and her mother advises against it. She writes Angel a letter but he never reads it, as it was hidden under his rug. She loses her courage and destroys the note. They marry.

On their wedding night, Angel tells her of a short city affair with an older woman. He asks for her forgiveness. She grants it. She then confesses her history honestly and asks his forgiveness, but he does not grant it. He is angry and feels betrayed. He abandons her. Tess returns to her home, and then seeks work. The work is hard and demeaning. Alec, to whom Tess' mother has written, finds her and offers to care for her and her family. Her father is unwell, and the family will lose their home when he dies. Tess rejects Alec, but he keeps returning. When the family is evicted following her father's death, they are forced to live in a tent, at which point Tess relents and becomes Alec's mistress.

Angel returns, unwell. When he recovers he seeks out Tess and asks her forgiveness, but it is too late. When he leaves, Tess is inconsolable and, when Alec berates her, she kills him and runs after Angel. He will save her, he claims, but in the end he cannot. The police find them and she is taken away to prison. Justice is done, and Tess is hanged.

The excerpt we will use is when Tess tries to tell Angel of her past before she agrees to marry him. Although she fails to tell him before the marriage, she is mindful of the need to enter into the marriage honestly, as admonished by the priest at the wedding ceremony. That night, after Angel's confession to her, she in turn confesses and loses him. He runs off to Brazil, abandoning Tess to her fate. This effort at honesty and the consequent abandonment will be the focus of our discussion about "Tess."

"The Pianist" (2002)

The last excerpt is from "The Pianist," which begins with the German invasion of Poland and ends when the war ends. "The Pianist" is Wladyslaw Szpilman (Adrien Brody), a world-famous pianist, a Jew who survives the war because Jews, Poles, and Germans, at different points through the war, have acted to save his life. The film is about Szpilman's survival, but it is also about all the losses he sustains. The sequence we will focus on is his effort in 1942 to secure work papers for his father. The effort only delays the inevitable—the deportation of the Szpilman family to a death camp. Eventually, Szpilman, his parents, and his three siblings are gathered at the train station with hundreds of others. Just when they are to be herded onto the transport train, a Jewish policeman pulls Szpilman from the crowd and encourages him to escape because he is a person worth saving. This is when he is torn away from his family, who is pressed onto the train. A German soldier rips the violin from his father's hands. This is the last time Szpilman will see his family. He helps another Jew cart bodies from the site and is overwhelmed with the grief of loss. Around him are the dead. He seeks out the small apartment where his family lived in the Jewish ghetto. Now it is empty but for the artifacts, and Szpilman is alone.

Text Interpretation

In terms of our experience of the director's idea, it is important that the state of aloneness be powerfully conveyed as we experience the main characters, their goals, and the power of the antagonists and plot to isolate the main characters, in short to victimize the main characters. To understand how the director's idea operates in Polanski's case, we need to explore for a moment the audience's relationship with his main characters and how a director can create empathy or identification with the main characters.

To encourage the audience to identify with the main characters, the micro strategies must be character focused and the macro strategies structural. The micro strategies have to do with the nature of the characters. Whether they are charismatic or flawed, there is an energy that emanates from the characters that engages the audience. Another strategy writers use is a private moment that reveals the true character. This strategy is appealing because the audience feels privileged when characters reveal themselves to them. The macro strategies essentially use plot and antagonists to victimize the main character. None of us likes to be victimized, and we hope that the character can avoid victimization. The strategy of victimizing the main character is the strategy Polanski uses. His characters do not manage to avoid victimization; instead, they are victimized by both the antagonist and the plot. Let's see how this works.

In "Rosemary's Baby," the plot is to have a normal woman bear the Devil's baby. Rosemary's goal is to have a baby, but the Castevets and her own husband Guy stand against her. They succeed in victimizing Rosemary, and in the end she bears the Devil's baby.

In "Chinatown," Jake Gittes' goal is to do his job effectively. The plot, to divert water from the city to the Valley and to profit from the appreciation of property values in the Valley, requires the death of anyone who is a barrier. The most prominent killing is that of Hollis Mulwray, and because Gittes has been investigating Mulwray for marital indiscretion, Gittes is pre-empted in his actions against Mulwray. He is out of the loop, used by bigger players with bigger goals than previous marital infidelity. He feels betrayed and doesn't understand why. As Gittes investigates the murder of Mulwray he bumps up against the why of it, the plot. He also begins a relationship with Mrs. Mulwray. The plot and this relationship bring Gittes up against the antagonist Noah Cross, Mrs. Mulwray's father. He loses Mrs. Mulwray, and Cross gets away with his scheme and his child by his daughter. Gittes is a victim of the plot and of the antagonist.

Tess d'Urberville is a victim of all three principal men in the story and ultimately is hanged for striking back at one of them. Her father, a drunk with pretensions, sends Tess off in pursuit of the well-to-do relatives. Tess discovers that Alec and his family bought the d'Urberville estate and name. Alec seduces Tess and she bears his illegitimate child. Angel, the love of her life, deserts her when, on their wedding night, she asks forgiveness for her relationship with Alec. Although Tess attempts to retain her dignity, in the end she is forced to turn to Alec to save her destitute mother and siblings from abject poverty. Throughout the story Tess, decent but poor, tries to retain her self-respect but the men in her life victimize her until she snaps, kills Alec, and is hanged for the murder.

In "The Pianist," the plot is the war against the Jews. Although the antagonist has many faces, we can say that the Nazis represent the antagonist and for the most part they are indiscriminately destructive of the Jews. Szpilman loses everyone as the plot progresses. In the end, all he has is his life and his music. He returns to play but he has lost so much. He has survived but his victimization has stripped him of all those he cared about—his family. In spite of the clarity of the main character's goal, the vigor of the plot, and the scale of the antagonist's goal, the interpretation remains that of a victim rather than a hero. We need only look at Spielberg's interpretation of Oscar Schindler in "Schindler's List" (1993) to highlight differences in the presentation of the main characters in the two films. Szpilman is neither a hero nor a romantic character, as Schindler is depicted; he is simply a human stripped down to the status of animal but trying to retain a shred of humanity—in short, a survivor.

A second feature of Polanski's text interpretation is the powerful sense of environment in his work—New York in "Rosemary's Baby," Los Angeles in "Chinatown," rural England during the Industrial Revolution in "Tess," and Warsaw, the cultural and urban center of Poland, in "The Pianist." Polanski's environments differ from those of John Ford in that Ford's environments do not test the characters and consequently elevate them. His work also differs from that of George Stevens in that Stevens' environments present a spiritual template for his characters. The environments in Polanski's films are neutral; they suggest that help should be available but none is. In this sense, the beauty of Polanski's environments is ironic because they offer little or no solace to his characters; they offer no protection from victimization. Cosmopolitan New York only serves to mask the primitiveness of the struggle between the forces of good and evil in "Rosemary's Baby." Similarly, the beauty of Southern California masks the primitive venality and greed operating in "Chinatown." In "Tess," the pastoral beauty of the countryside masks the ugliness of class and the exploitative nature of economic progress. In "The Pianist," the beauty and culture of civilized Warsaw can do nothing to protect its Jewish citizens. Again, the beauty of the environment masks the barbarity of its inhabitants.

Another feature of Polanski's text interpretation is his exclusion of the extraneous or, put another way, his documentary-like approach toward the progressive victimization of his main character. Detailing this progression requires the inclusion of specific details as markers. In "The Pianist," for example, Szpilman's finding a way to keep his father from being deported means securing a work permit. Szpilman secures the document, and his father can work, but this does not save the family—all will be deported. When the building is emptied and a woman asks where they will be going, she is shot by the German commanding officer. When the family is gathered outside the train landing, the father buys a caramel with all the funds left among them. He then splits the caramel with a knife and distributes the pieces to the family members. When the father is pushed onto the train, a German soldier grabs his violin from him. The father tries to hold onto his most prized possession, his last link with civilized culture and his work life. The soldier prevails and aggressively denies the father that last link. Upon returning to their home in the ghetto, Szpilman sees only bodies, mostly the young. All of these specific details create an authenticity to the barbarism of the war against the Jews and the struggle of the Szpilman family to retain a shred of human feeling and memory.

The details, the environment, the positioning of the main character, and the vigor of the plot work together to create the sense of aloneness of the main character. The performances of the actors deepen that sense of aloneness.

Directing the Actor

Polanski has always had a courageous approach to casting. He is very interested in type and in talent. Mia Farrow as Rosemary is the ultimate angelic victim in appearance; therefore, her tenacity in fighting her fate is surprising and speaks to her inner strength as an actress. Nastassja Kinski as Tess also comes across as a beautiful victim, although hers is a far more interior resistance. As a religious person, she is struggling with the dissonance between her own morality and the morality of others. In each case, the moral authority is vested in men who betray her. In the case of Adrien Brody as Wladyslaw Szpilman, Polanski has again cast for a surface vulnerability and expressiveness that imply the ultimate victim. Once again, though, the will to survive is a reflection of the inner conviction and drive of the actor. The talent to convey that inner drive for survival is the key to Brody's successful Oscar-winning performance.

Beyond casting, Polanski seems actively interested in sidestepping the "star" personality of some of his actors. He did not exploit the star image of Jack Nicholson as Jake Gittes; instead, he seemed to work against it. He worked Nicholson hard to create a sympathetic portrait of a man who has been emotionally wounded in the past and is trying to avoid a repeat. The result is a sensitive portrayal of a man trying to be honest in a dishonest world. Polanski did the same with John Cassavetes in "Rosemary's Baby." Working with Cassavetes' bad boy image, he made the character Guy a narcissist, an opportunist, a man willing to throw over his wife for his career. The portrayal in this case took advantage of Cassavetes' Hollywood image as being difficult and counter-Hollywood. By having a cynic play a narcissist, Polanski and Cassavetes created a role that is bigger in feeling than it would otherwise be.

Finally, Polanski gives each actor a specific note to play, a key to the performance. Rosemary is the mother or the wannabe mother throughout. The test for her is whether she will still be motherly when her baby is born. Jake Gittes is the professional with a heart of gold. In a sense, Polanski directed Nicholson as if he were a generous hooker, and of course Nicholson's character ends up paying the price for his heart of gold.

In the case of Tess, she is an innocent, a child in life forced into the cruel adult world. She tries to retain her innocence through all of her ordeals, but in the end the cruelty of the adult world drives her to murder and to her death. Szpilman is forever the musician. Music is the beauty in his life; it is what he holds onto until the end, and in the end his music saves him. In each case, these specific notes help the actors deepen their performances and strengthen the sense of their inner lives.

Directing the Camera

Polanski's director's idea, the aloneness of existence, goes to the heart of his camera placement and shot selection. Camera placement tells us whether or not we, the audience, should identify with the character. Subjective placement encourages identification. Proximity to the action suggests even more about the audience's relationship with a character. In Polanski's choice of a camera placement that is not only subjective but in effect placed so close to the action that it actually crowds the character, he is pushing us into identification as well as into developing a feeling about that character. The crowding creates an almost claustrophobic intensity around the characters. This placement has been an important dimension of Polanski's work since "Knife in the Water" and "Repulsion." In the films we have discussed here, Polanski used this placement to enhance our identification with Rosemary, Jake Gittes, Tess, and Szpilman. He also used the sense of proximity, or crowding, to create a sense of the aloneness of the character.

Aloneness requires context, and Polanski used the moving camera as well as the wide angle to contextualize how alone a character is. An example of the moving camera shot is the return of Szpilman to the streets of the ghetto, after he has lost his parents. The camera captures Szpilman crying, all around him the emptiness of the streets of the ghetto. All that is left is the artifacts of the removed Jews or the dead bodies of those left behind. Szpilman occupies only part of the frame and is seen as truly abandoned and alone.

An example of Polanski's use of the full frame of a shot for the same purpose is from "Tess." On her wedding night, in the foreground of the shot Tess is confessing her sinful past to new husband Angel. Polanksi held the shot for a long time. In the background, standing against the fireplace, is an out-of-focus Angel. He listens passively to her story. The gap between them is huge, and it telegraphs the outcome of the confession; the marriage is over before it has started. Tess is alone.

Point of view is always important, and point of view tends to be subjective. To punctuate a point of view, Polanski will use a strategic long shot. In the scene that leads up to the deportation in "The Pianist," Polanski has focused on the Szpilman family as well as young and old people. A young woman has suffocated her baby to avoid deportation. An old man counsels that they are not going to a labor camp—why would the Germans rely on women, children, and old men for labor? They intend to kill all of them. The Szpilmans try unsuccessfully to remain a family. During the rush to the train, Szpilman escapes. All of these scenes are detailed with close-ups. Once the train has pulled out, however, Polanski cut to an extreme long shot of the yard. We see only the artifacts, belongings abandoned by their owners—only things, no people. The long shot punctuates what has happened here, and it is as powerful as any close-up used elsewhere in the film.

Polanski achieved a similar result when he used long shots of the apartment in "Rosemary's Baby." The emptiness of the apartment and its coldness remind us of the absence of Guy, her husband. It also reminds us of the terrible events that have occurred in this building, events that contextualize what will soon happen to Rosemary. Beside the long shot, Polanski also relied on the powerful cutaway—in "Rosemary's Baby," the chocolate mousse that will transport Rosemary away from the rape experience to follow; in "The Pianist," the execution of a mother as she asks about the destination of the Jews; in "Chinatown," the broken tail light that will lead Gittes toward a sense of betrayal by Mrs. Mulwray; in "Tess," the jewelry of Angel's grandmother that he gives Tess just before her confession. The cutaway always introduces a new idea, but in Polanski's work that new idea always leads to the lonely space the character will soon occupy. If it conveys a sense of the optimistic, as in the jewelry shot in "Tess," the optimism does not last and in that sense the shot is bitterly ironic in the light of what shortly follows.

Polanski rarely relies on editing to convey the sensibility of dread and aloneness that permeates his work. More often he relies on camera placement and shot selection, including his powerful use of specific cutaways. He also tries to elevate his story to a mythic level. Consider the visual character of the rape in "Rosemary's Baby." Consider also the role of Chinatown as not only the location for the last scene but also a metaphor for the confluence of passion and

230

danger that ultimately leads to tragedy. In "The Pianist," Szpilman climbs out of a hospital under attack into a Bosch-like bombed-out Warsaw, the location of much of the last act of "The Pianist." In "Tess," the last scene is set at Stonehenge, dedicated to the spiritual gods of Celtic England. There, the police find Angel and Tess, and from Stonehenge she is taken to meet her fate. The use of these rather mythological scenes and locations after almost documentary-like treatments earlier in "The Pianist" and "Rosemary's Baby" raises the film experience to a deeper representational level. Because aloneness is physical for the most part, these scenes represent Polanski's elevation of the physical to the spiritual. They deepen the sense of his director's idea.

Although Polanski has ventured into parody in "The Vampire Killers" and "Cul de Sac," his strongest work has remained his genre films that in a rather orthodox fashion have transported his characters into a sense of their world, victimizing them and leaving them in a state of abandonment. Polanski is far from the romantic vision of modern life presented by his colleague Krystof Kieslowski in "Red" (1998). He is also far from the inevitable cynicism of his colleague Jerzy Skolimowski in "Deep End" (1968). He is also far from the political stance taken by his colleague Andrej Wajda in "Man of Marble" (1980). Perhaps he is closest to that other Polish-American artist, Isaac Bashevis Singer, in the sense that we are all alone, and the person a character will become is a secret to be revealed to that character when he or she has been abandoned and is alone.

Chapter 17

Stanley Kubrick: The Darkness of Modern Life

Introduction

Many theories of modern history were built on the model that as man works his way up from the animal world progress is made. That progress is an interpretation of human history which would be unmistakable if a historian based the interpretation on the work of Stanley Kubrick, who explored the darkness of modern life. That darkness—with regard to human frailty or something more sinister— is consistent whether Kubrick is exploring the future ("2001: A Space Odyssey," 1968), the past ("Barry Lyndon," 1975), or the present ("Eyes Wide Shut," 2000).

Although Kubrick made few films in a career that spanned almost 50 years, each of those films has had an enduring impact. Devalued in the Andrew Sarris hierarchy (see Sarris' *The American Cinema: Strained Seriousness*, University of Chicago Press, 1968, pp. 195–196), Kubrick's reputation among filmmakers and film enthusiasts has grown to the point where he today occupies a kind of exclusive, Olympian height reserved only for the gods of film-making, whomever they may be. As I mentioned early in the book, my goal is not so much to defend filmmakers as to try to understand what makes their work compelling and influential for the new generation of filmmakers.

In his career, Kubrick most often devoted himself to films about war, such as "Paths of Glory" (1956), "Dr. Strangelove" (1964), and "Full Metal Jacket" (1987); fables about human nature, such as "Lolita" (1962), "A Clockwork Orange" (1972), and "Eyes Wide Shut"; and genre films—crime films such as "The Killing" (1956), horror films such as "The Shining" (1979), science fiction films such as "2001: A Space Odyssey," and epics such as "Spartacus" (1960) and "Barry Lyndon." What all these films have in common, beyond their ambition, is a focus on the dark side of human nature. To cope with that darkness Kubrick used humor. Irony infuses "Dr. Strangelove," "A Clockwork Orange," "2001: A Space Odyssey," and "Lolita." And what is certain is that a character will lose a pound of flesh in the course of a Kubrick narrative. That pound of flesh may be spiritual or it may be physical. What is certain is the loss.

In order to articulate this loss Kubrick tended to focus on a particular human failing in each of his films. Before we examine those failings, what needs to be said is that there are particular bold, filmic qualities in Kubrick's work that pay off in much the same way as Sergei Eisenstein's work. It might be useful to highlight these qualities before we descend into the darkness that characterizes so much of Kubrick's work. His pay off can be categorized as the shot/scene as a visual metaphor and the set piece as a technical challenge.

Perhaps there is no other Kubrick scene as famous as the ape triumphantly throwing his bone weapon into the air, after which the camera cuts to a space station in outer space, continuing the movement albeit millions of years later. Almost as famous is Slim Pickens riding a nuclear warhead toward its target in "Dr. Strangelove." Complete with cowboy hat, he is riding the bomb as if it is a bucking bronco. A third example is the circular tracking shot of a master sergeant inspecting and humiliating his raw recruits in "Full Metal Jacket." Yet another example is Alex's beating of his male victim to the melodic sound of "Singin' in the Rain" in "A Clockwork Orange."

What is striking in each case is the visual metaphor Kubrick created, and in each case that metaphor drips with irony. In the victorious toss of the bone in "2001: A Space Odyssey," the metaphor is all about technology and progress. The irony here relates to whether the discovery of weaponry, with all its implications about proprietary rights and the disenfranchisement of others, is really progress. In the example from "Dr. Strangelove," the irony of the metaphor is much more apparent. A bomb that is about to kill hundreds of thousands of people is not likely to generate quite the same excitement and bravado of cowboy life. The third example, from "Full Metal Jacket," also deals with equating military values with societal values. The master sergeant is in charge of creating killing machines. This is his stated purpose, and in this scene he begins to find out who will and who will not become killing machines. The last example, from "A Clockwork Orange," is as ironic as the shot from "Dr. Strangelove." The "Singin' in the Rain" music suggests romance and love; however, the visuals are all about aggression and hate.

The set pieces are as audacious in their goals as are the shots/scenes; however, the goal is more complex. If the shots/scenes are impressive metaphors, the set pieces are rather like a rollercoaster ride where the viewer is in the hot seat. From thrills to nausea, the goal of the set piece is to give the audience a sense of being there. Because the sequences often pose a moral dilemma, the viewer will tend to feel queasy and uneasy.

Examples of sequences that have served as set pieces would include the execution of the three French soldiers for cowardice in "Paths of Glory." Here, the ritual of death is given a macabre dignity. The knowledge that these men are not cowards but are scapegoats for the failures of their commanding general makes the ritual and the soldiers' deaths painful beyond measure. A similar paradox infuses the sniper attack in "Full Metal Jacket." We will examine that set piece in more detail later in the chapter.

In "2001: A Space Odyssey," the single surviving astronaut's trip into deep outer space creates a sense that time and space are being obliterated. Kubrick offered his interpretation of what it might be like to approach the speed of light by shooting the passage as a light show, with changes in speed indicated by the increasing diffusion and refraction as the astronaut approaches his destination. Whether hallucination or reality, the trip is quite unlike any other film journey in nature or length. It is otherworldly.

235

Another set piece that is lengthy and almost unbearable to experience is the duel between Barry Lyndon and his stepson. Kubrick takes us into the inner emotional state of the hatred of the son and the ambivalence of the father. The set piece ends with a life shattered, that of Barry Lyndon, who has lost his leg and his status as a result of living a life of slipping morals and degradation. Barry Lyndon's fate is a caution to us all: To lift yourself above your station you must be able to pay the price.

We could include the attack on the ant hill in "Paths of Glory," the robbery in "The Killing," the final battle in "Spartacus," and Torrance's pursuit of his wife in "The Shining." Using a mix of camera motion and compositional acuity, each of these set pieces powerfully contributes to the Kubrick mythology. We turn now to the films and excerpts we will discuss in the remainder of the chapter.

"2001: A Space Odyssey" (1968)

We begin with the dawn of man sequence in "2001: A Space Odyssey." The film is presented as a history of mankind from the very beginning and well into the future. The focal point for the dawn of man sequence is the evolution and resulting primacy of the ape due to the development of weaponry. The focus of the balance of the film is on man's struggle for mastery over technology and the mysteries of the spiritual. The plot of the outer space sequence is the journey of astronaut Dave Bowman (Keir Dullea). The film concludes with his death and his rebirth. The dawn of man sequence begins in a timeless age. Eventually the ape appears and cohabits with other animals, but the quest for food means that the less powerful creatures are food for the more powerful ones. Night is a time of fear for the community of apes. Rivalries with other communities of apes, over water, seem to have no resolution. The stone is introduced. A deity of sorts, the stone is mysterious. The apes gather about it in curiosity and wonderment. A scene follows where an ape realizes that a bone can smash other bone. A cutaway to the stone suggests thought, association, perhaps learning and intelligence. The bone is effective in crushing other bone and other prey—food for the families. The formerly vegetarian apes gather at night to eat their meat. In another dispute over water, one group of apes armed with weapons kill the leader of their adversaries. They are victorious and take possession of the water hole. In this sequence, timelessness has passed into a progressive sense of time. Intelligence, learning, and possession have all come from the stone and weaponry. The dawn of man is over. Millions of years and man's history has been presented in a sequence that is less than 20 minutes.

"Barry Lyndon" (1975)

If a kind of progressive arrogance was at the heart of the dawn of man sequence, pride and its price are the core of the opening sequence of "Barry Lyndon." Barry Lyndon is a poor Irishman of noble birth. His father dies in a duel as the film opens, and Barry will become the victim of a duel with his stepson as the film ends. In between, Kubrick chronicles the life of a character whose choices in life, in Ireland and later in a career and marriage on the Continent, are increasingly immoral. In the end, Barry is a victim not so much of circumstance as of his own moral weakness. The opening sequence focuses on Barry's love and desire for his own cousin, Nora. Initially, she is seductive and encourages his affections. In the end, however, she chooses to marry a British captain who has the income necessary to restore her and her family to a more stable position. Barry does not accept her choice and feels that his honor is stained. He challenges the captain to a duel. A sham duel is staged that leads Barry to believe that he has killed the captain. He leaves home, never to return. This is the last sense of youthful innocence Barry Lyndon will experience.

"Full Metal Jacket" (1987)

The third excerpt we focus on is the sniper attack from "Full Metal Jacket" that occurs in the latter part of the film. The film breaks down into two phases: basic training and combat. In basic training, we watch Joker (Matthew Modine) and his fellow recruits become a unit of killing machines, as the master sergeant characterizes them. The sequence ends with the most continually humiliated recruit (Vincent D'Onofrio) killing the master sergeant and himself. Basic training is over. The film then shifts to Vietnam and primarily focuses on the Battle of Hue. The platoon has just lost its lieutenant and is now being led by Cowboy (Arliss Howard). The platoon is nervous and lost. A soldier is sent to scout a way forward and is wounded by a sniper. When he is shot again another soldier goes to his rescue, but he, too, is shot, and both end up dead because no tanks are available to come to their rescue. As the platoon moves up closer to the sniper's position, Cowboy is shot and killed. The rest of the platoon moves in for revenge. They wound the sniper, a young woman. As they gather around her they decide to let her die from her wounds. Joker is particularly conflicted because the young woman is now begging to be killed. Finally, he shoots her. The sequence ends as the remainder of the platoon returns to combat.

"Eyes Wide Shut" (2000)

The final excerpt I will use is the opening sequence of "Eyes Wide Shut" (2000). Screenwriter Frederic Raphael wrote an intriguing memoir on his work with Stanley Kubrick (*Eyes Wide Open*, Ballantine Books, New York, 1999). It offers insights into the Kubrick process and is especially meaningful as Kubrick died just as the film was released in North America in 2000. The film, provocative as any of Kubrick's works, is a cautionary fable about the limits of narcissism. William Harford (Tom Cruise) is a New York physician with a beautiful apartment and a beautiful wife, Alice (Nicole Kidman). His problem is a gnawing dissatisfaction with his life. Is his wife bored and keen on an extramarital affair? Why do his rich clients act out their sexual desires to the detriment of their relationships and in spite of their social position? Why do all the people he admires and cares about seek danger and thrills? Should he, too? He does seek out danger and thrills that threaten his marriage, but in the end he and his wife, almost in a state of resignation, opt to remain together.

The sequence we are concerned with begins with preparations for Victor Ziegler's Christmas party at his home, which looks like a museum. The Harfords know no one, but Alice seems to be taken up with looking at those who may or may not be looking at her. She seems to seek the looking, to need it. And she finds it. Bill is scooped away to rescue his host from potential embarrassment when his woman of the moment almost dies of an overdose. Alone, Alice is approached by a handsome Hungarian lothario who, as Alice continues to become more drunk, attempts to sweep her off her feet. In the end, after many dances, he proposes a tryst but she points to her wedding ring. He retorts that her ring should only liberate her to do as she wishes (in her search for pleasure). She waves goodnight but with a mixed message. She blows him a kiss. The evening concludes with a sexual encounter between husband and wife, but, as earlier, Alice looks away as if to see if anyone else is admiring her, besides her husband.

Text Interpretation

Kubrick's director's idea, the darkness of modern life, required a scale of narrative ambition that is rare in filmmaking. Only D.W. Griffith, Eisenstein, and Orson Welles have exhibited a similar level of ambition. Kubrick was always attracted to themes of scale. In some cases, the scale was so great as to defeat the project, as in the case of his Napoleon film, but even early in his career Kubrick was able to create epic narratives. In 1957, he made "Paths of Glory" from the Humphrey Cobb novel. Even a director of the stature of George Stevens had been unable to unlock studio support for the production of the Cobb novel. Kubrick was able to do it by securing one major star, Kirk Douglas. By making the film in Europe at the Munich Studios and by using B actors for the other roles, Kubrick was able to produce a film of enormous narrative ambition. Within three years he was making "Spartacus," a major Hollywood epic, and although he lost control of the film to its star/producer Kirk Douglas, the film remains one of the great epics to be produced by Hollywood.

Kubrick's narrative ambition grew exponentially. In 1962, he produced "Lolita," based on Nabokov's verboten love classic. He followed that film with his classic about nuclear holocaust, "Dr. Strangelove," and reached his pinnacle shortly thereafter with "2001: A Space Odyssey," a film about nothing less than all of human history and our future. Five years later, "A Clockwork Orange," his translation of Burgess' novel, seems less ambitious but only in comparison to his own "2001: A Space Odyssey" film. The film remains the ultimate parable about private aggression and public or governmental control of that aggression. The film ended his serious phase of films about adolescent angst. "Barry Lyndon" was of course a return to a larger palate. The tale of Barry Lyndon, or Redmond Barry, as he begins life is the basis for a more general narrative about 18th-century European life, particularly with regard to the role of money in the course of the life of the noble class. Thackeray and his film translator Kubrick proposed that money— its necessity, the means of acquiring it, and the means necessary to hold on to it—altered man's nature. It certainly did in the case of Barry Lyndon. The life of the title character allowed Kubrick to comment on the transitional period when romantic values were transformed into something altogether more modern, more dark.

"The Shining," "Full Metal Jacket," and "Eyes Wide Shut," all set in the here and now, are each specific in character but general in their implications of loss. Both "The Shining" and "Full Metal Jacket" articulate a loss of innocence. A writer isolated by his work as the custodian of a closed resort loses his mind in "The Shining." A writer, Joker, struggles to sustain his conscience and humanity in the midst of soldiering in "Full Metal Jacket." Finally, in "Eyes Wide Shut," it is the ample culture of narcissism that is under attack. The Harfords' life is materially rich—this is the specific. The generality enters when the search for spiritual richness is misinterpreted as the search for sexual gratification. No spiritual rewards here, only death and disappointment. Again, the specific was broadened into a generality as Kubrick looked for the large themes of modern life.

Important in the creation of scale are two other features of Kubrick's text interpretation. The first is the centrality of ideas in his narrative, and the second is his approach to character in his films. In "2001: A Space Odyssey," the narrative is remarkably ambitious, but essentially it conveys the idea that, although progress has been made, the arrogance produced by that progress has eroded man's capacity to be in the world. The erosion has made man nature's victim rather than its master. In "Full Metal Jacket," the creation of killing machines may seem necessary to further modern imperialism but the consequent loss in humanity and empathy for others more than offsets the gains. In "Eyes Wide Shut," the modern material world is a pretty empty, lonely place, instead of being a cornucopia of joy and well-being. All of the characters in "Eyes Wide Shut" are well off materially (except perhaps for the women in the sex-for-sale business), but the characters come across as depressed and spiritually flat.

In order to go from the specific to the general, a particular approach to character is required. When I discussed George Stevens and his approach to character in an earlier chapter, I noted the importance of the audience identifying with the characters and all that Stevens deployed to deepen that identification. The opposite is at play with Kubrick. He invites simply watching a character rather than empathizing with that character, and he tends to treat the character as a stereotype rather than as a three-dimensional person. Although we might admire Joker's antiauthoritarian streak, we never know enough about him to care more deeply in "Full Metal Jacket." When Cowboy dies, he is no more than Joker's friend and the platoon's nervous recent leader. His death is the pointless death of yet another soldier, the general case more than the specific. Whether the character is unsympathetic, as is the short-tempered Redmond Barry in "Barry Lyndon," or arrogant, as is astronaut Bowman in "2001: A Space Odyssey," the result is the same. We watch these characters rather than seeing ourselves in them. In this way they too become the general rather than the specific.

Another technique of Kubrick's was to position the main character as his own antagonist. This point is clearest in "The Killing" and "The Shining," but it is also the case of Redmond Barry in "Barry Lyndon." His treatment of his wife and her son moves him from protagonist to antagonist. In "2001: A Space Odyssey," Bowman's treatment of Hal the computer also raises the question of who is the protagonist and who is the antagonist. The computer seems victimized by the human, so Bowman, who eventually disconnects Hal because of his arrogance and his actions, is put in the position of antagonist.

Another important feature of Kubrick's interpretation was the narrative, and in his narratives we can identify distinct choices he made that promoted his director's idea. Kubrick's films have an almost overabundant plot as compared to the character layer of the film. One might suggest that people in Kubrick's films are not as important as the external events of the film. This was certainly Raphael's experience when he worked with Kubrick on the script of "Eyes Wide Shut" (see his *Eyes Wide Open*). In "Full Metal Jacket," coping with external events, basic training, and the Battle of Hue shaped the reactions of the characters, and in "Barry Lyndon," Redmond Barry is always reacting to external events—a duel, a war, his actions to come up with clientele for a mentor, his cousin's efforts to marry well, his mother's efforts to control his wife's assets— that all lead the character down the slippery slope that is his life. A robbery and its course shape the reactions of the main character and his colleagues in "The Killing." In "Paths of Glory," the attack on the ant hill causes the general to deem his men cowards and to designate three to die to restore the honor of the French army. Here, the main character who led the charge on the ant hill is called upon to defend the three men designated as cowards. Plot in each case is powerful and has a formative effect on the main character. The scale of the plot in each case overwhelms the main character.

Finally, in terms of tone, Kubrick deployed irony to distance us from the character and to amplify the power of the plot. I have already mentioned the scene of Slim Pickens riding a nuclear weapon toward its destination as if it were a bucking bronco, the ape discovering that a bone could be a weapon, the bravado of the platoon being filmed by a television crew with each acting as a performer, Alex dancing and beating his victim to the tune of "Singin' in the Rain"—all of these actions and scenes deploy irony, but none is on the level of Humbert Humbert in "Lolita" who marries the girl's mother to be nearer to the child. Kubrick brought the same sense of irony to the suburban American values in "Lolita." That same irony is at play in "Eyes Wide Shut" but with urban material values as its target. At times, the irony can be quite funny, particularly when Kubrick used comic actors, such as he did with Peter Sellers as Claire Quilty in "Lolita" and in such secondary roles as Dr. Strangelove in "Dr. Strangelove." It works less well when he used literal actors such as Tom Cruise in "Eyes Wide Shut." Nevertheless, an ironic tone is very important in a Kubrick film. It promotes distance from character and helps create a metaphorical space for Kubrick's views on progress, character, and modern life.

Directing the Actor

Kubrick relied a great deal on his casting decisions. Because he was dealing with characters ranging from outright unlikable to conflicted, his actors had to compensate by generating a certain energy within their roles; for example, Malcolm McDowell in "A Clockwork Orange" and Matthew Modine in "Full Metal Jacket" were capable of expressing rage in their roles. Another type of casting used by Kubrick was a "pretty boy" look that implied sexual ambiguity or a reliance on sex as the first line of personal endeavor, such as the casting of Ryan O'Neal in "Barry Lyndon" and Tom Cruise in "Eyes Wide Shut." In either case, the star persona fed the casting choice. A third dimension of Kubrick's casting was his casting of the male predator, where a combination of aggression and sexuality was necessary for the actor taking on such a role. Jack Nicholson in "The Shining" and Sterling Hayden in "The Killing" and "Dr. Strangelove" are representative of this aspect of Kubrick's casting. The look of the actor was another important dimension of Kubrick's films; for example, Keir Dullea looks perfect as the astronaut in "2001: A Space Odyssey."

Kubrick required his actors to operate within a very narrow range. Dullea played an astronaut who was the modern product of technology, so his emotional range was very limited. He seems to proceed without feeling, almost automatically, as if he were a robot. This narrow emotional range produces a lack of empathy or charm in his performance. Each actor in a Kubrick film uses a single extreme behavioral quality to drive the performance. Malcolm McDowell in "A Clockwork Orange" is always operating with aggression. James Mason in "Lolita" is always operating out of his desire. Ryan O'Neal in "Barry Lyndon" is always operating out of a shallow narcissism, as is Tom Cruise in "Eyes Wide Shut." This narrowness worked well with powerful actors such as James Mason and Peter Sellers in "Lolita." The strategy also worked well where the look of the actor had to imply the shallowness of a character. All the more remarkable, then, is the fact that the initial criticism of "Barry Lyndon" focused in good part on the casting of Ryan O'Neal. Now, 30 years later, "Barry Lyndon" is considered one of the great Kubrick films and the casting of Ryan O'Neal is no longer a source of criticism.

Notable is that all the actors and casting choices I have mentioned are men. This is because Kubrick's films are focused on the male characters and the male point of view. Although Shelley Winters gave a significant performance in "Lolita," as did Marie Windsor in "The Killing," Kubrick films are primarily about men, and "Full Metal Jacket" and "Paths of Glory" (at least until the epilogue) are exclusively about men.

Directing the Camera

Like Max Ophuls ("Lola Montes"), Orson Welles ("Citizen Kane"), Carol Reed ("Odd Man Out"), and David Lean ("Oliver Twist"), Kubrick was obsessed with what he could do with camera movement as opposed to editing a series of shots. And, like these directors, Kubrick was an aesthetic explorer into the possibilities and impact of camera movement as much as he was a narrative director telling a story. He chose to move the camera about the chateau in the interior scenes in "Paths of Glory" as much for the joy of the movement as for the benefit of the narrative. Kubrick also enjoyed using pop music as reference points in his films, as well as such technical challenges as using candle illumination for the interiors in "Barry Lyndon." These technical and aesthetic choices were the equivalent of Kubrick telling a joke—all are amusing but they are not the source of power in the Kubrick film.

In this section, we are looking for that mixture of a director's idea and camera choices that yields filmic power. Many such examples can be found in Kubrick's work. First, let's look at an editing idea: I need to transport the audience to a different time, so I am going to use the idea of time and how it is experienced as my editing idea.

In "2001: A Space Odyssey," the dawn of man sequence begins in timelessness. This translates into extreme long shots that are static and give little indication of a change in the time of day as we move from one shot to the other. The next scene introduces the ape as a vegetarian. The scene is shared with other animals, and the sequence ends with the ape becoming food for the leopard. The pace throughout the scene is even, with nothing to indicate a temporal shift. As we move through the next scenes, primarily mid shots are used to introduce new ideas, such as night implying danger. When we arrive at the introduction of the monolith, the camera angles shift and we have a shift in the power grid. Pace has entered, albeit modestly.

When we arrive at the discovery of the weapon much changes. Close-ups emphasize the importance of the bone. A cutaway to the monolith introduces a new idea—the power of the stone and the potential power of the bone. Once the potential for a weapon has been introduced as an idea, rapid cutting to the killing of animals and the primacy of the ape follows. Close-ups tell us that the importance of the discovery is understood. The rapid pace of the cutting indicates that a different sense of time has been established. The sense of time is totally changed from the opening scene at the dawn of time.

Turning to "Barry Lyndon," the idea once again was to transport the audience to a different time, to the different rhythms of the 18th century. To do so, Kubrick slowed down the pace of the introduction to "Barry Lyndon." He moved the camera physically but also used a zoom lens in order to lengthen the shots. The result is that, instead of shots lasting a few seconds, numerous shots last 30 to 60 seconds. By the time this first sequence is concluded, we are on 18th-century time, or at least Kubrick's version of it. He has via an editing idea transported us into another sense of time—the dawn of man in "2001: A Space Odyssey" and the 18th century in "Barry Lyndon."

A second idea Kubrick employed and tried to capture with the camera was the restlessness of the Harfords in "Eyes Wide Shut." He used the moving camera to represent that restlessness. When the film opens, Bill and Alice are preparing for a party. They leave their spacious Manhattan apartment to go to the museum-like residence of Victor Ziegler. The camera roams before them, recording their restlessness. At the party, when Bill is preoccupied by two beautiful women, the camera again records them moving. Whether the restlessness implied here equates movement with sexual desire or energy is open to interpretation. Once Alice begins to dance with the handsome Hungarian, the camera again moves, left to right, right to left, simulating the seductive movement of a dance. The movement also seems to center them to the exclusion of others at the party (except for Bill). The proximity of the camera to the dancing couple also raises the seductive quality of their proximity to one another. Again, the restlessness of the camera creates a feeling. In both of these scenes, the movements have a self-absorbed quality and a sexual quality. The camera movement furthers Kubrick's ideas about the source of the restlessness or the dissatisfaction of these characters. This restlessness, of course, goes right to the heart of Kubrick's director's idea.

Finally let's look at the sniper attack in "Full Metal Jacket." It exemplifies how Kubrick used point of view to convey the idea that war is all about killing and fighting to retain one's humanity. The sequence has two phases—the sniper's attack on the platoon and the platoon's attack on the sniper. In the first phase, Kubrick applied cinéma vérité strategies, such as the hand-held camera, the extensive use of camera movement, and the strategic use of close-ups, to give the audience a feeling of being under attack. During this phase, three members of the platoon, including its leader, Cowboy, are killed. The deaths are sudden and violent.

In the second phase of the attack, the attack on the sniper, the pace slows down and many static shots replace the moving shots. In this scene, only one person, the sniper, is killed. This scene has many more close-ups than the scene that preceded it. In this scene, Joker's decision about killing the young female sniper who wants to be killed is presented as intense and painful and in close-up. The aggression of the rest of the platoon toward the enemy contrasts sharply with Joker's conflicted feelings about killing. When he does shoot her it is his humane response to a suffering person rather than revenge against a hated enemy who moments before had killed his only friend in the platoon. By slowing down the scene and focusing on Joker's dilemma, Kubrick humanized the enemy and created a paradox for the viewer. If my enemy is human can he remain my enemy? This is the consequence of Kubrick's director's idea in "Full Metal Jacket." Modern war is the largest shadow cast over modern life. Killing is killing, whether in its modern version or a more ancient form.

Few directors are more powerful than Stanley Kubrick when he deployed the camera and the edit to his director's idea.

Chapter 18

Steven Spielberg: Childhood Forever

Introduction

Steven Spielberg's films tend to convey a certain "heaviness" with regard to adult life but joy and belief with regard to the children. He is at his most effective in his films that focus on childhood, such as "E.T." (1982) and "Empire of the Sun" (1987), and in films where the adults act like enthusiastic adolescents, such as "Raiders of the Lost Ark" (1981) and "Jurassic Park" (1994). His portrayals of adult life, on the other hand, are marked by destructive human behavior, such as "Schindler's List" (1993) and "Amistad" (1997), in which Spielberg constructed stories about such human tragedies as the Holocaust and a slave revolt in such a way as to create a hero. Oskar Schindler and Roger Baldwin represent the triumph of humanism over barbarism. These optimistic interpretations of two of the darkest moments in human history contrast sharply with the work of Stanley Kubrick, for example. Perhaps it is fair to say that Spielberg's director's idea requires that he find a romantic hero to align the dark material of "Schindler's List" and "Amistad" more closely with the core approach that characterizes his children's films.

That core approach has certain qualities that elevate his director's idea, and it is best that we take a moment to clarify those qualities to better understand how Spielberg articulates his director's idea. First and foremost, Spielberg uses plot to challenge his main character, and the plot is vigorous. An alien lands on Earth and wants to return home in "E.T." In "Saving Private Ryan," the challenge of rescuing the private behind enemy lines shortly after the D-Day landing is formidable, given the German hold on the French territory. A killer shark haunts the beaches of an island resort in "Jaws" (1975). The war against the Jews is the plot in "Schindler's List." A slave revolt and its aftermath comprise the plot of "Amistad."

Spielberg also deploys a substantial antagonist who is powerful enough to elevate the actions of the main character to a heroic level. Consider Amon Goeth (Ralph Fiennes) in "Schindler's List," those killer raptors in "Jurassic Park," and the overambitious French archeologist in "Raiders of the Lost Ark."

Spielberg also endeavors to create an otherwise ordinary hero who is much easier for the audience to identify with. Think of Elliott (Henry Thomas) in "E.T.," John Miller (Tom Hanks) in "Saving Private Ryan," Police Chief Martin Brody (Roy Scheider) in "Jaws," and Dr. Grant (Sam Neill) in "Jurassic Park." Each is earnest, even naïve, and none is a natural hero. (For a fuller discussion of this issue, see Chapter 5 in Dancyger and Rush's *Alternative Scriptwriting*, 3rd ed., Focal Press, 2002.) But when challenged by the plot and powerful antagonists, these characters act heroically. Spielberg also has a preference for genres that support his style of storytelling—specifically, action adventures, thrillers, and war films.

In terms of the filmmaking itself, few filmmakers pursue identification and the excitement of the medium as vigorously, but camera placement, camera movement, and pace have been used just as effectively by Alfred Hitchcock, Roman Polanski, and Luc Besson. Spielberg, like Hitchcock, is playful with the medium, unlike Orson Welles or Stanley Kubrick. That playfulness reinforces his director's idea and reflects the childlike joy and intensity present throughout much of Spielberg's work. From the outset of his career, he has pushed to challenge certain ideas about filmmaking. When he asked himself what he could do with the concept of a chase, his answer was "Duel" (1971), an entire film about a truck chasing the main character in his car.

Similar challenges mark many of the celebrated sequences in Spielberg's work—the D-Day landing sequence in "Saving Private Ryan," the clearing of the ghetto in "Schindler's List," and the openings of "Raiders of the Lost Ark," "Indiana Jones and the Temple of Doom" (1984), and "Indiana Jones and the Last Crusade" (1989). In each of the "Indiana Jones" films, Spielberg posed a different challenge for his hero to overcome. What is important here is that the identification and the excitement in the narrative merge with Spielberg's joy in filmmaking to yield a special experience for his audience. The most obvious result of this narrative and filmmaking confluence is that Spielberg is the single most successful commercial filmmaker in film history.

At this point, Spielberg's film career exceeds 30 years, beginning with "Duel" in 1971. Important markers include "Jaws" in 1975, the "Indiana Jones" series, 1981–1989, "E.T." in 1982, "Schindler's List" in 1992, "Jurassic Park" in 1994, "Saving Private Ryan" in 1998, and "Artificial Intelligence: AI" in 2001. Spielberg remains active as a director and as a producer. In order to capture the spirited approach Spielberg has taken to his director's idea, I have chosen the following four excerpts because they exemplify the director's idea, and they highlight Spielberg's virtuosity as a director. I should add that I could have chosen four or fourteen other excerpts and they would have made the same point.

"Jaws" (1975)

"Jaws" focuses on the efforts of a small-town police chief, Brody, to halt a killer shark that is terrorizing his island town. The town is a popular summer resort, and the mayor is pressuring Brody to minimize the danger and maximize economic activity on the island. The police chief's primary concern, however, is protecting human life. He is aided by an experienced fisherman (Robert Shaw) and by a shark expert (Richard Dreyfuss). The actions of the shark and the attempt to stop it are the plot. The conflict of material *versus* human values is the primary character struggle, particularly for the police chief. The film is a thriller and proceeds realistically from the shark's first kill to the killing of the shark. The excerpt we will focus on is a beach scene. Everyone is enjoying a sunny day at the beach except for Brody, who is sitting there watching for signs of the shark. The mood of the beachgoers contrasts sharply with the anxiety of the police chief. The shark does attack, and this time its victim is a young boy. The police chief can do nothing but herd people out of the water. The mother of the boy is in shock, and the other swimmers are panic stricken as they abandon the water for the safety of the shore. The scene has a powerful point of view—Brody's.

"Raiders of the Lost Ark" (1981)

"Raiders of the Lost Ark" follows the efforts of Indiana Jones (Harrison Ford), a youthful archeologist, to recover for the American government an ancient artifact, the Lost Ark of Solomon's temple, last housed in Jerusalem. Also in pursuit of the Ark is the Nazi government of Germany who is interested in harnessing the power of the Ark for their own purposes. The time is the 1930s. The search takes Indiana Jones from the United States to a Greek island where the fate of the Ark is resolved. Jones is aided by an Egyptian colleague (Jonathan Rhys-Davies). The sequence we will focus on takes place at a dig site in Egypt. The Ark has been found by Indiana Jones but has been stolen by a French archeologist working for the Germans. The Ark is being transported to its destination by truck. Indiana Jones finds a white stallion and begins his pursuit. In this sequence, Spielberg pits the old *versus* the new, brains *versus* brawn, and the result is one of the greatest chase sequences in modern film. Indiana Jones must catch up with the truck, mount the truck while it is in motion, and disable the guard and driver. The danger to all three participants is considerable. What is important in a sequence such as this is narrative clarity (what is happening and who is winning) and dramatic punctuation, as well as, I might add, a factor of excitement. This sequence has all of these ingredients and then some. It is a joyous tribute to the idea of the chase.

"E.T." (1982)

The third excerpt is from "E.T.," which begins with the extraterrestrial being left on Earth by accident. The arrival of a group of trucks forces the mother ship to leave without E.T. A wayward, intelligent ten-year-old named Elliott (Henry Thomas) is the middle of three children being raised by their mother (the father has abandoned the family). Elliott finds E.T., befriends E.T., and eventually helps E.T. return to his home. The trucks at the beginning of the film are in fact government authorities in pursuit of the extraterrestrial. They are essentially the antagonists of the film. Enlisting his older brother and his friends, Elliott helps E.T. escape from government possession and returns him to the ship that will take him home. The excerpt we will focus on is the opening scene when E.T. is abandoned on Earth. The sequence unfolds almost silently and without an emphasis on faces; that is, there is little identification of the humans and the extraterrestrials. The extraterrestrials are there for a purpose—refueling, perhaps. E.T. wanders off, curious about the city in the valley. Suddenly trucks pull up. We never see the faces of the humans but we do see keys and a badge. They are using flashlights and seem to be looking for the extraterrestrial. He is spotted, and they pursue him. As the agents approach the ship, the extraterrestrials draw up their walkway and take off, leaving E.T. behind. He eludes the humans and makes his way down into the valley, with the humans in hot pursuit. The sequence ends. Thus far, we have only seen E.T.'s hands and primarily the humans' feet. No discernable close-ups have provided any characterization or insight into why the pursuit is happening.

"Saving Private Ryan" (1998)

The final excerpt is from "Saving Private Ryan." Although the film begins with the grandfatherly Private Ryan visiting the Normandy Beach gravesite with his children and grandchildren, the bulk of the film takes place on June 6, 1944, and the few days following. The main character is Captain John Miller (Tom Hanks). The D-Day landing on the beach is the sequence we will focus on. Following this sequence, Captain Miller will be given the assignment to find Private Ryan, whose three brothers have died on the beach. General George Marshall has ordered Private Ryan be returned to his family as he is their only living son. The trouble is, he has parachuted behind enemy lines. To find him will jeopardize the members of Captain Miller's platoon. Is it worth it? This is the struggle for the main character, and in the end he will choose to sacrifice his life to save Private Ryan. The D-Day sequence is 24 minutes long and its intent is to put us, the viewer, on the beach and feel the danger, violence, and death experienced by so many American soldiers. (A detailed discussion of the editing of this sequence appears in my book, *The Technique of Film and Video Editing*, 3rd ed., Focal Press, 2002, pp. 197–201.) Using cinéma vérité techniques, hand-held moving cameras, many close-ups, and a shifting point of view from the American soldiers to the German machine gunners and back, Spielberg takes us to Normandy Beach on that fateful day. The sequence progresses as follows:

1. In the landing craft
2. In the water
3. At the edge of the beach (what do we do?)
4. Movement off the beach
5. Up the perimeter, marked with barbed wire
6. Gather weapons
7. Advance on the pill box and take the machine gun placement
8. Take the pill box and the surrounding environment
9. The beach is taken; stop shooting

What is important to Spielberg in this sequence is to give us the sense of being there, including the chaos, without confusing us. The sequence is impressive in its clarity and its characterization of the chaos of killing. The sequence illustrates the virtuosity of Spielberg's filmmaking skills.

Text Interpretation

In order to explore all the aspects of Spielberg's director's idea, we must first identify portions of the text that support that idea. Spielberg tends to explore the various aspects of childhood and adulthood and uses filmmaking to visualize his ideas about childhood and adulthood. This point is important here. Spielberg is such an active proponent of the joy of filmmaking that the process of filmmaking itself almost becomes a character in his work. We will save this part of the interpretation for the camera-edit discussion later.

When I speak of childhood, I am referring to a more romanticized view than we found in the work of François Truffaut. Whether dealing with the loneliness of childhood or the joys of childhood, Spielberg presents the child as expressive, energetic, curious, and always creative. His presentations of adulthood, however, are not filtered by the same romantic prism; instead, he depicts all the limitations, disappointments, and loss of idealism characteristic of adults. Think of the adult as a disappointed child who is capable of overcoming that disappointment, and you have Spielberg's version of adulthood.

In Spielberg's interpretation of the main character, the child is not isolated or alone as he or she might be in Polanski's work. Elliott may be quirky or unusual in "E.T.," but he is part of a community comprised of his two siblings and his older brother's friends, as well as a tall blonde in the classroom who is clearly more interested in him than she is in the classroom activities. Let's call it the community of childhood. Even when the main characters are adults, they are part of a community that includes children. Police Chief Brody, for example, in "Jaws" is often seen with his two sons or worrying about his two sons. In "Indiana Jones and the Temple of Doom," Indiana's community is a beautiful blonde and a little boy. They are in effect his sidekicks and together they stand against the antagonist.

A second feature of Spielberg's interpretation is that although the antagonist is great enough to make a hero of the main character, the antagonist tends to be cartoonish or one dimensional, such as the misguided French archeologist in "Raiders of the Lost Ark," the single-minded shark in "Jaws," and the persistent raptors in

"Jurassic Park." Amon Goeth in "Schindler's List" and the German soldier in "Saving Private Ryan" represent a departure in Spielberg's work. Both are studies in evil and consequently far more dangerous as antagonists.

The role of plot is crucial to Spielberg's work, and not just to serve as a challenge to the goal of the main character. For most of the directors we have examined thus far, plot rarely became an element of its own, taking precedence over character. Think of John Ford, for example. Plot could be vigorous, but we never forget in "The Searchers" that plot is an expression of Ethan's revenge. In Polanski's "Rosemary's Baby," the plot is related to Rosemary's greatest wish to be a mother. Her worst nightmare would be to see her child as evil but this is precisely what occurs. In Spielberg's work, the plot becomes the most powerful narrative element. It stands above and beyond character. It is the true source of challenge and allows Spielberg to be playful. How else are we to understand the vigor of the chase in "Raiders of the Lost Ark"? Indiana Jones is victorious, but the excitement and joy are created by the idea of Indiana Jones on horseback overtaking a truck and coming up with its contents. The same can be said of the D-Day beach sequence in "Saving Private Ryan." The twists and turns in the action on that beach are more important than the fate or psychology of the main character at that point. Spielberg's enjoyment of plot and plotting is evident in each realization of his director's idea.

Finally, I should offer a comment on the tone that supports the director's idea in Spielberg's films. Tone is very much about the visual details that create the mood Spielberg is after. The excerpt from "E.T." is useful here. Imagine that a spaceship from outer space has landed. Menace, malice, and mischief can all be motivations, but the details Spielberg provided indicate none of these intentions. Instead, the details reflect a sense of curiosity. E.T.'s curiosity about the lighted valley below and a plant he digs up, his response to being left behind, the lights that flicker from the frontal heart region of the extraterrestrial—all of these details suggest a benign, even kind nature. Although the look of the extraterrestrial is strange, his actions are not. Indeed, they are childlike and considerate. Humans in this excerpt are portrayed as aggressive and rather mysterious. They pursue. We see their lights, their

253

keys, their badges. The association here is that these humans mean to do no good. The extraterrestrials are childlike and potential victims, and the humans are adult and victimizers. This revised perception of aliens is accomplished without words and without close-ups.

Directing the Actors

Casting is critical in the Spielberg film. Main characters are often cast for their ordinary look. They should not stand out in the crowd. Harrison Ford in the "Indiana Jones" series, Tom Hanks in "Saving Private Ryan," Sam Neill in "Jurassic Park," Dennis Weaver in "Duel," and Roy Scheider in "Jaws" each has an everyman appearance. Neither heroic nor intimidating, these actors project decency. Women are cast for their youthful spunkiness, not Katharine Hepburn sophistication nor Barbara Stanwyck sexuality. These actresses have a look that is compatible with the rather ordinary-looking actors they play opposite of. Spielberg understandably casts and works with children more often than most directors. As ordinary as the adult main characters seem to be, all of Spielberg's child characters seem extraordinary—think of Henry Thomas and Drew Barrymore in "E.T." and Joel Haley Osment in "Artificial Intelligence: AI."

Spielberg always casts at least one larger than life character—Robert Shaw in "Jaws," Denholm Elliott in "Raiders of the Lost Ark," Sean Connery in "Indiana Jones and the Last Crusade," and Richard Attenborough in "Jurassic Park." These characters provide the charisma lacking in the other adult main characters.

In terms of the performances themselves, Spielberg keeps them in the low key to charming range, like a young shy boy trying to please. In this way, they do not undermine the dynamic plot, and they do not complicate the audience's response to the character. Examples of performances or characters who invite a more complicated response would include George Clooney as a charming criminal in Steven Soderbergh's "Out of Sight" and Tom Cruise as the contract killer in Michael Mann's "Collateral." Occasionally, Spielberg will try a more complex characterization, such as Richard Dreyfuss in "Close Encounters of the Third Kind" and Ralph Fiennes in "Schindler's List." The results are mixed principally because Spielberg has moved away from the romantic character arc so fundamental to the majority of his films.

Directing the Camera

Spielberg tries to achieve a number of goals through his use of camera placement, camera motion, and pace. The guiding principles seem to be:

1. Keep the story clear.
2. Keep the story moving.
3. Identification with the main character is important.
4. Specific details should advance plot and character.
5. Keep it exciting.
6. Pace and point of view are the key.

We will deal with each of these in turn. Keep in mind that each of these features is important to the joy of filmmaking. Above all is Spielberg's ability to project this joy in his films. It is this joy that buoys up his director's idea. Keeping the story clear is about visual signposts. The excerpt from "Jaws" will serve to illustrate this clarity. Police Chief Brody and his family are sitting on the beach. The beach is crowded. Children are playing with their toys in the water, teenagers flirt, and older people are just trying to keep cool on a hot day. While Mrs. Brody is busy enjoying the day and watching her two sons, Brody is worried. He is focused on the danger of another shark attack. His point of view is all about watching the water. When Spielberg wants to remind us about this concern, he momentarily blocks Brody's line of sight line to the beach. More tension is built when Brody spots a sudden movement in the water. It looks like a shark's fin but it proves to be an elderly man's swimming cap. The next false start is a sudden violent eruption in the water when a teenager lifts his girlfriend up and out of the water. She screams in delight rather than terror.

Potential victims of the shark are put into position. A teenager playing with his dog throws a piece of driftwood out into the ocean, and the dog goes after it for its master. A woman guides her youngster and his inflatable yellow raft out to water's edge, and the boy paddles out toward the horizon. The first warning of danger is the teenager looking for his dog and a cutaway to the driftwood floating. No more dog. As Brody is being given a shoulder rub by his wife, the young boy on the raft is attacked by the shark. A bloody geyser rises from the ocean. What Brody has feared has happened. He rushes to the edge of the ocean to help get the panicked swimmers out. When everyone is out the mother is still looking desperately for her son, but all that is left is the shredded bloody yellow raft. The sequence has been focused and clear. The signposts were there and the worst has happened.

This sequence proceeded with a minimum of dialogue. The next sequence, which keeps the story moving, also proceeds without the benefit of dialogue. Since "Duel" it has been clear that Spielberg loves pure action. The opening of "E.T." is presented as pure action, and it proceeds very quickly. From a narrative point of view, there are three important elements of this scene—a curious E.T. has strayed from the spaceship, the human pursuers are looking for visitors from outer space, and the spaceship leaves E.T. behind because they must elude their human pursuers. The key to this sequence is movement—the camera moves, E.T. moves, the human pursuers and their vehicles move, the flashlights move. Throughout the scene, the emphasis is on movement. The few still shots (the rabbit reacting to E.T., E.T.'s removal of a plant, the mushroom-like pods in the spaceship) are unusual in the sequence. Screen direction keeps clear who is chasing whom and creates the sense of conflict in the scene.

Identification with the main character is critical. In the "Jaws" sequence, it is Brody's point of view. In much of "Saving Private Ryan," it is either Captain Miller's point of view or the point of view of the German machine gunners. In the "Raiders of the Lost Ark" sequence, it is Indiana Jones' point of view or the guard or driver of the truck. Point of view allows us to identify with Indiana Jones or Captain Miller or Police Chief Brody.

Spielberg understands the importance of details to advance the plot or characterize. The shot of the piece of driftwood tells us in "Jaws" that the dog has become a victim of the shark. The shark is out there. The punctured yellow raft tells us about the fate of its young occupant. Lifting the plant from the ground tells us E.T. is a benign presence. A soldier kissing his cross before he shoots a German machine gunner tells us so much about the soldier in "Saving Private Ryan." Spielberg uses these specific details for plot and characterization purposes.

Maintaining a level of excitement in a film is a by-product of the subject as well as the dynamism of the filmic approach taken. All four of these excerpts are exciting to watch because they get the adrenalin flowing. Excitement is created by camera movement combined with action paced for emotional punctuation. Few sequences are as exciting as the chase in "Raiders of the Lost Ark." Because the odds are obviously against Indiana Jones, the thrill of his overcoming them is added. Overcoming such odds, however, must be plausible, so Spielberg carefully takes us through each step. A simple, logical progression is not enough, though. Each step has to be more dangerous than the last, each adversary more skilled than the last. In the "Raiders of the Lost Ark" chase, the commander is the strongest and most dangerous adversary for Indiana Jones, so he is saved for the last. Close quarters and Indiana Jones' injury all raise the stakes for this final confrontation. This is a great action sequence in that it is exciting in much the same way as a child's surprise checkers victory or a high school sports victory is exciting. Nothing is as thrilling as a childhood victory in an adult world. This is precisely what happens when Indiana Jones takes over the German truck.

Finally, the combination of pace and point of view is key to an affecting film experience. Few sequences are as powerful as the 24-minute D-Day landing sequence in "Saving Private Ryan." I have already mentioned the narrative progression of the scene earlier in the chapter. Here, we focus on a few of Spielberg's ideas in the sequence. The first is the chaos of the landing experience. To create a sense of chaos, Spielberg used a lot of camera movement. Some movement, as in the landing craft, is fluid from the back of the craft to the front. On shore, the movement becomes more chaotic. Spielberg used handheld cameras with lots of jostling in the movement to establish the pace and a sense of danger on the beach. Jump cutting, lots of close-ups, and sharp changes in sound levels all contribute to the sense of chaos.

Spielberg's next idea was to suggest that that the beach was not simply dangerous but rather was a killing field where the majority of the landing troops did not have a chance. Here, the point of view from the German machine gun placement establishes a long perspective on the beach/killing field. Moving in closer, we have many subjective mid and close-up shots of death and dying. In fact, Spielberg made a point of cutting to numerous images of torn limbs and disemboweled soldiers. Dying was not only prevalent, it was horrific.

A third idea that Spielberg worked with was medics trying to do the impossible—save lives in the midst of a killing field. These scenes illustrate the frustration of medics who were able to save the lives of their comrades only to witness them being killed by incoming enemy fire. The most powerful sense emanating from these images is the dedication but ongoing frustration of the medics who tried to help but to little avail. There are so many dimensions to this sequence. Point of view and pace provide a pathway to interpretation and feeling—a feeling of being as overwhelmed by the sequence as the landing troops were by the awesome danger of their mission. The sequence is reminiscent in its power of Elem Klimov's "Come and See" (1987) and is one of the most powerful in the history of filmmaking.

It is in his use of the camera and the edit that Spielberg most effectively animates his director's idea that childhood is forever, and if it must fade in adulthood, as it does on those beaches at Normandy in "Saving Private Ryan," we are all the less for it.

Chapter 19

Margarethe Von Trotta: Historical Life and Personal Life Intersect

Introduction

Margarethe Von Trotta was one of the German writers who were active and important in what has come to be called New German cinema of the 1970s. The filmmakers were very different in intent and style but like the New Wave ten years earlier they energetically pursued a creative agenda very different from the filmmakers of the previous generation. Rainer Werner Fassbinder embraced melodrama as his genre of choice. Wim Wenders favored existential narratives that mixed realistic characters with fable-like events or fable-like character with real events. Werner Herzog was only interested in the fable, while Margarethe Von Trotta and her partner/husband Volker Schlondorff were most attracted to a radical or political treatment of events or people.

Von Trotta has been an important filmmaker for 30 years. Her work initially was principally as the writer of Schlondorff's films, such as "The Sudden Wealth of the Poor People of Kalmbach." In 1975, she co-directed with Schlondorff "The Lost Honor of Katharina Blum." She appeared in a major role in and co-directed with Schlondorff "Coup de Grace" (1980). In 1977, she solely directed "The Second Awakening of Crista Klages." She directed her most famous film, "Marianne and Juliane," known as "The German Sisters" in Europe, in 1981. Since then she has made numerous theatrical and television films, the most prominent being "The Sisters of Happiness" (1985), "Rosa Luxemburg" (1994), "The Promise" (1995), and "Rosenstrasse" (2004).

Because her base of operation shifted from Germany to Italy, she has somehow received a treatment similar to the Polish filmmaker Agnieszka Holland, a kind of snub that has made each filmmaker a "European" filmmaker or an "international" filmmaker rather than a German or Polish film director. I attribute such treatment to each being a female director. Roland Emmerich and Paul Verhoeven have not had the same kind of experience although they went to Hollywood. They are still accepted as German and Dutch directors as well.

Before we look at a number of excerpts from Von Trotta's work, a few observations will contextualize her director's idea. First and foremost is the observation that Von Trotta, like Billy Wilder before her, is principally a writer and it is her writing that shapes all other directorial decisions. That writing must emotionalize the personal story and provide the historical story intersection points so as to raise the stakes within the personal story. Another way of considering the two narrative elements is to see the plot as the historical story and the personal story as the character layer, the traditional means of emotionalizing the story. An example will illustrate the point. In "Rosenstrasse," the personal story is about a contemporary German Jew who has grown up in New York. She is engaged to a gentile. When her father dies, her mother becomes very disapproving of her fiancé. To understand why, the daughter returns to Germany to learn of her mother's past. What she discovers is that during World War II in Germany her mother, a Jew, lost her parents and was hidden by a German non-Jewish woman who at that time was fighting for the life of her husband, a Jew. Her husband has been rounded up by the authorities for transport east. The historical narrative has two aspects—the gentile woman caring for the Jewish child and the gentile woman fighting to rescue her Jewish husband together with like-minded women whose husbands have also been taken. The daughter learns her mother's history by interviewing the woman who had saved her, now old and living mostly with her memories. The personal history and the historical fate of those women and their Jewish husbands during World War II blend to influence how a young woman today will make a decision about her gentile fiancé.

A second take on the schism between the historical and the personal is that they are like the spokes of a wheel; they surround the core of the story. Parents in the Von Trotta narrative represent history while children represent the personal. An authoritarian pastor and his quiescent wife are the parents of the two daughters at the core of the story in "Marianne and Juliane." Another schism in that story is the male/female divide. The men are needy and weak, and the two women are strong and goal directed; consequently, the men quickly fracture. "Marianne and Juliane" opens with Marianne's former husband, Werner, leaving their child with Juliane and committing suicide. Near the end of the film, Wolfgang, Juliane's boyfriend of ten years, abandons her because Marianne's corpse is between them. In terms of the key relationship between the sisters, they are presented as bonded and allied since childhood; nevertheless, they are opposites of one another. As children, the older sister (Juliane) was responsible, the younger one irresponsible; the older less sexual, the younger highly sexual; the older political, the younger more imaginative. When the sisters become adults, their differences become more intense, and they take opposing political positions— older sister Juliane becomes a political journalist and younger sister Marianne becomes a political terrorist. Yet, the most important person for the other is her sister. It is the generational, gender, and character fault lines in the work that generate the historical–personal director's idea.

Each of Von Trotta's stories unfolds in the shape of a riddle with the answer telling us who will survive. In "Sisters, or the Balance of Happiness" (1979), again the story of two sisters, it is the older sister who will survive the suicide of the younger. She survives by creating a replacement relationship. A young secretary at work, who looks like her sister, becomes the new sister. Although the strategy is not permanent, it does help the older sister cope with her loss. In "The Second Awakening of Crista Klages" (1977), a woman who robs a bank to raise money for her childcare center loses her male accomplices but when finally taken by the police is rescued by the female bank employee whom she held captive during the bank robbery. The employee denies Christa was the robber, and Christa is given her second chance.

Finally, Von Trotta emphasized character, the personal, over plot, the historical. "Marianne and Juliane" is the story of a 1960s political terrorist, Marianne, yet we do not see the bank robberies or the bombings. Instead, the focus is on Marianne's relationship with her older sister, Juliane. There is a high point that expresses the love in their relationship. Marianne is in prison, and Juliane is visiting her. A male records their conversation. Two matrons watch to contain the two women if necessary, and there is an armed guard present. We are very aware of the level of intervention, the lack of privacy. At the moment of saying goodbye Marianne asks her sister to swap sweaters, a throwback to an adolescent desire to be close to the other. Without hesitation the two strip off their sweaters and swap them and then embrace. Their intimacy with the other at a moment when they have four strangers in the room is personal and touching. All that matters at that instant is the bond between them. Everything else is excluded. It is a moment of intense love and revelation about the personal.

In terms of excerpts, I am going to alter our approach slightly. Rather than particular excerpts, I will examine the characterization of the key relationships in four of Von Trotta's films. This approach will give us insight into how Von Trotta dramatically prioritizes her historical–personal idea. It will also lead us to a more particular set of visual choices that support her director's idea. The films we will refer to are "The Lost Honor of Katharina Blum," "The Second Awakening of Christa Klages," "Marianne and Juliane," and "Rosenstrasse."

"The Lost Honor of Katharina Blum" (1975)

In "The Lost Honor of Katharina Blum," the main character, Katharina Blum (Angela Winkler), is a decent working-class woman of high moral character and a rather shy woman, as well. She is seen fraternizing with a known terrorist and is considered an accomplice in helping him elude police. The police collude with a tabloid journalist to destroy her reputation. As they proceed to systematically destroy her, Katharina (the most decent person they know, say her employers) is forced to act to defend her dignity. In the end, she kills the journalist whose reports have misrepresented her and who has thrived on her public destruction. The terrorist she protected and loved succeeds in eluding the authorities. The sequence we will focus on is the opening, when the terrorist Ludwig Götten (Jürgen Prochnow) is eluding the police who are in close pursuit. He meets Katharina (the "nun," according to police reports) at her cousin's party, where they are all under surveillance. Katharina returns to her apartment with Ludwig and they spend the night together. In the morning, a police task force enters her apartment. Ludwig is gone but the police consider her to be an accomplice, continually insulting her in her own home. They treat her not only as a suspect but also as if she were a prostitute. She insists upon respect, as they are in her home, but none is forthcoming. The police and the prosecutor, both men, take an authoritarian and demeaning attitude toward Katharina. This is in marked contrast to the behavior of Ludwig toward her. He, the terrorist, is kind and considerate, while the authorities are aggressive and accusatory even though they are in her home.

"The Second Awakening of Christa Klages" (1977)

In "The Second Awakening of Christa Klages," Christa (Tina Engel), a childcare worker, robs a bank. Acting with two male accomplices, she takes a bank employee hostage (Katharina Thalbach) and holds the woman while the men take the money. The hostage, Lena, becomes more important in the story as she begins to obsess about Christa. One of the robbers, Wolfgang (Friedrich Kaiser), is quickly captured by the police while Christa and the other robber, Werner (Marius Müller-Westernhagen), escape by train. They begin a journey to find a friend who can launder the money so they can turn it over to the daycare center so they can continue to care for the children. First, they visit Hans (Peter Schneider), a pastor. Hans refuses to launder the money, although he is quite taken with Christa. They visit Ingrid (Silvia Reize), a school friend. Ingrid is willing to help, but the daycare center will not take the money. In the meantime, Lena has begun looking for Christa and will do so throughout the film.

When Werner is killed by the police, Hans helps Christa leave the country using Ingrid's passport. Ingrid joins her in Portugal. The townspeople who are conservative interpret their close relationship as a lesbian relationship and consequently turn against them. Returning to Germany, Christa is picked up by the police, and Lena is brought in to identify her as the female bank robber. She denies Christa was the robber and the film ends. Christa is free. The excerpts we will focus on are the scenes of Christa with Lena in the bank and, at the end, Christa with Ingrid and Christa with her daughter. What characterizes all of these scenes is the closeness of the females, one with the other. It is a man's world, and, whether it is Werner or Ingrid's husband, men are more selfish and in the end they support one another rather than their female lover or partner. It is the women who help one another. That was the motivation for Christa to rob a bank. Daycare is an issue for women. Men care about cars, money, and having sex. They are not very generous to women. Although Hans is kind, his interest in Christa seems to be sexual, and he is the most principled of the men in this film!

"Marianne and Juliane" (1981)

"Marianne and Juliane" is the story of two German sisters. The film begins with the son of Marianne (Barbara Sukowa) being delivered to her sister Juliane (Jutta Lampe) for safekeeping. The film ends with Juliane trying to take care of Marianne's son. By now his father, Wolfgang, has committed suicide, as has his terrorist mother. And the child has been immolated, a cruel prank, because he is his mother's son. Between the narrative bookends provided by the son, we focus on the story of the two sisters. A historical thread traces their history from young children to adolescents. The family history focuses on the father, the compliance of Marianne, and the rebelliousness of Juliane. The contemporary story is a total reversal, with Marianne now a bank robber/terrorist and Juliane a committed leftist journalist. Juliane has a ten-year relationship with an architect but no marriage and no children. Marianne enters and exits Juliane's life with some frequency and chides her sister for not being more like her—action over words. A third of the way through the film Marianne is taken by the police, and further scenes between the sisters take place in prison. The second third of the film focuses on this period. The visits alternate between being angry and affectionate. On one of the last visits Juliane brings their mother.

When Juliane and Wolfgang are away on holiday in Italy, Juliane sees news of her sister on television. She calls home to discover that her sister has hanged herself. The last section of the film focuses on Juliane's obsession with proving that her sister was killed rather than committing suicide. Her obsession fractures her own personal relationship with Wolfgang. In her commitment to raise Marianne's son, Juliane is becoming closer to her dead sister. The scenes that we focus on are the childhood/adolescent scenes of the two sisters. As children they seem inseparable. Their father is a pastor, and prayer and compliance are demanded in his home, but Juliane is rebellious. The father insists that her dress code of black jeans must be set aside if she is to attend a dance. She is rebellious and asserts her right to dress as she pleases. The father rejects her and her rights. Only Marianne's intervention leads to Juliane attending the dance. Even at the dance, though, Juliane is nonconformist. On a wager, she dances a waltz alone, and all of the students gape at her. In a later scene, the adolescent Marianne and Juliane watch concentration camp footage with their classmates. Marianne leaves, ill. Juliane joins her, in solidarity with her sister. These scenes together portray the personal relationship of the sisters and how they stood together against the past. The father represents that past, and he and what he represents is actively rejected by Juliane. On the other hand, Marianne insists that you must work with the past— father and religion and the Nazi ideology about family—in order to get by and to get your way. It is here on the matter of history that the sisters differ.

"Rosenstrasse" (2004)

The last film we will focus on is "Rosenstrasse." Earlier in the chapter I described the narrative, the story of three women—the contemporary story of Hannah Weinstein (Maria Schrader); the 1943 story of Ruth Weinstein (Jutta Lampe), Hannah's mother; and the 1943 story of Lena Fischer (Katja Riemann), the gentile woman who rescues Ruth. Each of these women suffers a loss that ruptures her life. That historical loss is directly embedded in the historical plot, the war against the Jews. Can a gentile save a Jew? In the contemporary story, that gentile is Lena. Hannah, a young woman, is disturbed by her mother's rejection of her gentile fiancé, Luis. If she can discover her mother's history perhaps she can move forward. Lena, now 90, tells Hannah about her mother, Ruth's wartime personal history. The second story is about Ruth as a child. Early in the film she loses her mother in a Berlin sweep of Jews. A young man pulls the Jewish star from Ruth's vest and following her mother's advice she asks a gentile woman outside Gestapo headquarters to take care of her. The German women gathered there have Jewish husbands who have also been rounded up. It is Lena who saves Ruth. The third story, also set in 1943, is Lena's story. From a noble family, Lena has chosen to marry Fabian, a Jewish musician. She and Fabian were a creative couple—she on the piano and Fabian playing the violin. Lena also was a Von Essenbach, the daughter of long-standing respected German aristocrats. She suffered her father's rejection for her marriage to a Jew. When Fabian is picked up in the 1943 sweep of Jews, he is taken to a Gestapo holding area on Rosenstrasse. Lena and other gentile wives of Jews protest in front of the building. She appeals to her family to intercede but her father remains intransigent. She is no longer his daughter. Only her war-injured officer brother tries to help her. She finally offers herself to the SS leadership to secure Fabian's release. In the end, her efforts bear results. She secures his release together with that of many other Jewish husbands of gentile wives.

In "Rosenstrasse," we focus on the 1943 relationships of Lena with her husband, Fabian, and with the young Ruth. In these scenes, Von Trotta is interested in creating the motivation for Lena, a motivation that will make her risk humiliation, even death, in order to secure her love relationship with the Jew, Fabian, and also create a mother/child bond with Ruth. These scenes proceed in the light of insult from Gestapo officers (Lena is "a Jew-loving whore"), the rejection of her father, and the prostituting of herself with the SS hierarchy. All of these commitments are measures of self-sacrifice for love.

Text Interpretation

Margarethe Von Trotta is above all a political filmmaker. I use the term *political* in the sense that her stories are about personal transformation and political action, not in the formal sense, but the actions of an individual to change her interaction with the society. Von Trotta has made films that are more literally political, a film such as "Rosa Luxemburg," for example, about the Spartacist leader killed by the German army during the 1918 workers' revolt against the government of post-World War I Germany. Each of the four films I talk about in this chapter focuses on personal and political action. In "The Lost Honor of Katharina Blum," Katharina, a shy, modest woman with firm middle-class values, becomes a murderer to defend herself against an exploitative journalist and the police and legal officials whose authoritarianism is all about their empowerment to the detriment of the rights of an individual such as Katharina Blum. Von Trotta sidesteps the love story, the melodrama of a woman trying to make her way in Germany, and the terrorist's story, to focus on Katharina's transformation.

In "The Second Awakening of Christa Klages," Christa takes action to subsidize a daycare center and its children. Clearly, the daycare center has been forsaken by conventional government funding and the fate of the children has become precarious. Transgression on behalf of children comprises the political action in "The Second Awakening of Christa Klages." In "Marianne and Juliane," both sisters have already taken political action as the film begins. Marianne is a terrorist wanted by the government. Juliane is a leftist reporter focusing on women's issues and environmental issues. The deeper political action, however, moves away from the paternalistic model that is religious and conservative. The authoritarian model of their pastor father is the basis for the deeper political action taken by "Marianne and Juliane." They are rejecting the father and all that his generation stood for.

In "Rosenstrasse," the political action is about the preservation of life and relationships—specifically, the life of a Jewish girl, Ruth, and a Jewish musician, Fabian. Lena, a German aristocrat and a woman, stands up against the paternalism of her family, of the army, and of the State in 1943 Germany. Her actions are pro-life rather than anti-Nazi, but in acting as she does she is also anti-Nazi. Although "Rosenstrasse" is closest to being a war film, Von Trotta minimizes the plot and stays very close to Lena and the other characters in order to highlight and personalize Lena's political action. Which brings us to the next feature of Von Trotta's text interpretation. The character arc at the core of each of these films is a journey, a journey of transformation from what the women were when we meet them to what they become in the course of the film. The journey may be a political or personal journey; often it is both.

For Katharina Blum, it is a journey of realization that one cannot hide behind the veneer of one's personality and values. When we meet Katharina she is shy and modest—as her cousin describes her, she is a "nun." The implication is that Katharina is in retreat from life. When she is attacked, her home is invaded and her life and the lives of her family are destroyed to feed the press' appetite for gossip, negativity, and notoriety. A modest woman is transformed into a monster. Katharina reacts to protect her inner core. She transgresses and takes action. By the end, she has become engaged with society on its own destructive terms.

For Christa Klages, the transformation is different. She begins as a person of action, a transgressor, on behalf of her beliefs. The actions of Ingrid, her friend, on her behalf as well as of Lena, her captive, who lies to save her from prison, suggest that women can and should help one another. This feminist take on a male society—it does not act to save its children but rather cares more for cars and other material goods and money—transforms a political activist into a more caring woman. She cares for her daughter, for Ingrid (battered by her husband), and for Lena, who identifies with her as a woman rather than with her male employers at the bank. Also, Lena sees the male policemen persecuting another woman, in this case Christa.

For Juliane, the leftist reporter, her transformation through her commitment to her dead sister (another politically active woman) transforms her into a woman who can be a caregiver, a mother. At the end, she will care for Jan, Marianne's son, and patiently raise him, at the very least to understand his dead mother. Juliane is a very different woman when the film ends than she was when the film began.

The transformation in "Rosenstrasse" is principally Hannah's transformation. By developing a relationship with Lena, Hannah learns about her mother's history, her mother's loss in 1943 of her own mother, and her finding a surrogate mother in Lena. When we meet Hannah she is angry with her mother, Ruth, who at the funeral of her husband rejected Luis, Hannah's gentile fiancé. Should she, too, reject Luis? She is unsure. Until she knows her mother's history and therefore her own she is unsure how to proceed so she avoids Luis.

Only when she is given her grandmother's ring by Lena (who has held the ring since 1945 for Ruth) does she realize the depth of the loss her mother experienced. She returns the ring to Ruth, who now feeling acknowledged by her daughter, offers it back to Hannah. This symbolic piece of Ruth's own mother then binds the generations and Hannah has permission to move on. The film ends with her marriage to Luis. The life cycle can begin again for Hannah who will contribute to the continuity of her family.

Directing the Actor

In terms of casting, Von Trotta is very particular about the look of the actors. The women tend to have a strong look—Angela Winkler's innocence in "The Lost Honor of Katharina Blum," Tina Engel's forcefulness in "The Second Awakening of Christa Klages," Jutta Lampe's strength in "Sisters" and "Marianne and Juliane," and Barbara Sukowa's charisma in "Marianne and Juliane" and in "Rosa Luxemburg." The women are not Marilyn Monroe beautiful, but their faces are interesting and their beauty grows as we become more familiar with them as characters. It is safe to say that Von Trotta is above all interested in strong women. That is not to say she does not cast against type. Katja Riemann has a very feminine, soft look but her role as Lena in "Rosenstrasse" required her to be very forceful. The softer, more sexual side of Lena is an important presence in her character.

Beyond the look of the actor, Von Trotta looks for a reservoir of passion. All of the characters described here are believers. Marianne believes in revolution, Christa Klages believes that transgression in the name of a principled position is right, and Katharina Blum believes in middle-class values and an orderly society until she is pushed to change. Passion that can lead to action is a fundamental dimension of each of these performances.

Another dimension of these performances is that each of these women takes risks; she goes to the edge. If they succeed they live, but each knows they may have to go further and put their lives at risk. This willingness to take risks has to be part of the performance. It certainly goes to the heart of Barbara Sukowa's performance as Marianne, the terrorist. We believe she can kill or be killed or kill herself. When she argues with her sister she is always pushing her to join her and risk it all. The performance is striking with regard to Sukowa's risk taking as an actress. She is never still and is always moving, ever on the edge of explosion. *Fierce* is the word that comes to mind about her performance.

Von Trotta always brings such characters into her films. The journalist who pushes Katharina Blum, for example, is a volcanic, egotistical media star who eats his subjects for breakfast. In "Rosenstrasse," it is the adult Ruth who is about to erupt and destroy, so deep is her despair regarding the loss of her husband, the final loss in a life of too many losses.

Finally, the performances have to explore all the dimensions of a relationship—friendship, love, jealousy, anger, envy, and sexuality, so we can experience the danger and warmth in each relationship. This is very clear in the performances of Jutta Lampe and Barbara Sukowa as Juliane and Marianne, the two German sisters. One expects the relationship of siblings to be either supportive or rivalrous. The Von Trotta version is neither. I would call the two sisters symbiotic. They are together, they need each other, they support each other, and yet there is intense anger between them as well. And there is intense love. I described the sweater exchange earlier in this chapter. It is a moment of intimacy, partially sexual. The goal of these performances was to evoke all the dimensions of the relationship. The consequent complexity of the sisters' relationship is the subtext for their performances. It was Von Trotta's ambition for her actresses and her challenge in modulating their performances.

Directing the Camera

"Rosenstrasse" begins with a montage of New York. "Sisters," unusually beings with a tracking shot into the woods. This abstract image will recur throughout the film. The visual metaphor is unusual in Von Trotta's work. More often she is straightforward with the images. Her narrative agenda is so considerable that she needs to devote the visuals to carrying us from narrative point to narrative point. In this sense, Von Trotta is not flashy visually but rather functional. She shows us what she needs to show us in order to follow the narrative. All else is excluded. Another quality of her visuals is that she prefers to focus on the performances rather than the visual power of a shot. Substance in her work triumphs over style.

Her approach to the camera is natural rather than fancy, direct rather than subtle. In "Marianne and Juliane," the scenes that characterize the girls growing up focus first and foremost on their relationship, their closeness. The past is dominated by one person, their father. In those scenes, the focus is on the father's authoritarian style *versus* the girls' wrath, Juliane's outrage, and Marianne's conciliatory moves between father and the rebellious Juliane. All else, including the mother, is contextual, background. Marianne, Juliane, and their father are shown in close-ups, the others primarily in long shots.

Similarly in the classroom scene where the adolescent girls are shown concentration camp films, the focus is on the two girls and the footage. The teacher and the other students are background or simply omitted. A feature, then, of Von Trotta's style is her focus on only the principal characters and letting all else fall away or blend into the background context. Associated with this quality is a focus on character over plot; when plot is introduced, as in the effort to free Fabian in "Rosenstrasse," it is within the context of one of the principal characters — in this case, Fabian's wife Lena. There are shots of Fabian being threatened with death by the Gestapo, but these shots are there to remind us of what is at stake (Fabian's life), as well as the power of the Gestapo over the lives of the Jews being held.

Another quality of Von Trotta's visual choices has to do with the editing. Because she is telling multiple stories, such as in "Rosenstrasse," transitions are necessary to suggest moving from modern times to 1943. A piece of music or a bowl of soup can provide such a transition. Equally important is Von Trotta's use of parallel action. "Rosenstrasse" has three main characters and occurs over two time periods. Moving between time periods and from one character to another, as well as maintaining the momentum of the story and its tension, are serious editing challenges. Rather than rely on pace to create an emotional arc, Von Trotta keeps the fate of the two men (Fabian in 1943 and Luis in 2003) uncertain until the end. The narrative tension consequently keeps the audience wondering and worrying if all will work out for Lena with Fabian and for Hannah with Luis. Narrative clarity and dramatic emphasis were the editing goals. Generous use of close-ups keeps the emotions high, and the periodic use of camera movement further energizes the narrative.

One element that Von Trotta does reinforce visually is the link between the historical life and the personal life. Adding to the chauvinist maleness of the Nazis are the swastikas, Jewish stars, Nazi salute, and personal embraces. The Nazis see Lena—the aristocrat, the wife, the surrogate mother of Ruth—not as another human but rather as another sexual opportunity. By embedding the historical pathology of the Nazis in such a simple personal encounter, Von Trotta allows the audience to experience the director's idea dramatically and in a highly emotionalized way. It is this kind of deep directorial decision that raises the bar for Von Trotta's audiences. Just as her characters risk it all, Von Trotta herself is an ambitious narrative risk taker. And when the risk pays off, as it does in each of these four films, we witness the power of passion and commitment in directing.

Chapter 20

Lukas Moodysson: Empathy and Its Limits

Introduction

The opposite of empathy is contempt, and you can find both in the brief but powerful career of Lukas Moodysson. "Together" with Tom Tykwer of Germany and Catherine Breillat of France, these film-makers represent a powerful new voice among directors. Bold, uncompromising, experimental, each of these filmmakers has quickly made a mark comparable to that of Martin Scorsese in the United States and Wong Kar Wai in Asia. In this chapter, we will look at the four films made by Moodysson in Sweden: "Fucking Åmål" (called "Show Me Love" in North America; 1998), "Together" (2000), "Lilja 4-Ever" (2002), and "A Hole in My Heart" (2004).

In terms of the director's idea, Moodysson is examining in each of these films extreme characters, and in each film he is looking for a way to empathize with that character or characters. Before going into the characters and the films, a discussion about empathy would be useful. Of the other directors I have described, probably the most similar to Moodysson with regard to empathy are Ernst Lubitsch and Margarethe Von Trotta. In George Stevens' work, the goal was to have the audience merge with the character, which is something beyond empathy. In the work of John Ford, the characters are iconic, larger than life—easy to admire but difficult to identify with. Creating empathy was not a goal of either of these directors.

Both Lubitsch and Von Trotta deeply care about their characters, and they do not mind flaws in them. In fact, the flaws are important to convey a complexity, a realism to the character. This is what I mean by empathy, which can be found in realistic characters that we can recognize and find either contemptible or admirable—characters operating with strengths and weaknesses and a passion. These are the qualities we find in the characters of Lukas Moodysson.

There are limits to empathy, however, and those limits begin to translate as soft satire when they are mildly expressed and downright anger and contempt when they become forceful. In Lubitsch, we see the soft satire in nearly all the films. The married couple—the great actor Joseph Tura (Jack Benny) and the even greater actress, his wife Maria (Carole Lombard)—in "To Be or Not To Be" are both credible and empathic—he in his jealousy and she in her guile; both are the source of Lubitsch's soft satire about the narcissism of actors. Similarly, Von Trotta empathizes with the older sister (Jutta Lampe) in "Sisters" and at the same time blames the character for being overly controlling with her younger sister and with the surrogate younger sister after the former's suicide. For both Von Trotta and Lubitsch, the more negative views translate differently than they do in Moodysson. Von Trotta veers toward a cerebral, serious approach in "Rosa Luxemburg." The consequence is a neutralization of the film's impact in spite of Barbara Sukowa's earnest portrayal of Rosa. In the case of Lubitsch, he becomes serious and pedantic in "The Man I Killed," blunting the impact of the film. Moodysson, on the other hand, just keeps going in "A Hole in My Heart," looking for empathy while bathing us in the contempt his characters feel for themselves, each other, and their world. More on this later in the chapter.

Before we turn to Moodysson's work we need to contextualize him as a filmmaker of the 21st century, as a European filmmaker, and as a Swedish filmmaker. As a Swedish director he works in the shadow of Ingmar Bergman, the director who dominated Swedish film for 30 years and who even today casts a giant shadow on Swedish theater. What is important about Bergman's films is his range and his willingness to take filmic risks. He could be literary ("The Seventh Seal"), experimental ("Persona"), classical ("Fanny and Alexander"), or genre oriented ("Hour of the Wolf"). Above all, he was visceral in his approach to his characters. Portraying honesty, revelation, manipulation, and creativity was his goal, as it is for Moodysson.

In Europe, as in the United States, there is an impulse to go with young directors and young themes, young ideas; consequently, the Dogme movement that developed around Lars Von Trier in Denmark in the mid-1990s was important. Dogme was a reaction against the high-tech, special-effects, big-budget direction of filmmaking, and it has resonated for directors around the world. Genre filmmaking has been a focus for Belgian filmmakers such as Luc Belvaux ("The Trilogy") and for Italian directors such as Emmanuele Crialese ("Respiro"). And throughout Europe there is an impulse to innovate in response to the dominance of the Hollywood film. The upshot has been the rise of filmmakers such as Pedro Almodovar in Spain, Mathieu Kassovitz and Jacques Audiard in France, and Lynn Ramsay and Danny Boyle in the United Kingdom, all of whom have influenced Moodysson.

Finally, the globalization sensibility has promoted voice, a national voice that has used voice-oriented genres to become a global director. Xiang Yimou ("Hero") and Wong Kar Wai ("In the Mood for Love"), both of China, focus on style over content and have been a profound influence on young filmmakers all over the world. Although this movement began with Quentin Tarantino and "Pulp Fiction," global directors have not followed the same path. Each has adopted a powerful style but made individual choices about their approach to content—specifically, whether it should be stylized or more emotionally available. (For a discussion of voice-oriented genres and the ascent of voice see my earlier book, *Global Scriptwriting*, Focal Press, 2001.) This globalization has been a powerful influence on Moodysson and his approach to his work.

"Fucking Åmål" (1998)

"Fucking Åmål" refers to the exclamation of the main character, Elin (Alexandra Dahlström), who makes the statement to her sister, Jessica: "Why do we have to live in fucking piss and shit Åmål?" (Åmål is a small town in Sweden.) Elin is a beautiful 14 year old. She is popular with a bad reputation for being easy with the boys; nevertheless, Johan (Mathias Rust) is obsessed with her and thinks he is in love. Elin thinks she will be Miss Sweden but her older sister tells her she is too short. Elin is bored with it all ("I hate my life") and she needs the stimulus of sex, drugs, and rock and roll. She is looking for a change.

Agnes (Rebecka Liljeberg) is turning 16. Her concerned parents want her to be happy and popular, so her mother cooks meat for a party to which Agnes, a vegetarian, is uncertain if anyone will come. Her father is concerned and heavily identifies with his daughter. She is new to the neighborhood, and her parents hope that a party will make her feel that she belongs. Agnes knows this will not happen. The reason why she feels like an outsider is because she is gay and in love with Elin, but the aggressively heterosexual Elin does not even know Agnes exists.

Elin's mother does not want her daughter to go out; she considers her provocative dress to be a prescription for disaster. Agnes' party seems safe, though, and Elin's mother allows her and Jessica to go off to Agnes' party. They and a girl in a wheelchair are the only guests. During the party, Agnes suggests a wager between the sisters. To win the bet, Elin kisses Agnes. After a quick glass of wine, though, Elin and Jessica leave. Agnes is so despondent that her father fears she may commit suicide. After leaving Agnes' house, Elin and Jessica make their way to another party, where Johan waits impatiently for Elin. He is earnest but she is clearly not interested. Growing drunker, she considers hitching into Stockholm but instead returns to Agnes' house, and she and Agnes have a sincere exchange during which they kiss again, giving Agnes hope.

The next day at school Elin intentionally ignores Agnes' feelings for her. Elin has decided that Agnes' notion of a lesbian love relationship may just be a cure for her boredom, and she thinks Agnes is more authentic than the other girls. Johan is crushed, but the story ends with Elin and Agnes celebrating their nonconformist status in school, as lesbians. Both, for the moment, seem to have what they want. Agnes has Elin and Elin has a notoriety earned not on the normal terms ("how many boys have you slept with?") but on her own terms ("how many of you have slept with a girl?"). In "Fucking Åmål," we will focus on the opening, which introduces Agnes' problem, Elin's problem, and Johan's desire. Each narrative thread comes back to Elin. How Moodysson manages multiple characters, goals, and stories energizes the opening of the film.

"Together" (2000)

"Together" is also a multiple-character narrative. It takes place on a commune in November 1975. The film opens with the news that Franco is dead. All the members of the Swedish commune celebrate as if it is New Year's Eve. The film follows Elisabeth (Lisa Lindgren), who is not a commune member. Elisabeth decides to leave her husband, Rolf (Michael Nyqvist), who has beaten her while drunk. She and her children, Eva and Stefan, will find refuge at Together, her brother Göran's commune.

The commune is made up of a divorced couple, Lasse (Ola Norell) and Anna (Jessica Liedberg). Anna has decided that males are oppressive and has declared herself a lesbian. They have a 4-year-old son, Tet. Göran (Gustav Hammarsten) has a girlfriend, Lena (Anja Lundqvist), who is self-centered and very interested in open sexuality. Göran is conservative, idealistic, and very sweet. He seems to be the leader of the house. Klas (Shanti Roney) is gay and in love with Lasse. Eric (Olle Sarri) is doctrinaire and very Marxist. His father is a wealthy banker. Signe (Cecilia Frode) and Sigvard (Lars Frode) and their son, Måne, round out the population of the commune. They seem the most antisocial of the group, always complaining about the behavior of others.

When Elisabeth and her children arrive, the others are gathered in the living room arguing about personal *versus* collective rights. Lasse is outraged that his ex-wife, Anna, stands around with no pants, dress, or underwear and is naked from the navel down. He is distracted by her state of undress. She asserts that a fungal infection has dictated her state of undress. This is her interpretation of freedom, but Lasse feels imprisoned by her freedom. Elisabeth and the children are shocked.

The film follows the conservative Elisabeth as she tries to adjust to her new life. Anna pursues her as does her husband, Rolf. Her children try to adjust, Eva finding a male friend next door. They are alike because of the thickness of their eyeglasses and their eccentric tastes in music. Stefan wants his father back. Lasse wants Anna back. Klas wants Lasse. Lena wants Eric, and so it goes. In the course of the story the collective characters become more individualistic, and the individualistic or conservative characters become more collective. Elisabeth and Rolf get back together and leave the commune. Lasse and Anna get back together. Göran throws the self-serving Lena out. The collective falls apart. The sequence we will focus on is the opening, which energetically introduces all the characters, their agendas, and their conflicts. As in "Fucking Åmål," Moodysson quickly focuses on his characters and juggles multiple story lines. Rather than confusing us, the multiple story lines clash and energize the charming set of characters of "Together."

"Lilja 4-Ever" (2002)

"Lilja 4-Ever" is an altogether different kind of story. The first half of the film is set in contemporary Russia, the second half in Sweden. After a prologue in Sweden, the film opens as a mother announces to the 15-year-old Lilja (Oksana Akinshina) that she is leaving for the United States with her new husband. She will send for Lilja when she is settled. Having been abandoned by her mother, Lilja is promptly thrown out of her apartment by her aunt. She must live in a run-down apartment, and the aunt will live in what was Lilja's apartment.

The school front is no better. Lilja walks out of school angry at all adults, but primarily her teacher. The friend situation is little better. The boys see all girls as hookers and act accordingly. A girlfriend

279

invites her out to a club, picks up a man, gets paid for sex, and promptly gives the money to Lilja. Her own father would kill her if he knew the truth. Lilja's reputation is tarnished for prostituting herself even though it was not her. She throws away the money given her. The world continues to close in on Lilja even though she has tried to be a 15 year old with a self-respect and morality absent in her peers and the adults in her life.

All she has on her side is one friend, a younger boy named Volodya ("glue and vodka"). Volodya (Artyom Bogucharsky) and Lilja form a friendship without sex, a friendship that is for each their only shield against total abandonment. Volodya is clearly abused by his family and persecuted by a gang of boys who roam the neighborhood. As if Lilja's situation was not bad enough, she receives a formal letter via the welfare authorities that her mother has given up all rights and responsibilities for Lilja. She is devastated and without means. The electricity is turned off in the hovel that is her apartment.

At this stage she turns to selling herself to men for money. She uses the money to buy a basketball for Volodya, an act of kindness toward an otherwise suicidal young boy. At this stage, she meets a young man in a club. The man treats her with kindness and she believes that, at last, someone will be kind and caring. But he is leaving for Sweden to work. He invites her to go with him.

Believing this is the beginning of a better life, she agrees. She says goodbye to Volodya who after she leaves feels totally abandoned and commits suicide. At the last minute, Lilja's young man tells her he cannot leave today but has arranged a flight and papers for her. He will soon follow. She goes to Stockholm.

In Stockholm, she is picked up at the airport but quickly discovers the young man's true intentions—a prisoner, she must now work as a prostitute. She rebels but is beaten into a life of imprisonment and prostitution. She is never let out of the apartment except to turn tricks. Life has become even more despairing. Without friends, without means, without dignity, Lilja tries to run away but fails. Her last act of self-respect is to take her own life. She is visited by Volodya with wings and the two play together, now both winged and free at last in death. The excerpt I will focus on is the last 10 minutes of the film, the events leading up to Lilja's suicide and liberation.

"A Hole in My Heart" (2004)

"A Hole in My Heart" is Moodysson's darkest film. There are four characters, and the ostensible plot of the film is the making of a pornographic film in urban Sweden. A father and son live in the apartment where most of the action takes place. The son, Eric (Björn Almroth), is long haired and has a birth defect—his right hand is claw-like. He seems depressed and escapes into his music. A rope hangs in the foreground of his room and seems to question whether he will continue to live. The father, Rickard (Throsten Flinck), is an alcoholic, rather dissipated, overweight, adolescent-like male. He will make a pornographic film today in the apartment. He invites Eric to watch but Eric is repulsed by what his father does. Eric, more conservative than his father, is rebellious against his father. When his father asks for a glass of water, Eric gives him water from the toilet bowl.

Geko (Goran Marjanovic), who will be the male in the film, is young, muscular, and angry. He oozes hate and aggression. Tess (Sanna Bråding), a 21-year-old woman appearing in the film, is there because she is bored and the only enthusiasm she has in life is for sex.

The through line of the film is the making of the porno film, but as the performers and director get bored with what they are doing they seek out more and more sensational actions for the film and for their own personal needs to remain engaged and stimulated. Those actions are increasingly about harming each other and themselves. Although violence is threatened, the actions remain on the level of humiliation and the loss of dignity. From a viewer's point of view of the film, however, these actions have not been replicated in commercial or artistic film since Pier Paolo Pasolini's "Salo." And they are a graphic representation of what is being shown on screen is creatively exploitative while at the same time critical of the human behavior depicted.

In the midst of all this, Moodysson introduces a human heart operation to save life while toys and sex scenes show exploitation of life functions/behavior. These cutaways provide Moodysson the opportunity to introduce his views on society and progress. To humanize his four characters he has them at different points confess to us their deepest aspirations and fantasies. In the case of Geko, the least sympathetic character, he cuts back repeatedly to Geko's pastoral fantasy (an escape from his behavior). His fantasy is escapist and pastoral—to run away to golden fields, assume the fetal position, and immerse himself in another reality. In the case of the other characters, their dreams are less humanistic, more regressive and aggressive. Only Eric remains the most human of the four characters, and the film ends with a close-up of him and Tess together. Rickard and Gcko seem to be victims of their own anger and disappointment in life. The two youngest, Tess and Eric, suggest a modicum of hope for the future; both proceed wounded but less scarred by their experiences. The excerpt I will use from "A Hole in My Heart" is the opening. As the four characters are introduced, Moodysson uses a jumpy style to capture the fractured nature of the four lives of the characters that will populate "A Hole in My Heart."

Text Interpretation

The director's idea, empathy and its limits, gives rise to the presence of empathy and contempt in Moodysson's character interpretations and the pressure points of plot and character that prompt change. In a sense, the director's idea creates a pathway into the narrative. In "Fucking Åmål," the main character, Elin, is bored. She is attractive and energetic and passionate. Her openness and her insensitivity commingle to make us wary of empathizing with her. In the progression of her relationship with Agnes we can see her shift from poseur and experimentalist to a more authentic person. Her energy and authenticity make Elin an empathic character. To elevate that sense of empathy Moodysson communicates a gentle contempt toward the well-meaning parents, toward the cruelty of adolescent boys, and toward the need to conform found among the school population at large.

In "Together" Moodysson is most empathic to Eva and Stefan. It is the children who suffer most in a family breakup. The gentle contempt is amply spread around the adult population. Göran is chided for his idealism, Lena for her promiscuity, Anna for her exhibitionism, and Eric for his rigidity and his anger. The contempt is not so great as to squeeze the charm out of these characters, but it is a presence.

Empathy is at its most poignant for Volodya and Lilja in "Lilja 4-Ever," and contempt is at its height when aimed at Geko and Rickard in "A Hole in My Heart," but both empathy and contempt are operative in each of these films. What is clear is that Moodysson is empathetic toward children, even a grown one like Eric in "A Hole in My Heart," and he views adult behavior as contemptible. The men in both "Lilja 4-Ever" and "A Hole in My Heart" are hateful and abusive toward children and women. This view of character permeates all of Moodysson's work.

To understand the why of the children/adult fault line in Moodysson's work we need to think of him as a moralist embracing a set of values in his work. Although values are central to the work of Moodysson's fellow countryman Lasse Hallström ("The Cider House Rules") and the independent filmmaker Alexander Payne ("Sideways"), they are not a central focus for most directors.

To highlight his exploration of values Moodysson has opted to utilize two genres that put a clash of values at the core of the narrative: situation comedy and melodrama. Because situation comedy and melodrama can be considered to be opposites, this choice becomes even more understandable. In "Fucking Åmål" and "Together," the dramatic arc is typical of a situation comedy. In comedies, the clash of values emanates from child *versus* adult and conformist *versus* nonconformist conflict. Moodysson uses a melodrama story frame for "Lilja 4-Ever" and "A Hole in My Heart." In the melodrama, the clash is exclusively between the child and adult. The powerless children Lilja and Volodya struggle for their dignity and a sense of power over their lives. In the melodrama, however, the outcome is dark and unyielding. Only death provides a playfulness and dignity absent in the lives of these two children. The clash of values and the morality/immorality implications are clear and foregrounded in Moodysson's films.

To support his interpretation of and empathy for his child characters, Moodysson opts for transformation via relationships. Agnes transforms Elin in "Fucking Åmål" and Göran is transformed by living with his sister Elisabeth in "Together." Plot is a barrier that has a negative impact on Lilja in "Lilja 4-Ever" and on Eric and Rickard in "A Hole in My Heart." Interestingly, both plots have to do with exploitation—the prostitution of Lilja in Sweden in "Lilja 4-Ever" and the making of the porno film in "A Hole in My Heart." For the most part, plot occupies the adult tier in these stories and the character relationships for the most part occupy the child tier. Moodysson the moralist is embedding empathy in relationships and contempt within the plot.

Directing the Actor

In casting his films, Moodysson casts for a look that will support the director's idea. For the adolescent roles in "Fucking Åmål" and "Lilja 4-Ever" the look has to elicit empathy, which means it must be appealing, expressive, and energetic. It also must be a natural look. In "Together," the children Eva and Stefan must look like obvious outsiders, and the adults (who so often act like adolescents) who belong to the commune must look like earnest, intense young adults committed to the communal idea. Only Elisabeth and Rolf look like real adults. To convey the contempt in "Lilja 4-Ever" and "A Hole in My Heart," the adults must look like they have no heart.

Beyond the look of the adolescents, children, and adults in Moodysson's films, the actors (similar to Kazan's sense of performance) have to key off of a single characteristic and then explore it in every way in their performances. Geko has to explore every aspect of his aggression, including the murderous dimension of his rage, in "A Hole in My Heart." Rickard has to explore every nook and cranny of his self-pity. In the case of Lilja in "Lilja 4-Ever," the young actress Oksana must hold onto every last morsel of her dignity, whatever the circumstances she finds herself in, and dignity must clearly be what her character values most. In "Together," Rolf must explore every dimension of his addiction to alcohol and its consequences. The courage and the humiliation provided by the alcohol have to be fully a presence in his performance. Moodysson's performers have to, in effect, risk it all because that is what their characters do.

The best way to capture Moodysson's approach to directing actors is to view his performance goals as being akin to those of Peter Brook, who is experimental in his efforts to achieve performances that go for a spiritual as well as a material presence. Although the word *existential* comes to mind, its implication is too academic for the Moodysson performances. They are raw and go far in generating a feeling equivalent to that of Brook's work, an edgy mix of the material and the spiritual.

Finally, there is a declarative dimension to the performances. Whether this is about a state ("I am so bored") or whether it is about a goal ("I love Elin") that obsesses the character, the outcome is the same. The performances gain an urgency that energizes the need of the character to find a solution. Lena tells Göran that she wants to sleep with Eric because he's so troubled. Afterward, she also tells Göran that she has had her first ever orgasm. All the ones she had with Göran were fake. Of course, her admission could be viewed as her character opening up, which might be true on the surface. In the performance, however, we also need to see her self-serving promiscuous urges. This is a girl who just wants to have fun. Think of it as the declaration and the revelation. Moodysson seeks both in the performance.

Directing the Camera

An examination of Moodysson's camera and editing choices should begin with what he omits. Moodysson does not open convention-ally. He opens without the benefit of establishing shots. To put it another way, he throws us into the middle of his story at the outset. The purpose of the establishing shot, whether it is an extremely long shot or a long shot, is to locate the action and its time and place; it is an establishing shot that provides context for the story to follow. Moodysson provides us neither context nor narrative link to consider where he is taking us.

In "Fucking Åmål," we are immediately introduced to Agnes and Elin. In "Together," we are introduced to Göran and Lena and the commune as the death of Franco is announced and the commune members celebrate by chanting, "Franco is dead." "Lilja 4-Ever" opens with Lilja running down a Swedish street toward the bridge she will use to commit suicide, "Meine Herz Brent" pulsing to the strings of a hard rock beat. "A Hole in My Heart" opens in the morning as Rickard awakens and Eric contemplates whether he will make it through another day. In each of the films, we simply move right into the characters. All are caught at a critical moment in their lives. For Agnes, it is her 16th birthday. For Lilja, it is the last moment before she ends her life. Moving right to the characters, Moodysson is telling us what is important in his stories—the characters, not the context.

To bring us closer to the characters, Moodysson favors the close-up. Rather than mid shots and long shots, he generally opts for the close-up. The films are not exclusively shot in close-up, as Carl Dreyer does in "The Passion of Joan of Arc," but close-ups are used enough to push us closer to the characters. No context means we have only the relationship with the characters as we are introduced to them and observe them.

A second visual dimension that enhances our relationship with the characters is Moodysson's use of a hand-held camera. Not as extreme as the Dogme use of the hand-held camera, Moodysson nevertheless has in the progression of his work opted increasingly for hand-held shooting. The danger here is that hand-held shooting brings a devil-may-care attitude to the formal qualities of composition, opposite that of Ford or Eisenstein. I believe that Moodysson has chosen the hand-held camera to get closer to Lilja and Volodya and Tess and Geko, and nothing formal should interfere with our access to these characters and their availability to us.

Another dimension of Moodysson's visual style is that he does not favor the wide-angle lens. Consider Roman Polanski for a moment. In "The Pianist," the camera is placed close to the main character and a Warsaw street or a rail station is fully in focus in the background. The placement puts us close to the main characters, and the lens choice gives context and a sense of how alone that character is. When Moodysson chooses a normal or even telephoto lens, context collapses and we feel that all that exists is the character. Placements seem dictated by the limits of space but they also seem to be about getting close to the character under any circumstances. Although Moodysson gives up the aesthetic bonus of beautiful framing, he is giving us a clear sense of his priorities: Get close to the character under all circumstances. The close-ups, the hand-held camera, and the lens choice all support his push to establish empathy for the main character and the other characters.

In terms of his editing choices, they are as distinctive as the camera choices. The first thing one notices is that Moodysson is interested in multiple characters; consequently, he utilizes parallel action editing. In "Fucking Åmål," he introduces Agnes and her obsession with Elin and Elin and her obsession with boredom and being somebody, and he intercuts their stories with Johan and his interest in Elin. The three stories then proceed, intersecting as we move into the narrative. Similarly, in "Together" we move between the commune and Elisabeth and Rolf's breakup. The intercutting continues until Göran brings Elisabeth and her children to the commune. Another thread that is introduced in the midst of these two storylines is Elisabeth's younger child, Stefan, and his sense of being an outsider among his own peers. The various story strands and the use of parallel editing energize these character-driven stories.

Moodysson also uses the jump cut to energize the narratives. Jump cutting on hand-held movement in the opening of "Lilja 4-Ever" propels us into the story of a character we meet in motion. The jump cutting gives us a sense of Lilja's internal chaos and the external violence of her life situation without spelling either out. The soundtrack of "Together" makes the scene powerful and overwhelming. The jump cut makes an important contribution to that feeling.

In "A Hole in My Heart," the jump cut and the sense of a lack of control implies the need for control in the lives of its four characters. Here, the jumps are disruptive rather than energizing. Also disruptive is Moodysson's choice of straight cutting from scene to scene. There is no softening via fades or dissolves. Blunt cutting results in a few seconds' lag before we begin to realize we are in a different location with different characters.

Finally, Moodysson is very sophisticated in his use of sound, particularly his juxtaposition of different types of music tracks. He moves from hard rock to atonal music to bass ambient noise in the opening of "A Hole in My Heart." As in the case of jump cutting, the result is disruptive and disorienting. In a sense, he is using a sound jump cut. The overall feeling of the opening of "A Hole in My Heart" is that we are caught in a series of MTV moments, unreal in the feeling that they are manufactured. Given the subject matter, the making of a porno film, this approach to the sound design gives the film opening of "A Hole in My Heart" an artificial feeling, a manufactured feeling. Like canned laughter on a television sitcom, the sound design emphasizes the artificiality of the experience to come. It does not come as a surprise that making the film is not spiritually nurturing for any of the characters involved.

Returning to the director's idea of empathy and its limits, we can see that Moodysson uses a variety of visual strategies to move us closer to his characters and another series of visual and sound strategies not so much to distance us as to alienate us, to move us into the soft and sometimes intense contempt he feels toward the characters and the situations they have placed themselves in. Both camera and editing strategies are operating to draw us close (empathy) and repel us (contempt). Quite where this young filmmaker will take us with his fifth film is anybody's guess. We look forward in eager anticipation to that next chapter.

287

Chapter 21

Catherine Breillat:
The Warfare of Sexuality

Introduction

Catherine Breillat wrote her first novel at 17. By the time she made her first film, "A Real Young Girl," in 1975, she had written three other novels and a stage play. Although her writing career continued she did not direct another film until 1988, when she made "36 Fillette," based on her novel. Not until 1999 with "Romance" was her international reputation established. Since then she has made films almost annually, including "Fat Girl" (2001), "Brief Crossing" (2001), "The Housekeeper" (2003), and "Anatomy of Hell" (2004).

All of Breillat's films focus on sexuality from the point of view of a girl or a woman. All are sexually explicit, and all of the films portray the obstacles women face, such as men in pursuit of sexual satisfaction. The challenge for Breillat is to avoid being aggressively pedantic or exploitative about her subject. She has to reveal as well as surprise us with her subjects, and the work has to succeed as a film experience. These are notable challenges, given the way in which Breillat pursues her focus on women and their sexuality. Characterization plays a role and is implied through what appears to be an obsession with sex. Conventional plot focuses only on the sexual act, such as the commercialized sex in "Anatomy of Hell" and the making of a film in "Sex Is Comedy" (2002). The consequence is a conscious sidestepping of the conventional narrative tools. This does not make Breillat's films any easier to watch; on the contrary, it makes the films all the more brave but difficult or provocative.

To understand Breillat and her approach, her work must be considered within the contexts of women as directors (and women as directors in France) and women as representations of culture. It is telling that of the fourteen directors I discuss in the book only three are women. (I have addressed this appalling statistic elsewhere; see *The Technique of Film and Video Editing*, 3rd ed., Focal Press, 2002, pp. 175–181.) Whether the reason is the politics of film or the economics of the industry, the fact is that far fewer women than men become film directors. Many who do tend to make assertive films about the plight of women, such as Margarethe Von Trotta ("Rosenstrasse"), Agnieszka Holland ("Olivier, Olivier"), Clara Law ("Floating Life"), Deepa Mehta ("Fire"), Julie Dash ("Daughters of the Dust"), Amy Heckerling ("Clueless"), and Angelica Huston

("Bastard Out of Carolina"). Other female directors deal with a broader band of narrative material in their films, including Ida Lupino ("The Burglar"), Diane Keaton ("Unstrung Heroes"), and Kathryn Bigelow ("Point Break").

In France, Chantal Ackerman ("Nuit et Jour") Claire Denis ("Beau Travail"), Josiane Balasko ("French Twist"), Agnés Jaoui ("The Taste of Others"), and Coline Serreau ("Chaos") have made important films from the point of view of women. Generally, these films have taken a political position but they essentially use voice-oriented genres such as the melodrama, fable, experimental narrative, and docudrama to humorously point out the shortcomings of men in the war between men and women. More often, French films have neatly divided French womanhood among coquettes (Brigitte Bardot), hookers with a heart (Simone Signoret), independent women (Jeanne Moreau), and suffering mothers (Catherine Frot). This was the context for Catherine Breillat as she moved from a career as a novelist to a career as a novelist and film director.

Although some of the filmmakers mentioned here share Breillat's passion for the equal treatment of women in society and outrage about the inequities bred in their respective societies, none has opted exclusively for the sex act as a narrative focal point. But Breillat cannot be put into the Russ Meyers and Tinto Brass category of filmmakers who make sexuality the narrative focus of their work. Breillat is far more interesting and, might I add, daring in her approach.

To move more deeply into Breillat's work, a number of observations are necessary. First, Breillat is as interested in the inner life of her characters as she is in their sexuality. She is very interested in exploring how a younger sister who is fat feels about having a beautiful but impulsive older sister in "Fat Girl." How does she feel being the scapegoat for the three other members of her family? How does a woman director, Jeanne, work, and why does she have such mixed feelings toward her male actor in "Sex Is Comedy"? How does sexual frustration push a schoolteacher to experiment with a variety of pleasure-seeking encounters in "Romance"?

Breillat seems interested in a woman's sense of dignity and is willing to set up undignified or humiliating situations in order to explore the dignity/humiliation paradox in human sexuality. This is the core issue in "Anatomy of Hell," in which a woman has an encounter with a homosexual and hires him for four nights of sexual exploration. In "Fat Girl," an older sister has her first sexual encounters in a room where her younger, obese sister is trying to sleep. A teacher explores sadomasochism with her headmaster in "Romance."

Breillat is also interested in exploring the role of women as sexual predators, role reversal in a sense. Fifteen-year-old Alice is curious and sexually aggressive in "A Real Young Girl." In "The Anatomy of Hell," a woman is the sexual initiator of a paid relationship with a homosexual. Indeed, Breillat is also interested in turning other sexual stereotypes on their head, such as the homosexual participating in a heterosexual encounter in "The Anatomy of Hell," the sexual desire of an obese teenager in "Fat Girl," the anti-stud behavior of the male actor who has to perform a sex scene in a film in "Sex Is Comedy." Breillat is challenging all of these stereotypes.

Having suggested the ambition of Breillat in her work, I feel we need to also point out how she has set many limitations on the narrative and speculate as to why. "Anatomy of Hell" has in essence two locations—a club where the two characters meet and a house by the sea where they have their nocturnal encounters. "Sex Is Comedy" has two settings—the beach, where an exterior scene is being filmed, even though the weather is the opposite of what one might expect, and a set where the interiors are being filmed, which seems almost summer-like. "Fat Girl" is set in a southern resort town off-season. Half of the screen time for this film is spent in the shared bedroom of the two girls. The second major setting is the car, a Mercedes, which the mother uses to transport her daughters in the second part of the film to their home outside Paris. The limited number of settings is used to position the films as interior narratives rather than as stories about characters out in the world. Breillat also limits the settings in order to create a sense of ritual or metaphor for her characters. The opposite, seeing her characters in a more varied, normal diversity of circumstances, would normalize our sense of the characters. They would be safer, more familiar. As it is, the characters present as strange, even menacing. I believe Breillat would consider them more pure characters.

This is an appropriate point to return to Breillat's director's idea. Her films are about sexuality as a power struggle between men and women. In her films, therefore, there has to be a sexual goal. It might be pleasure, it might be pain, it might be biological, it might simply be about procreation. It is rarely about what so many songs have been written about, love. And, because it is a power struggle, there is an antagonist. It might be the self as in "Anatomy of Hell." More often, though, it is men—the actor in "Sex Is Comedy," the boyfriend in "Romance." The antagonist might also be society's preference for beauty, such as in "Fat Girl." Often, the outcome of the power struggle is provided—the violent deaths of the mother and sister in "Fat Girl," the rape in "Fat Girl," the death of the boyfriend in "Romance." Breillat's films may be all about sex, but they are also about the emotional and physical violence that so often accompanies power struggles. Breillat views the sexual act as a power struggle for primacy, for satisfaction, and for satisfying the many needs of her characters.

"Romance" (1999)

"Romance" is the story of Marie (Caroline Ducey), a young teacher who has a boyfriend who is a male model. Since they have been living together he has backed away from having sexual relations. Although she craves sex he is turned off by the thought and abstention is their current sexual status. She seeks out sexual encounters while remaining in the relationship with her boyfriend. She picks up someone in a club and they plan an encounter the next day. Her headmaster seems supportive, but that support evolves into a sado-masochistic encounter with him. She also has a casual encounter on the street on her way home one day. After all of these encounters she has returned to the boyfriend. For her encounter with the headmaster, she dresses in red. Until this point white had been her color of choice. Whether it is the dress or something else, the boyfriend wants to have sex and she becomes pregnant from the one encounter. At the doctor's office, all the residents (male and female) as well as the doctor give her a vaginal examination. This scene seems violent, or at least a violation. In her relationship with her boyfriend, the violence takes on an emotional character. At a club one night, the boyfriend dances sensually with others, totally ignoring her, and that makes her angry. When she leaves in the morning he is asleep. She turns on the gas and after she has left the apartment it explodes and burns. Marie goes into labor. The headmaster is present and is passing himself off as the father. We see the birth, and for the first time Marie feels and expresses visually a different kind of pleasure. In our discussion of "Romance" we will focus on the birthing scene that concludes the film.

"Fat Girl" (2001)

"Fat Girl" is in some ways Breillat's most shocking film. Two sisters are on vacation in the southwest with their parents. It is off season. The main character, Anaïs Pingot (Anaïs Reboux), is the fat girl of the title. She is the younger sister and clearly suffers because her sister, Elena (Roxane Mesquida), is beautiful. Elena is impulsive in love. She picks up a young Italian law student, Fernando (Libero De Rienzo), and proceeds into the relationship as if he were the love of her life. Elena is cruel to her sister, blaming Anaïs and belittling her for her eating, all the while forcing her to eat to shut her up. Anaïs is also the scapegoat for her mother and father. The height of Elena's cruelty is the fact that she invites Fernando into her bed while sharing a room with Anaïs. Her sexual initiation with Fernando is witnessed by Anaïs. When Elena loses her virginity to Fernando, Anaïs is again a witness. There is no end to the emotional torment of her older sister. All the while, Anaïs is curious about her own developing sexuality. A family crisis develops when Fernando's mother arrives to reclaim a ring Fernando gave Elena to coax her into bed with him. Anaïs' father has already returned to work, and her mother retreats from the humiliation by cutting short the vacation and returning home. The mother is particularly punitive to Anaïs, who becomes car sick on the way home. The car ride is long, and the number of trucks on the road seems to make the ride more dangerous. The mother passes many trucks, but as night falls she tires and pulls into a rest stop to sleep. A truck also pulls into the rest stop, and the driver eyes them. Later the driver attacks them in their car. He axes Elena to death and chokes the mother to death. Anaïs witnesses the killings and tries to escape, but the killer takes her into the woods and rapes her. The film ends with the police recovering Anaïs and her denial of being touched. The scene we will focus on is the drive toward home, the killings, and the rape. The end of the film can be experienced as the culmination of the war between men and women for power, in this case on the road. The scene can also be read as a projection of Anaïs' anger toward her sister and mother for their persistent persecution of Anaïs. She has not caused either of them any harm but they still hurt her.

CATHERINE BREILLAT: THE WARFARE OF SEXUALITY

"Sex Is Comedy" (2002)

"Sex Is Comedy" is a film about making a film. The film director is a woman (Anne Parillaud) and her focus seems to be on the sex scene where the two actors will consummate their relationship. The film begins on the beach. The two actors, young and clearly stars, seem to hate each other. The young woman (Roxane Mesquida) is agreeable and vapid, and the young man (Grégoire Colin) is disagreeable and utterly neurotic. It is cold and about to rain but the actors and extras have to pretend it is a summer day at the beach. Finally, though, the rain ends the day's shooting. Jeanne, the director, is very cerebral and confides in her assistant director (Ashley Wanninger) all of her thoughts and feelings. The scene shifts to a studio for the interior shots. Because the actor is so neurotic, Jeanne had a number of prosthetic penises made for the actor but nobody told the actress about them. The focus of the rest of the film is on the filming of the nude scene. The director spends a lot of time trying to develop a relationship with the actor. It is clear, however, that she despises him. She also keeps changing her mind about how she wants the 15-page sex scene shot. Conversations with the cinematographer, set designer, and costumer continue but only in her scenes with her assistant does the director seem at ease; otherwise, she seems as high strung as the actor. All works out, and she films the scene (prosthetic and all). What is clear to the audience, at least, is that making a film is the equivalent of having sex—anxious moments followed by a joyous feeling of happiness and release. In "Sex Is Comedy" we will focus on the beach opening of the film. The scene provides Breillat with the perfect metaphor of artifice and reality, acting and feeling, beauty and boredom.

"Anatomy of Hell" (2004)

Finally we will look at the opening of "Anatomy of Hell." "Anatomy of Hell" follows four nights of a sexual encounter between a woman (Amira Casar) and a homosexual (Rocco Siffredi). The end of the scene acknowledges the possibility of sexual intercourse between this man and woman, but their exchange of true feelings occurs in the opening. The woman is at a club. She is alone and seems unhappy in the midst of the sensual noise and dancing. She goes to the bathroom, where she slices her wrists. The homosexual enters and intervenes. He takes her to a doctor, who bandages her arms. She offers a kind of payback by performing fellatio upon him. The fact that he could be aroused encourages her to make her four-night proposal. This scene has violence and feeling. The four nights that follow show the woman objectified, naked and passionless, and raises the question of whether a homosexual can choose to become heterosexual. The ending leaves itself open to numerous interpretations.

Text Interpretation

It is clear that Breillat has strong views about women in society and that she has chosen sexuality as her prism for examining that issue. Implicitly, she wants to empower women but as can be the case with artists she is offering a challenge to prevailing social stereotypes that women are passive and demure about their sexuality, that sexuality is biological and instinctual, and that sociological and psychological discussions about sexuality (the intellectualization of sexuality) have created an aura of pathology around sexuality that she feels is simply wrong. Breillat also is interested in linking paradoxes to sexuality—pleasure and pain, man and woman, self and other, propagation and non-purposeful sexuality.

In order to get us to think about the ideas in her films as well as to feel engaged in a film experience, she uses her text interpretation to distance us from her characters. She tells us very little about Marie in "Romance." For example, does she have parents or siblings? All of her history is stripped away and we are left with a young woman trying to deal with her boyfriend. The austere narrative, focusing only on sexual encounters, also distances us from Marie. Ironically, Breillat focuses on Marie in the most intimate of moments, sexual encounters, and yet we do not really understand Marie.

This characteristic is taken to an extreme in "Anatomy of Hell," where both the woman and the man she hires have an abstract quality. They are simply a woman and a man. Information about the woman is implied. Clearly, she is a woman of means, as she hires the man and they meet at a villa by the sea. Again, Breillat strips the characters down to essentials, to stereotypes, rather than creating complex characters, to further her ideas about sexuality and the power struggle between the woman and this man.

A second characteristic of Breillat's interpretation is to make a main character passive, watching rather than actively working toward achieving a goal; instead, the action is focused on other characters. In "Fat Girl," Anaïs observes her sister. She does act out her sexual curiosity and eat, but the action is driven by her beautiful older sister and her sexual relationship with Fernando. Anaïs even observes the killing of her sister and mother as if she is outside the action of the film. In "Sex Is Comedy," as a director, Jeanne is in a similar position. The actor and actress will perform for the camera, and the cameraman and art director and costumer are all essential to the film being made. They all have active roles to play, and Jeanne struggles with how to make the film her own, to materialize her vision. She manages in the end but she is for the most part a person watching and trying to capture the energy of all the other participants, particularly the actors.

Finally, Breillat resorts to shock to make her point about sexuality and the warfare between men and women. When I use the term *shock* I mean it in the same way I used the term *narrative exaggeration* earlier. Kubrick often used narrative exaggeration to make his point, as did Bunuel. Breillat's metaphors are not as elegant as the cowboy riding a nuclear bomb to its target, but they are equally powerful. In "Anatomy of Hell," the woman mixes a cocktail—part blood-red tampon, part water—and the two characters drink it. I have earlier mentioned the penis prosthesis in "Sex Is Comedy," and the multiple vaginal examinations Marie is subjected to in "Romance" are another example of the Breillat shock tactic. These moments are all presented in a visually pleasing surround that is every bit as light and beautiful as watching an Almodovar scene.

Directing the Actor

Breillat casts for a particular look—an obese 13 year old and her beautiful 15-year-old sister in "Fat Girl," a film director who has a sensual as well as a cerebral look in "Sex Is Comedy," a boyfriend who is better looking than his girlfriend in "Romance," and an actress and actor who are sensually beautiful, archetypically so, in "Anatomy of Hell." Breillat does not invite her actors to work within a wide range of emotions. Anne Parillaud in "Sex Is Comedy" is an

exception; because Breillat was working with performers as characters in that film, both the director and the actors worked within a
greater range than displayed in the performances in the three other
films discussed in this chapter. More typical is the pain to passive
range of Amira Casar in "Anatomy of Hell." Caroline Ducey as
Marie in "Romance" had a similar range, although in both films
there is a change in the last shot. Not quite pleasure, but perhaps an
openness to pleasure, is expressed by Amira Casar as "Anatomy of
Hell" ends. Caroline Ducey is less ambiguous when Marie's child
is born. Marie seems to have some hope for the future, whereas
until this point she had been obsessively focused on the moment
and anticipation of release or relief.

Finally, an important element of the performance is for actors to
imply or project a feeling about their own sexuality. That feeling
might be benign as in "Anatomy of Hell." It might be curiosity as in
"Fat Girl." It might be obsession as in "Romance." Whatever the
dimension Breillat is trying to capture, it is far from the heavy
breathing and glazed eyes that so often pass for performance and
sexuality in many films.

Directing the Camera

The visual look of Breillat's work tends to be romantic. The opening of "Sex Is Comedy" and the opening of "Romance" both have
an aesthetically pleasing set design, as does "Anatomy of Hell." But
this is where performance and visuals begin to collide. The actors
are miserable on the beach in "Sex Is Comedy." Marie is profoundly
frustrated with her boyfriend in "Romance." A woman attempts suicide in "Anatomy of Hell." In this sense, the visual look of the films
makes the unhappiness of the characters ironic. And we are curious
as to why.

A second visual component is that Breillat saves close-ups for
vital parts rather than vital dramatic moments; otherwise, her visual
style does not emotionalize scenes. On the contrary, her intent
seems to be to objectify her characters and objectify the sexual act.
Longs shots tend to objectify rather than emotionalize. When Marie
gets undressed in front of her boyfriend, we can see her disrobing in
the same shot that registers her boyfriend's indifference.

What does draw Breillat to close-ups is violence. In the last scene of "Romance," which focuses on the birth of Marie's child, Breillat uses close-ups. The head of the baby as it emerges from the vagina is an intense close-up that is followed by the full emergence of the baby. As presented, this moment is about birth as violence to the mother's body.

The kiss of actor and actress on the beach in "Sex Is Comedy" is shot as a close-up that illustrates the hatred of one character for the other. Similarly, Breillat used a close-up to reveal the breast of the actress on the beach. Given the temperature, this shot implies not passion but cold weather. The depiction of violence and its partnership with acts of intimacy, even love, supports Breillat's director's idea and does not yield insight into her characters.

Breillat also uses camera placement and editing to create a sense of violence. In "Fat Girl," the editing style up until the drive back to Paris was very relaxed, but then the style shifts abruptly. The mother is very angry with the older daughter, Elena, but seems to save all her ire for Anaïs. The shots from the point of view of Anaïs or the mother are of the traffic, particularly the trucks. Often their Mercedes seems surrounded by trucks. The sequence also focuses on the mother's anger. She is smoking almost continually. She does not turn on the radio when Anaïs requests it, but later she turns on the music very loud, much to the annoyance of Anaïs. Anaïs purchasing food, eating, and being sick—all are visually included. Elena seems exceedingly worried whether her mother will tell her father what happened and whether they will force her to be medically examined. By jump cutting, by focusing on the number and proximity of the trucks, Breillat creates a sense of impending violence. Consequently, the trip seems almost unbearable and dangerous. When the mother stops the car at night to rest, it is almost a relief. This momentary peace does not last long, however. Elena goes to the restroom, and a truck pulls in. The driver eyes them and then smashes the window with an axe and does the same to Elena. The violence continues unabated until the police find Anaïs. In this sequence, Breillat used camera placement and an editing strategy to prepare us for the violence.

In tying murder and rape to a narrative about an obese girl who is the scapegoat of her family, Breillat created her most overpowering realization of her director's idea. Here, sexuality is at the core of

the narrative. Exerting power, whether the sexual power of an adolescent over her sibling or the male–female power struggle, always
leads to the same place—the violent resolutions of conflict
that affirm that women are the victims of men rather than their
partners. "Fat Girl" takes us as far from romantic love as we can
travel. We are left with the director's idea to ponder our own ideal-
izations and demonizations of sexuality. This is where Breillat's
films take us.

299

Chapter 22

Mary Harron:
Celebrity and Banality

Introduction

Mary Harron has directed interesting series television such as "L Word" and "Homicide," and she is now completing her third feature film. Unlike the other case studies in this book, she has only two feature film credits at the writing of this book, yet I feel that her films are so distinctive that I am concluding the book with an examination of her work in those two films because her director's idea is so compelling. Mary Harron's directors idea is to link celebrity and banality. I will discuss those two films, "I Shot Andy Warhol" (1995) and "American Psycho" (2000) shortly.

First, an explanation about celebrity and banality, her director's idea. Other filmmakers have made films about the epicenters of celebrity, Hollywood and television. Most often those films have been satires, occasionally melodramas. The satires include Robert Altman's "The Player" and Sydney Lumet's "Network." The melodramas include Elia Kazan's "A Face in the Crowd" and Paul Thomas Anderson's "Boogie Nights." Other filmmakers have taken the more benign approach of situation comedy, including Sydney Pollack's "Tootsie," James Brooks' "Broadcast News," and Woody Allen's "The Purple Rose of Cairo." All of these films, in ways critical and less critical, address the issue of celebrity and values. Those values range from the social and political to the ethical. All portray a tradeoff between celebrity or narcissistic values and humanistic or altruistic values.

Mary Harron's work differs from the above mentioned in an important respect. Her characters are not celebrities but rather narcissistic characters that identify with celebrity. They want and need their 15 minutes of fame, and her work explores their desperate obsession with those 15 minutes. In this sense, her characters are a part of a new phenomenon, new at least since Christopher Lasch wrote about the culture of narcissism in his book *The Culture of Narcissism* (1979). That culture has elevated popular music and its stars, popular art and its stars, and fashion and its stars to iconic levels. The upshot today is reality television and its centerpiece, "American Idol." This is the cultural terrain that Harron's characters occupy. They are intense wannabes. The inner life of these characters clashes with their outer reality. Their major talent is their desire and here they merge with the superficiality of celebrity.

Harron finds the common ground to be the banality of both celebrities and the wannabes.

Whether this perception makes Harron a satirist of celebrity or whether she is simply an interested observer, she does seem to be able to take us into her character's inner need for celebrity and into the pathology generated by the clash of inner need and outer reality. For her the gold of celebrity glitters preciously but at the same time it is false, fool's gold. This is the tragedy of her characters. Their efforts lead only to despair and to destruction. The fact that she can achieve feeling for these unattractive characters is part of Harron's gift as a writer and director.

In order to understand Harron's director's idea, it is important to examine her work within the context of a woman directing in America at the end of the 20th century and into the next. Earlier chapters examined the work of Margarethe Von Trotta and Catherine Breillat, both of whom are political filmmakers in that their subject is women in a world of men. Von Trotta focuses on the lives of her characters, while Breillat focuses on the inner life as expressed in sexual behavior. Harron is far more American (although she is Canadian) in her sociological focus. It is not the war between men and women that interests her, nor is it class. It is a different divide between the have-nots and the haves. The haves are celebrities, the Andy Warhols, while the have-nots are the Valerie Solanas characters of the society.

Among the other women directors working in America today, Alison Anders focuses on women trying to make their way in a man's world in "Gas, Food and Lodging." Amy Heckerling examines fashionista life for females in the fast lane of high school in "Clueless." Mo Ogrodnik is interested in adolescent sexuality in "Fresh." Patty Jenkins is interested in female pathology and its genesis in male/female relationships in "Monster." Mira Nair is interested in celebrating her Indian roots in "Monsoon Wedding." The Sprecher sisters are interested in exploring post-9/11 ennui in "Thirteen Conversations About One Thing." The perspective in all of these films is modern and feminist. How Mary Harron differs from these filmmakers is principally in her choice of genres. "I Shot Andy Warhol" is a docudrama. "American Psycho" is a moral fable or hyperdrama. (For a discussion of hyperdrama, or the moral fable, see the book I co-wrote with Pat Cooper, *Writing the Short Film*,

3rd ed., Focal Press, 2003.) Both docudrama and hyperdrama are genres that elevate voice. (See the chapters entitled "The Centrality of Metagenres" and "The Ascent of Voice" in my book *Global Scriptwriting*, Focal Press, 2001.) These genres of voice require that the director distance us from the characters and here lies the risk of these genres. These genres have a strong voice, but they do not invite us to identify with their characters. And so we watch Valerie Solanas in "I Shot Andy Warhol" and Patrick Bateman in "American Psycho," but we do not identify with them. Indeed, they are characters we do not care for at all. By using the melodrama structure, Patty Jenkins invites us to identify and care about Aileen, the serial killer who is the main character of "Monster," as intensely as Allison Anders does with the young daughter in "Gas, Food and Lodging" and as Amy Heckerling does with Emma in her situation comedy, "Clueless."

To compensate for this loss of identification Harron has had to undertake compensating strategies that strengthen the experience of her films. These strategies include the use of irony and humor with regard to her characters and the environment that nurtures their narcissism. Another strategy is to have a powerful sense of time and place. In "I Shot Andy Warhol," 1960s New York with all its subversive hedonism, is as much a character as the empty glamour of a gentrified New York of the 1980s is in "American Psycho." Finally, Harron adopts a distinctive style that is vigorous and in line with the genre she has chosen.

Docudrama is a fiction film that looks like a documentary. A place, a character, or an issue is organized around an idea about that place, character, or issue. The organization of the narrative is the equivalent of a case for or against. The character at the center of the narrative is the vehicle for the case. "I Shot Andy Warhol" suggests that celebrity appeals to a character who is utterly marginalized by her family history and by society's values. In the case of Valerie Solanas, celebrity is both attractive and overwhelming. She wants it but she is afraid of it, and in the end her resulting paranoia brings her the celebrity she so desperately sought. She will forever be known as the woman who shot Andy Warhol. Here, Harron used the docudrama story form to condemn the celebrity culture and its root cause, the culture of narcissism.

In "American Psycho," the issues are similar. This time, the issue is the emptiness that the culture of narcissism yields. Patrick

Bateman is a Harvard graduate, a vice president in a corporation whose function is to market. He is by society's measure a success, but inside he is empty. As his narcissistic needs grow he fills himself with a hateful, murderous inner life that totally disconnects him from the real or external world. The moral of the story is that the culture of narcissism is empty on the inside but looks great on the outside. For Harron, that culture is destructive and she chose the moral fable to shape her cautionary tale. It is notable that "American Psycho" was released in the same year Stanley Kubrick released his cautionary fable, "Eyes Wide Shut." The difference is that Kubrick's treatment is genteel compared to the nightmare Harron has created. Both, however, are cautionary tales about the dangers of the narcissistic culture.

Before I describe the excerpts I will use to illustrate the director's idea, let's examine the strategies Harron uses to embed the director's idea in the narrative. These strategies will contextualize the discussion to follow. If the director's idea requires a linkage between celebrity and banality, Harron must make each appealing and repellent. In other words, she must embed in the character of celebrity an allure as well as a banality. In the banality there is so much desperation for a wish of celebrity acknowledgment that pathos for the character is created. To do so, Harron takes a paradoxical approach to character and place in her two films. Specifically, New York is an exciting as well as callow and cruel environment in "I Shot Andy Warhol." In "American Psycho," the environment is all about the power of steel and affluence as well as superficiality, the plastic quality at the center of narcissistic consumerism. Its very coldness is what makes New York dangerous for its inhabitants in "American Psycho."

Similarly, in her approach to character she includes both negative and positive characters. The negative characters occupy the celebrity status in "I Shot Andy Warhol." They are the occupants of the Factory, Andy Warhol and his hangers-on. The publisher of pornography, Maurice Girodias, is another negative character. The positive characters are the lesbians around Valerie Solanas, including the transsexual Candy Darling. Their desire for recognition and their marginal status positions them as opposites of the celebrities and would-be celebrities. Valerie herself is the narrator and witness to both sides. She provides the baseline entry into the world of celebrity in the New York of the 1960s.

In this world of celebrities and non-celebrities, extreme behavior is the norm, as reflected in "American Psycho." If anything, the behavior becomes more extreme throughout the film. In "American Psycho," the celebrity/non-celebrity line is constantly being redefined. On first appearance, Patrick Bateman might be considered a celebrity. He has the job, the money, the clothes, and the attitude that suggest it. But something as simple as his colleagues' having more elegant business cards is enough to push him into the category of non-celebrity. In "American Psycho," there is no sympathetic group; rather, the characters could be divided into groups of unpleasant and more unpleasant. Only the prostitutes Patrick uses summon a modicum of sympathy. Although Patrick himself acts as narrator, it is his secretary, Jean, who gives the film an emotional baseline. In her vulnerability and in her sense of having a moral compass, she is different from all the other characters in the narrative. She rather than Patrick is the character we are invited to stand with. In terms of linking celebrity and banality, all the characters that surround Patrick, both men and women (fiancée, mistress), are banal and well positioned enough to be considered celebrities, but their status is conditional. Each is aware of the vulnerability of that status, aware that it could be withdrawn at any moment for any reason.

Celebrity and banality are at the very heart of the characters in both "I Shot Andy Warhol" and "American Psycho." And, in both, the place (New York) becomes an active character that breeds the desire to be or to be seen as a celebrity. Not to be a celebrity in New York is not to be seen at all. In this sense, New York acts as a metaphor, the geographical pinnacle that represents celebrity.

Finally, the voice-oriented genre Harron chooses must be combined with her approach to character and narrative incident. That approach fluctuates between sincerity and irony, inside the character and outside the character. The consequence is the creation of a satiric frame where Harron is free to shift between standing with the character and gazing at the character. The genre frame enables Harron to be gently and not so gently satiric about the world of celebrity around New York and Andy Warhol in "I Shot Andy Warhol" and about the shallow narcissistic world around the affluent Patrick Bateman in 1980s New York in "American Psycho." For our discussion of these two films, I suggest that we use the openings and closings of each film as the basis of our exploration of the director's idea.

MARY HARRON: CELEBRITY AND BANALITY

"I Shot Andy Warhol" (1995)

"I Shot Andy Warhol" begins with the shooting of Andy Warhol (Jared Harris) in the late 1960s. It then moves back in time to tell the story of Valerie Solanas (Lily Taylor), the shooter. The flashback is framed as a case study with the examining psychologist as the lead narrator. Eventually Valerie herself will become the principal narrator. In docudrama style, the early part of the film mixes home movies of Valerie together with a filmed, stylized interview with Valerie, who reads from her manifesto, *SCUM*. This early portion of the film focuses on her sexual history—the fact that she was sexually abused by her father, the fact that Valerie has declared her preference for women, the fact that she made it her mission to be aggressive toward and rejecting of men, the fact that she earned tuition for college by prostituting herself.

After college studies in psychology in Maryland, Valerie moves to New York and it is here that the balance of the film takes place. It is the 1960s. New York is edgy and attractive. Valerie affiliates with a subculture of lesbians and transsexuals. She panhandles and prostitutes herself to pay her way. She sees herself as a writer. First she writes a feminist manifesto, *SCUM*, and then a play titled "Up Your Ass." Both are virulently anti-male.

Life is lively but marginal. Through her own efforts she meets Maurice Girodias (Lothaire Bluteau), a publisher of pornography. She also meets Candy Darling (Stephen Dorff), a transsexual who has begun to act in Andy Warhol movies. Valerie feels confident that Warhol will produce her play, but he doesn't. When Girodias offers her a contract for a book she accepts but immediately begins to come apart at the seams. The pressure of performance makes Valerie paranoid and she becomes threatening to the key men in her life, Girodias and Warhol. Already marginalized by Warhol's hangers-on, Valerie takes it out on Warhol and shoots him. This brief description does not do justice to the sexual/psychological portrait of a marginalized woman and the vivid portrait of the edgy celebrity scene of the Factory, Warhol's window on his world, and the New York it made famous.

The opening of "I Shot Andy Warhol" begins with Valerie Solanas having shot Andy Warhol. The gun is empty. A colleague of Warhol suggests that she leave. Valerie's father sees his daughter on television, arrested for the shooting. She claims the reason for the

306

shooting is complicated and suggests that the reporter read her manifesto to understand why she shot Warhol. Andy Warhol's acolytes are interviewed about the shooting. His wig is retrieved. The next scene focuses on Valerie being interviewed by the police. What follows is Valerie's personal history until she goes to New York following college. The history is described by the prison psychologist.

The film's ending follows a series of sharp short scenes. Candy Darling, Valerie's friend Jeremiah (Danny Morgenstern), and Valerie watch and editorialize about the Miss America pageant. The next scene is a television interview with Valerie (remember that Valerie has yearned for celebrity). The interview set up by Jeremiah proves to be a disaster. A right wing host looks only to belittle Valerie for her lesbian appearance and radical political views. He baits her and finally she physically attacks him and walks out on the interview; subsequently, she beats Jeremiah and Candy. She then threatens Girodias and threatens Stevie (Martha Plimpton) with a gun. Stevie throws her out. She visits Girodias' office and tells his secretary that the next time she sees him she will kill him. She waits for Warhol on the street level of the Factory. She joins him on the elevator and enters his apartment. He takes a call, ignoring her. She takes out her pistol and shoots him and a colleague. When she leaves she announces to a policeman she is wanted, that she shot Andy Warhol. The scene that follows shows both Warhol and Valerie hospitalized. An epilogue explains the fate of Candy Darling, Andy Warhol, and Valerie Solanas. The film ends with a statement by Valerie on the lack of need for reproduction and future generations.

"American Psycho" (2000)

"American Psycho" opens on an elegant meal in an elegant restaurant. The food is shown being prepared, arriving at the table, and being eaten. The preparations are elegant and beautiful but somehow violent. So, too, is the consumption of the meal. Patrick Bateman (Christian Bale) and his colleagues are elegant but aggressive. They talk, the conversation is elevated in its sophistication, but it doesn't go anywhere. We are aware mainly of the aggression each hurls at the other. They continue on to an expensive club where Bateman, our main character, is abusive verbally but she, the bartender, doesn't respond. Was it an imagined conversation? It seems to be.

Patrick Bateman, the main character, narrates. He provides superficial information, including his age. We see his menacing preparations to get ready for work (morning ritual—exercise, shaving, bathing). He is all surface. Later, at work again, he is obviously superficial. He holds the position of vice president for mergers and acquisitions at Pierce & Pierce. His secretary flatters him, clearly under his influence, but Patrick could not care less about her.

We learn that Patrick has a fiancée, Evelyn (Reese Witherspoon) and a mistress, who happens to be his colleague's fiancée, Courtney (Samantha Mathis). We also learn that Patrick can talk the talk (social concerns over materialism) to his colleagues, but in practice he is a fraud. He feels that he is "simply not there" and that his day-to-day life is out of alignment with his internal life, which seethes with aggression and need (he sees himself as a sexual and societal predator). Outwardly, however, his colleagues are far more predatory and effective.

At the top of the peer group is Paul Allen (Jared Leto), who does not even recognize Patrick. He mistakes him for someone else, a colleague who wears similar suits and glasses and goes to the same barber. Patrick's crisis occurs at a meeting where he presents his business card to claim his status in his peer group. David Van Patten (Bill Sage) and Timothy Bryce (Justin Theroux) present their cards and each is a blow to Patrick. The final blow, however, is the obvious superiority of Paul Allen's business card. Patrick has been put in his place. The business card incident is his Waterloo. From this point on, Patrick falls apart; he is crushed and the balance of the film is concerned with the consequences of this blow.

What follows is Patrick's descent into a kind of mad rage. First, he encounters a homeless person. Initially patronizing, Patrick ends up killing the man. This killing is followed by an encounter with Allen. They arrange to have dinner, but Allen still mistakes who Patrick is. Later, at Allen's apartment, Patrick murders Allen with an axe and gets rid of the dismembered body. Patrick meets periodically with Detective Donald Kimball (Willem Dafoe), who is looking into the disappearance of Allen. The purpose of these scenes is to put pressure on Patrick for his murderous actions. Patrick's sexual appetites grow. He alternates between his mistress and prostitutes. His fiancée seems increasingly demanding and unloving. His resentment of her grows. When Patrick engages two prostitutes for an evening, it ends murderously when he kills one with a chain saw. Patrick's blood lust continues. He kills numerous low-level security employees at work. He tries to sleep with his secretary, but cannot do it. He lets her go. He breaks with his fiancée. He confesses murder to his lawyer. Bloodlust and overwhelming turbulence bring Patrick to the breaking point. By now Patrick is essentially in a state of emotional collapse. When he tells his secretary that he cannot come into the office that afternoon, she tells him that his colleagues are expecting him to meet them for drinks after work. He does not think he is up to it, but he does go. Meanwhile, his secretary looks through Patrick's desk and finds his personal diary. She is shocked by the violent sketches it contains.

At Harry's Club, Patrick meets up with his colleagues. He seems anxious and distracted. They are concerned about getting a reservation for dinner. When Patrick sees his lawyer, he approaches him, but the lawyer mistakes him for David Van Patten, another client. Patrick asks how he felt about his telephoned murder confession. The lawyer says he was amused. Patrick tries to correct his identity and verify his murderous activities, but the lawyer no longer thinks it is funny. When Patrick persists the lawyer tells him that what he is saying is untrue because he had dinner twice with Allen in London, only 10 days ago, after Patrick says he killed him. Patrick has no response.

When he rejoins his friends, Patrick is clearly deflated. The film ends on Paul's self-deprecating inner monologue about no more barriers to cross, about how his pain is constant and sharp and his punishment continues to elude him. The confession has meant nothing. Clearly, the murders have been fantasies and Patrick Bateman's life is empty if he cannot even be known (become a celebrity) for the abundant violence he has committed.

The opening of "American Psycho" introduces the environment, a restaurant where status and taste outweigh human values. Here, the characters are the expression of their menu choices and their restaurant choices. Only later does the main character, Patrick Bateman, introduce himself. He does so by introducing us to his elegant apartment and his precise morning routine to hone his physical appearance. He exercises and applies sundry lotions, including an herb/mint facial mask. Patrick's focus on brand-name gels, scrubs, and cleansers implies, as he tells us, that "there is no real me, I'm simply not there."

MARY HARRON: CELEBRITY AND BANALITY

He arrives at his office to the beat of "I'm Walking on Sunshine." Here, too, the image is all surfaces with no substance. He comments not on the workday but rather on restaurant reservations and makes suggestions regarding his secretary's appearance. At that moment, her surface is more important than anything else. The opening of "American Psycho" establishes the main character's priority (celebrity or nothing) and the tenuousness of celebrity status.

The ending of "American Psycho" focuses on the puncturing of Patrick's violent delusions. They are real on paper, as his secretary witnesses. They are, however, a fantasy, as Patrick's lawyer attests. Harry's Club is banal, and Patrick's colleagues are not content; in fact, they are quite discontent as they want to be having dinner or at least have a reservation for dinner. Once Patrick realizes that his murderous rages are fantasies, he deflates. The film ends with his narration, and the camera moves in on him, closer and closer, as he confesses that his confession has meant nothing. Not even the celebrity of murder is left him. He is banal and empty and he is in pain. There is no catharsis for this narcissistic character.

Text Interpretation

Celebrity can be seen as power, and the desire for celebrity can be interpreted as the desire for power. For Harron, banality is not a state of powerlessness; rather, she regards Andy Warhol and those around him, including the media, as banal, empty icons who have created a modern mythology of material fortune and fame together with a spiritual emptiness. Patrick uses the very word *emptiness* to characterize himself in "American Psycho." In this sense, Harron is a critic of celebrity and of banality. Her characters are desperate for a better life but settle for celebrity because they know nothing else. As I mentioned earlier in the chapter, Harron's use of voice-oriented genres, the docudrama in the case of "I Shot Andy Warhol" and the moral fable in the case of "American Psycho," is her most important narrative decision.

A second decision that enables us to grasp her interpretation is her choice to illustrate the dissonance between the inner voice and the outer action. Both Valerie Solanas and Patrick Bateman act as their own narrators, the inner confessional voice of their narratives. The actions of the two characters, on the other hand, aggressively pursue actions that increasingly marginalize them, psychologically and socially. That is not to say that Harron wants to portray these characters as losers but rather as perennial outsiders. They are like the rest of us in a celebrity-obsessed society, outsiders looking in on what they imagine they want. It is Harron's twist to point the emptiness she sees inside celebrity society. This ordinariness and its meanness rob the celebrity society of its romanticism, and the films suggest that perhaps Solanas and Bateman are at least feeling people as opposed to the zombie-like visitors to the Factory and the 1980s glamorous New York restaurants.

A third strategy Harron uses in the text interpretation is to pepper her tragic narratives with humor. Foreign journalists interview Factory hangers-on about the shooting of Andy Warhol. The remarks, tinged with irony, point out the interviewer's pompousness and the interviewees' envy of Warhol's status. The readings of Solanas from her manifesto are so inflammatory that they seem unintentionally funny, which makes them even funnier. Bateman's retort to his racist, sexist colleagues makes him seem to be New York's last moralist. Both the comments of his colleagues and Bateman's moralizing are wildly funny given that in his mind Bateman is a killer of blacks, women, and vice presidents in his company.

Finally, a sense of time and place is critical in Harron's text interpretation. There would have been no Valerie Solanas without the sex- and drug-obsessed New York of the 1960s, and there would have been no Patrick Bateman without the "greed is good" philosophy of 1980s New York, a time when junk bonds and brand names in all things from soap to suits were the epitome of making it. Harron weaves the sense of time and place throughout her films; indeed, they transcend individualism and the love–work nexus that Freud placed at the center of his interpretation of happiness. The culture of narcissism that thrived in the 1960s and 1980s is about as far away from the positive goals and attainments of those eras as is possible. And these are the worlds of Valerie Solanas and Patrick Bateman.

Directing the Actor

Mary Harron set herself quite a challenge in the characters of "I Shot Andy Warhol" and "American Psycho." The task was to make these eccentric, unappealing characters sufficiently energetic and engaging to keep us engaged in the movies. Here casting helped. In both films, Harron cast very good young character actors. In "I Shot Andy Warhol," she casts Lili Taylor as Valerie Solanas and Jared Harris as Andy Warhol and proceeded to surround them with the crime crème de la crème of New York actors: Martha Plimpton, Steven Dorff, Lothaire Bluteau, and Jill Hennessy. All are charismatic character actors. She cast "American Psycho" in a similar way by surrounding Christian Bale with Reese Witherspoon, Samantha Matthis, Chloé Sevigny, Jared Leto, Josh Lucas, and Willem Dafoe. Again, individual charisma was key. The casting was for look, range, and energy and always for individualistic presence.

Working with her cast, Harron set the bar high. Both Solanas and Bateman had to appear as eccentric, strange, inaccessible people who operate just below the radar. This quality gives each character a remote, alienated quality. From this base, Harron encouraged energy. Solanas is always moving. She spits out bullets for words. Whether she is aggressive or anxious, movement gives her performance physicality, yet Solanas speaks with a flatness of affect that contradicts the words themselves, signaling her internal struggle. The lack of affect also implies Valerie's disconnect from the world around her.

Playing Patrick Bateman, Christian Bale had to move between his character's self-absorption and his aggression. Bateman watches himself in a mirror as he's making love to a woman. His body rather than hers is his love object. Vanity, watching people watch him, creates the internal values of this character. He couldn't care less about anybody else, and this goes to the nub of the character's problem. He is contemptuous of others.

Harron juxtaposes these main characters with the theatricality that surrounds them. In "I Shot Andy Warhol," Candy Darling and the acolytes around Andy Warhol are each over the top in their falseness; they are poseurs hoping that hanging around Andy Warhol will elevate them to a celebrity that will distinguish them from the crowd. In "American Psycho," Bateman's peers are each over the top in their aggression and their contempt for the rest of humanity. This theatricality surrounds the main characters and challenges them to join if they can. In each case, whatever poignancy these characters generate emanates from their inability to be accepted by the poseurs who are closer to celebrity than they are.

Directing the Camera

If the director's idea is to link celebrity and banality, how does Harron frame her shots and organize her images to support that idea? The first notable visualization of the idea is the opening of each film. Humanity and the humanness of her characters are notably absent in the opening of "American Psycho." Instead, we see a series of close-ups of sliced duck breast surrounded by raspberries. Other close-ups of beautifully prepared food follow. The camera looks down from above on these dishes. The cutting makes the scene aggressive rather than aesthetic. The cutaways to mid shots of waiters reciting the exotic special of the day present the point of view of a paying customer who is distant and disdainful. The images distance us from the people and focus on an aggressive, disembodied aesthetic—Harron's version of the culture of consumption.

Although "I Shot Andy Warhol" opens with the shooting of Andy Warhol, the scene lacks any humanity. Replacing narrative continuity and causality are shots of the Factory, the cowboy boots of the wounded Andy Warhol, Valerie in mid shot with gun in hand, and her leave-taking having expended all the bullets in her gun. It is a scene of consequences of actions rather than the actions themselves. The result is unstable and unnerving in its jumpy detailing. Harron quickly follows with a fragmented biography of Valerie. Home footage, black-and-white interview footage, and staged university scenes characterize Valerie as a good student who has been sexually abused. Although declaring herself gay, she could be heterosexual when she needed to be. Valerie's notion of sex as currency is quickly established, as is her hatred of men. Jump cutting and camera movement give the scenes an observational rather than involving quality.

In both sequences, the visualization works with the idea of celebrity and banality in a particular way. Andy Warhol's blonde wig merits a close-up; his wounded body does not. Valerie's response to men, her anger, is worthy of a head-on mid shot, as is her promiscuous desire for a female instructor in college. The shooting of Andy Warhol, however, is not worthy of moving in this close. Similarly, in "American Psycho," we only move into a close-up of Patrick Bateman when he applies gels and masks to his face. When we later see Patrick with his fiancée in a car, the camera shot is a mid shot. We are not even introduced to Patrick in the earliest shots of the film. The focus is on the food in the restaurant.

Harron also seems to take an almost musical approach to these introductions. Details are punctuated by other details. A tone is created, a very impressionistic one, but a character is not introduced. The result is that events supersede the character. Inanimate objects such as food supersede character, and the environment also supersedes character.

In terms of the editing, Harron prefers short, quick scenes, cutting slowly. She prefers movement rather than rapid cutting. The result is a kind of character inertia rather than a dynamic character in action. Looking at the narrative content of "I Shot Andy Warhol," it is strange as the film opens with the shooting having just taken place. The mid and long shots of Valerie further distance us from what has just happened. In "American Psycho," Harron chose to open with the food and eating close-ups and eventually moved out to mid and long shots of the characters. She gradually moved in on Patrick Bateman, opting for moving the camera rather than fast cutting. She closed the film in the same shot pattern.

Above all what has fleshed out her camera choices is the need to conform to the genre—the docudrama in "I Shot Andy Warhol" and the fable in "American Psycho." Camera placement and shot choice in "I Shot Andy Warhol" have a captured as opposed to composed look. On the other hand, the images in "American Psycho" are utterly composed, even stylized, a look suitable for this stylized fable of the 1980s.

Celebrity and banality, desire and the emptiness of those who seek it—these comprise the director's idea deployed by Mary Harron in "I Shot Andy Warhol" and "American Psycho." The challenge Harron faced was to make us care about Valerie Solanas and the 1960s in New York and Patrick Bateman and the New York of the

314

1980s. By opting for genres that have a distinct style and consequent aesthetic payoff in spite of troubled and troubling main characters, Harron has displayed a courage not often seen among film directors. It is in this spirit that I commend her work to you. It is worthy of your consideration, in more than one way.

315

Chapter 23

Conclusion

The central idea of this book has been that the director of a film must have a concept, an interpretive idea that I have called the director's idea, to determine an effective approach to the text, the performances, and the camera. With a clear director's idea, the film will be deeper, more layered, and more powerful. Without the director's idea, the film can still be made, but the audience's experience of the film will be flatter. In this sense, the director's idea is the path to better directing, possibly even great directing.

I suggested in Part I that directors fall into particular categories: competent, good, or great. Competent directing is the baseline for directing. This category is characterized by a particular view. The examples that I used, "King Arthur" by Antoine Fuqua and "The Lighthorsemen" by Simon Wincer, have taken a singular approach of featuring heroes in war and their adversaries (*i.e.*, the enemy). These films deploy the romantic idea that men who go to war, whether they embrace the mission or not, are inevitably romantic heroes. This romantic idea of heroism was realized by the director's camera choices, the performances he drew out of his actors, and his interpretation of the narrative. These choices applied to all the characters in the films—those helping the main character as well as those opposing the main character. The experience of these films is singularly romantic, and the films are entertaining. Competent directors, such as Antoine Fuqua and Simon Wincer, are effective in what they set out to do.

When discussing the good director, I used the examples of Adrian Lyne and Claude Chabrol. Lyne remade Chabrol's "Une Femme Infidele" into "Unfaithful." Lyne's film focuses on the woman as the main character and views the murder of the lover as an accident, the results of which must be addressed by husband and wife. The film proceeds as a story of desire and its tragic consequences. In Chabrol's film, the main character is the husband and his motivation is jealousy. He has a beautiful wife and assumes she is bored with him, but he remains overwhelmingly in love with her. That love takes him from suspicion to painful discovery to murderous rage and back to the stasis of love and acknowledgment of guilt. The character in the Chabrol film has a powerful inner life, and Chabrol used feeling and irony to make his motivation seem both understandable and poignant. There is no such understanding about the husband in Lyne's version. He is simply overcome and surprised by the arrival of his rage at the moment of murder. For the purposes of our discussion, Lyne represents a competent director and Chabrol a good director.

The good director adds value to a project through his text interpretation, direction of the actors' performances, and camera deployment, creating surprise and a subtext that deepens our experience of the film. In Chapter 4, I focused on the work of Anthony Mann, a director known principally for his Westerns. In Mann's "Winchester '73," the surprise is the dynamic deployment of the environment to reveal how morally ambiguous the main character has become. The classic Western positions the main character as a moral hero and the antagonist as morally reprehensible, but this dynamic does not operate in "Winchester '73," as both the main character and his antagonist are humanized. The humanity of each is compelling, and the genre expectation shifts. The subtext in Mann's work is rather modern compared to the classical pastoral sense of the West; consequently, the film proceeds toward resolution without the optimistic sensibility of the classic Western. To compensate for this shift, Mann provides a visual aesthetic that is dynamic and powerful. The real hero of his films is the artist, Mann himself, who takes us on a visual rollercoaster ride that is quite unforgettable. He does so in his war films as well as his film noir films. Visual power and disappointed characters are a potent mix in the experience of a Mann film.

If the good director uses a counterpoint approach to layer our experience of the film, the great director deploys his own voice to transform our experience of the film. The vehicle for that voice is the director's idea. As I mentioned in Chapter 5, particular characteristics mark the work of the great director. The level of passion in the work of the great director is unusual. The great director stakes out a distinct position on a subject or character in the film, and there is a simplicity in his approach as well as economy in the narrative. Much is achieved in a single shot. Finally, there is a distinctive style in the work of the great director.

A useful comparison of good directors and great directors is provided by the two versions of "The Manchurian Candidate." I suggested in Chapter 4 that the more recent example of "The Manchurian Candidate" directed by Jonathan Demme is an example of good directing. By deploying an aggressive, intense camera,

Demme was able to portray the madness of creating two assassins for political gain. The antagonist in Demme's version is the corporate/industrial complex seeking dominance. Although this version is layered, the performances are realistic, which relegates this "The Manchurian Candidate" to an entertaining cautionary tale.

On the other hand, the original "The Manchurian Candidate" directed by John Frankenheimer exemplifies great directing. In this version, Cold War politics provides the core struggle. Communists create an assassin to help them take over the United States, their capitalist rival state. The Cold War plot is transformed into an emotionally compelling nightmare by positioning the struggle inside one family. Raymond Shaw, the main character who is brainwashed to be an assassin, is forever the powerless son. The antagonist is his mother, who presents herself as a patriot but is in fact the communist mole who controls Raymond and moves him toward his assignment of killing the presidential candidate. Her power over her son destroys his life, and this personal tragedy becomes a national tragedy. Made in 1962, this film illustrates how politics and personal life can clash to the detriment of the family and the nation. Frankenheimer's visual style and ironic deployment of visual observations about race relations, interpersonal relations, and national rivalries even between Allies make "The Manchurian Candidate" a powerful example of what great directing can be.

The director deploys three tools to create the director's idea: text interpretation, direction of the actors' performances, and camera choices that create editing opportunities to realize the director's idea. Let's look at each of these individually.

In Chapter 4, I described how Michael Mann in "Collateral" interpreted Los Angeles as a city where individuals are alone. They cannot count on people or organizations within the environment to help them. This is a more neutral presentation of Los Angeles than Robert Altman's in "Short Cuts," and it is more neutral but in the opposite direction than the view set forth by Stanley Donen and Gene Kelly about the city of dreams in "Singin' in the Rain." My point here is that in his interpretation of the text in "Collateral," Mann used his depiction of the city to make his main character, a taxi driver, even more defenseless against the hit man who is a passenger in his cab. Mann's depiction of the city is an interpretive strategy that deepens our experience of the narrative.

In terms of the performance of the actors, in Chapter 4 I described Elia Kazan's strategy in "Splendor in the Grass." The text is all about sexual desire and the powerful inhibition parents can have on their children. Deanie and Bud are in love. Her parents are poor. His father is a self-made man. Deanie's mother says sex before marriage is wrong, and sex is not pleasurable for women anyway. Bud's father says sex is necessary but marriage is about consolidating wealth and power, not love. He is implying that Bud should marry with an eye on climbing the social ladder, not for love. Kazan stages consecutive scenes between the children and their parents. The text says "don't," but in each scene Kazan's staging communicates the opposite. Deanie physically clings to her mother as she offers her daughter advice. Bud's father physically pummels Bud, albeit both aggressively and affectionately, while he advises him. In both cases, the physical (desire) outweighs what is being said (delay desire; go for power). The directorial choice is empathetic to the desire both Bud and Deanie feel; here, performance tells us about the director's idea.

In Chapter 3, which discusses camera placement and how the elements of the shot are organized to convey the director's idea, I mentioned the bombing shots from "Pearl Harbor" and "Dr. Strangelove." In "Pearl Harbor," the bomb from a Japanese airplane is dropped on a ship below. As the bomb drops toward the ship, the camera takes the view of the bomb. The image is conceptual but in the end it simply elicits a sensation rather than deeper feelings. I compared this shot to the nuclear bomb being dropped from the B52 in "Dr. Strangelove." Slim Pickens' character has opted to ride the bomb to its destination. Wearing a cowboy hat, he rides the bomb as though it is a wild bull. He is all excitement trying to tame the bomb/bull. Whether we view the shot ironically, whether we consider the character to be demented or a macho cowboy to the end, the image stays with us long after the film has ended. Kubrick transformed a narrative action—bombing the target—into another level of meaning. Whether we view it as an anti-war or anti-cowboy mythology and mentality, the shot is transformative. It has become more than the sum of its narrative parts. Good directing and great directing use the camera, the performances, and the interpretation of the text in just such ways.

It has not been my intention in this book to create a hierarchy of directors, but it has been my intention to suggest that great directing can move in numerous directions. The tools—text interpretation, direction of the actors' performances, and direction of the camera shots—are applied through the lens of the director's idea. I would like to close this book by reconsidering how these tools are used and to what purpose. Specifically, I would like to suggest that great directors often use the tools preferentially to achieve a level of feeling that underpins the director's idea. A director such as Sergei Eisenstein, for example, uses interpretation and camera more than he relies on performance, while a director such as Elia Kazan relies on performance and interpretation more than on the camera shots and editing style. Both are great directors.

In this book we have looked at 14 directors. Let's review those directors who focus on text interpretation and performance in their films. I would like to suggest that there is an underlying purpose for such an approach. In the case of Margarethe Von Trotta and Catherine Breillat, that purpose is political. Both Von Trotta and Breillat have staked out a specific position in the war between men and women for equal rights in society. In the case of Von Trotta, the text interpretation focuses on political action in the community. A woman commits robbery to save a child daycare center in "The Second Awakening of Crista Klages." One sister becomes a terrorist while the other acts for the environment and women's rights within the law in "Marianne and Juliane." The bedroom is the battleground for Catherine Breillat; whether we look at "Fat Girl" or "Anatomy of Hell," the struggle between men and women can be boiled down to a matter of getting what you want sexually.

Because the stakes are so high in the work of Von Trotta and Breillat, much pressure is put on the conviction of the actors. They have to make the audience believe that their very existence is at stake. The political dimension of the narratives of these filmmakers must be communicated by the performers, so charisma as well as conviction are at the core of the actors' performances in these films. In both cases, despite the provocative dimensions of the narrative, the visuals must follow or take a subordinate position to text interpretation and performance.

If politics is the goal in the work of Von Trotta and Breillat, the goal is energy in the work of Elia Kazan and Mary Harron. Kazan and Harron both favor performance and text interpretation but for a different purpose. I have already mentioned Kazan's performance work in "Splendor in the Grass." His work with Jack Palance and Zero Mostel in "Panic in the Streets," Raymond Massey and James Dean in "East of Eden," and Marlon Brando and Rod Steiger in "On the Waterfront" produced legendary performances by mythologized performers. All of the performances are driven by the conflict between the character trying to achieve a goal and the vigor of the forces opposing him. The interpretation keys the performances. The clash of drama and psychology, so forcefully utilized by Kazan, highly energizes these films.

The same holds true for the work of Mary Harron in "I Shot Andy Warhol" and "American Psycho," where the energy is generated by the performances of Lili Taylor and Christian Bale. The characters' inner and outer lives are at war, and the battlegrounds—haves *versus* have-nots, celebrities *versus* non-celebrities, men *versus* women— energize these films. From an interpretive point of view, Harron's choice of genres—docudrama and fable—adds her own contrarian views that conflict with those of the characters. In both films, the characters want celebrity, but Harron illustrates the emptiness of their goal by displaying the banality of Warhol and his acolytes, as well as that of the corporate vice presidents. Her voice conflicts with the characters' goals, and the intentions of the characters are presented as ironic rather than as something we can identify with or care about. In these films, neither Solanas nor Bateman gains happiness or understanding as a result of their actions, but Harron has put their actions to good purpose to energize her dark narratives.

If politics is the key transformative device in the films of Breillat and Von Trotta and energy is the key transformative device in the works of Kazan and Harron, it is the romantic subtext that is transformative in the work of Ernst Lubitsch and Billy Wilder. Again, performance and text interpretation propel the subtext deeper into the films. Because Lubitsch specialized in romantic comedy, on first glance my claim may seem confusing. Let me explain. Although the films follow the course of a relationship between a man and a woman, the course of that relationship is always underpinned by the subtext. In "Trouble in Paradise," the lovers in the end have more in common with one another than the challenger Madame Colet could ever hope for, and the fact that both of the lovers are thieves saves the romantic relationship. In "To Be or Not To Be," the shared narcissism saves the relationship of Joseph and

Maria Tura. In "The Shop Around the Corner," idealism and the need for idealism fuels the relationship of Klara and Alfred. Finally, in "Ninotchka" the joy of romance fuels the relationship of Leon and Ninotchka and helps each overcome their political differences.

To highlight the subtext, the performances are keyed toward opposites attracting. Leon is portrayed as a hedonist, so light he might just float away, and Ninotchka is portrayed as serious and somber, weighed down by her heaviness. It is the joy of finding each other that transforms Leon into a man who can make and honor commitments and Ninotchka into a woman who can laugh and take pleasure in the small things, such as a hat or a Moscow dinner party with her friends, all of whom have been banished from where their hearts are—Paris. The performers had to be able to capture the pleasure and the pain, the seriousness and the lightness. And this is precisely where Lubitsch brought the performances. In each case, they are the focus of his text interpretations.

Billy Wilder also focused on the romantic subtext in his films. Lost hope is the subtext of "Double Indemnity." Lost dreams are the subtext of "The Lost Weekend." Lost ambition is the subtext of "Sunset Boulevard." Lost moral values are the subtext of "The Apartment." Using text interpretation, Wilder amplified hope and its destruction in "Double Indemnity," in which a single character—the woman of Walter Neff's dreams, Phyllis Dietrichson—was responsible for both. In a sense, two women represent Joe Gillis' relationship with ambition in "Sunset Boulevard." Norma Desmond represents the collapse of Joe's ambition for himself; with her, he is a kept man. With Betty, the story analyst, Joe regains the sense that he may be a good writer. His relationship with her represents the hope that he might regain that ambition.

Critical to the performances of the actors is that we need to see their self-contempt for losing their ambition and we need to see the desire, the hope, that the ambition can live again. This requires a labile performance swinging from cynicism to anticipation to love. William Holden's performance as Joe Gillis does not disappoint, nor do the other actors in Wilder's films. Both Ray Milland in "The Lost Weekend" and Jack Lemmon in "The Apartment" were recognized with Oscars for their acting. Portraying the swings between moral confusion and clarity in no small part contributed to Jack Lemmon's performance in "The Apartment." Performance together with text interpretation created romantic subtexts that lifted Wilder's director's ideas to remarkable heights.

Not all directors use the same mix of tools to elevate their work. The directors we have discussed thus far used a mix of text interpretation and performance to power their work. The next group of directors uses a different mix, that of performance and the camera. In the case of George Stevens and Steven Spielberg, they have deployed camera and performance to highlight the humanity in the characters portrayed in their films. Both Stevens and Spielberg have had as their goal that the audience will recognize themselves in their characters. This attentiveness to character can seem manipulative but in their work the focus is on first a recognition of the humanity of the character and eventually an invitation to see ourselves in that character. There is no other way to understand the power and poignancy of the character of George Eastman in "A Place in the Sun" or of John Miller in "Saving Private Ryan." For Stevens, humanity required an emotional complexity. When Angela Vickers meets George Eastman in "A Place in the Sun," he is playing pool alone. We understand why he is alone. He has tried to mingle with the guests at the Eastman party but even his cousin has failed to acknowledge his presence. When Angela sees him she is impressed by his acumen at pool. She asks him why he is alone. Is he feeling blue, or is he simply antisocial? In a sense, he is both. He has been rejected by his peers, so, alone, he is both blue and antisocial. This acknowledgment by Angela immediately penetrates his mask, and his wanting to be alone turns into anxiety, and this feeling, too, is acknowledged. In this brief exchange of the soon-to-be lovers, George Eastman has been acknowledged and portrayed as emotionally complex and very human. Later, when his desire clouds his judgment and he considers killing his working-class lover, Alice, it is his humanity, and hers, that prevents him from carrying out the murder. At this point we can see ourselves in George Eastman—basically decent but conflicted about desire and our feeling guilty for having that desire.

To characterize the humanity of George Eastman, Stevens relied principally on performance and his direction of the camera. The performances of Montgomery Clift as George Eastman, of Elizabeth Taylor as Angela, and Shelly Winters as Alice can be categorized as either masked or emotionally open. Both Angela and

Alice are emotionally open and expressive, which requires above all an honesty in the presentation of these characters. The actresses portraying these characters are admirable in their projection of the transparency of their characters. Montgomery Clift, on the other hand, is more masked; he feigns directness but all the while masks his feeling. When Angela unmasks him in their first meeting, we get a glimpse of his vulnerability. For Clift, this required a more internal performance and he, too, performed admirably.

In terms of camera choices, Stevens relied on two styles of shots to depict the humanity of his characters. The close-ups of George and Angela in the scene where they meet captures the openness of Angela and the mask of George. Later close-ups of George in the boat with Alice are not able to illustrate his murderous intent. The lighting produced shadows on his face, particularly his eyes, which masked his intent from Alice but suggested his intent to the audience. The other shot Stevens relied on was a slow tracking shot. As Angela and George begin to dance in the scene that follows their meeting in the pool room, the camera discovers them and moves in on their growing intimacy. The slow tracking shot creates an anticipation of their growing desire and the culmination of their desire to be together.

In the case of John Miller, Spielberg introduced him in "Saving Private Ryan" as a capable officer who is serious about his job. Like the police chief in "Jaws," Miller is decent and effective in his work. In both "Saving Private Ryan" and "Jaws," the plot challenges the character. For Miller, the plot is to find Private Ryan behind enemy lines. This means putting his men in harm's way. Is it worth it? This will be Miller's struggle. In the case of "Jaws," the police chief unequivocally stands for shutting the beaches and eliminating the human food supply for the shark. In both cases, the humanity of the main character is highlighted and challenged by the plot.

In terms of performance, the key was to convey an idea of the characters being caring and effective. Both Tom Hanks and Roy Scheider worked within these parameters. Spielberg also gave each main character a private moment—the police chief with his wife, Miller with platoon members who are trying to find out about his private life—where the vulnerability of each character is clearly on display. As in the case of Stevens, Spielberg allows secondary characters to be expressive while the private side of them remains more

CONCLUSION

hidden, masked. Spielberg does this to provide a transparency to their professional effectiveness. The personal is private, masked, so it will not get in the way of the characters' conduct of their work. As in the case of Stevens, Spielberg relies on the close-up and camera movement to articulate the feelings, professional and personal, of his main characters.

Both Stevens and Spielberg have defined humanity in terms of the other—a couple, a platoon, a community. Roman Polanski and Stanley Kubrick, on the other hand, have focused on the individual, the solitary self being pummeled and punished by another. Their focus is on the existence of the self and its quality, based on challenges by the actions of others. Both Polanski and Kubrick have used a mix of performance and camera to evoke this punishing dynamic. Whether the two directors were or are pessimists or realists is a matter of interpretation. What we experience in their work, however, is a transformation of the narrative into its most basis struggle, the self struggling to survive under the most ferocious attack from social, political, even spiritual antagonists.

Polanski uses the camera to highlight or focus upon the individual—Tess, in Hardy's adaptation of "Tess," and Rosemary, in "Rosemary's Baby." These women's perspectives on the world are represented by a subjective camera that is so intimate that it crowds them, revealing the anxiety they feel about their state of aloneness. Their performances are attenuated to their communities. They want connectivity but all they are offered is the traditional female position of powerlessness, of being used for other agendas and then abandoned. In this sense, the performances focus on their vulnerability. Casting and the shape of the performances emphasize their openness and their vulnerability. The consequence is that they are disposable, having served the agendas of powerful men in society. Their existence is in the service of others.

In the case of Kubrick, the camera roams, focusing on the narcissism of a New York doctor and his wife or on the callowness of a young Irish nobleman. In "Eyes Wide Shut" and "Barry Lyndon," the characters are held up for examination. The camera is the witness to their feelings. In terms of performance, Kubrick's characters are enacting a habitual state. They are dissatisfied and trapped in that state. Ryan O'Neal, Tom Cruise, and Nicole Kidman seem self-conscious about their unheroic characters. Their discomfort lies in their flawed characters. The performances are keyed to that discomfort and to its unheroic nature. They are restless rather than objects of satire, disillusioned rather than unhappy. The performances focus on the restlessness of the characters, characters who do not understand, characters struggling for meaning. Finally, both Kubrick and Polanski use the moving camera to a greater extent than most directors. It is a searching camera, a probing camera, and its restless movement raises questions about existence and meaning.

If Polanski and Kubrick used the camera and performance to explore the issue of existence, François Truffaut and Lukas Moodysson have used the camera and performance to subvert and challenge norms, the baseline of social and psychological existence. That subversion can also be used to turn those norms over to reveal new and stimulating alternatives. Truffaut in his embrace of children, viewed rebellion as the expression of individuality, eccentricity as a creative norm, relationships as the litmus test of aspiration and happiness. To do all this, Truffaut peppered his narratives with mischievous performances. Jean-Pierre Léaud as Antoine Doinel is Truffaut's alter ego. As the unreliable narrator of "Love on the Run," Léaud's performance subverts the authenticity of the memoir of Doinel in his sundry relationships past and present. The camera movement between Doinel and his son and Colette in the train station, their sighting of each other, and their eventual coming together on the train after Colette has been reading about herself in Antoine's *roman à clef* links the characters together in a random rather than urgent manner. The consequence is that the camera lowers expectations for an eventual encounter. In a sense, Truffaut used the camera to alter the traditional result of parallel editing, the coming together of the two parties, in a more dramatically satisfying and expected manner.

In the case of Lukas Moodysson, subversion is also achieved through a mix of camera and performance. The characters in "Together" could be characterized as straight or conservative (*e.g.*, Elisabeth and her children) or unconventional (*e.g.*, her brothers and fellow hippies). Key to the performances is that Elisabeth and her children provide a baseline for behavior. Their presence unmasks the conventionality of the others. By the time she leaves the commune, the hippies have been transformed, their ideals subverted into a more practical approach to life. Also key to the performances is developing this capacity for subversion without making the change farcical. In fact, Moodysson handles the change believably. The camera is direct and close to the characters in order to capture the changes. Because the characters' arcs are similar, there is no confusion in the editing. The shot selection is similar in "Lilja 4-Ever," although the character arc is more intense, as in the end Volodya and Lilja choose to end their lives. The subversion here is that in nature Lilja and Volodya are decent, moral friends. It is the people around them who undermine the life force and move these characters toward their deaths.

We end this chapter by looking at the two remaining directors, Sergei Eisenstein and John Ford. Both preferred to use the camera and text interpretation to create the distinct styles central to their work. Their distinctive styles transformed their films from a tale well told to an altogether different level of experience. Many filmmakers have opted for including political or historical material in their films but none has matched Eisenstein in the formal power of his imagery. Composition and the juxtaposition of light within a frame and between consecutive shots go to the heart of depicting the conflict and transformation typically found in Eisenstein's work. The vigor of Eisenstein's style elevates "Ivan the Terrible" from a portrait of an important monarch to an operatic tragedy of a man abandoned and betrayed by all those around him. The transformation of a man into someone who has earned the surname "Terrible" is tragic because of Eisenstein's operatic interpretation. Francis Ford Coppola used the same operatic interpretation to transform "The Godfather" into an iconic American tragedy.

As much can be said for John Ford. His politics may seem old fashioned and his narrative rambling, but his style turns nostalgia, romance, loss, love, and revenge into poetry. Few filmmakers have been able to summon the power of style in such a manner as Ford did in "The Grapes of Wrath" and "The Searchers." The poetry he created suggested a larger-than-life quality or deeper soul within his characters. Ford exemplified the capacity for greatness in us all. Westerns and poetry—these are the legacies of John Ford.

The path to great direction is a varied one. By choosing a particular mix of tools, a director can formulate a director's idea that will realize his vision.

Appendix: Finding the Director's Idea

HOLLYWOOD

PRODUCTION

DIRECTOR

CAMERA

DATE   SCENE   TAK

This appendix is intended to offer you practical guidelines for finding the director's idea for your project. We begin with a deep reading of the script.

Strategy for Reading the Script

Three crucial questions should emerge from the first reading:

1. *What is the genre or story form?* Each story form has a different dramatic shape and presentation of character and deployment of plot.
2. *Who is the main character and his or her goal?* There should be a distinct main character with a clear goal.
3. *What is the character arc, or, to put it another way, how will the experience of the story change the main character?* You should be able to identify the state of the character at the beginning of the story and how the character changes as the story unfolds.

Upon a second reading, another set of questions should be answered:

1. *What is the premise of the story?* The premise—sometimes called the spine, central conflict, or engine—of the story is best understood as the two opposing choices facing the main character. Often these two choices concern important relationships presented in the narrative.
2. *Is the premise consistent with the main character and his goal?* It should be. If, for example, the main character in the "The Verdict" is a successful lawyer, then the premise of restoring dignity to a dissipated life would not resonate. There must be a link between the premise and the main character.
3. *Does the main character transform in such a way that his or her transformation is credible, meaningful, and emotionally satisfying?*
4. *What is the plot in the film, and how is the plot used?* Ideally, plot works most effectively when it puts into place forces pitted against the main character's goal. In "A Very Long Engagement," a young woman cannot believe her fiancé has

been killed in World War I. The lethality of the war as well as the plot to find him and restore the relationship seem closer to fantasy than a realistic likelyhood. Unless plot puts some kind of obstacle in the way of the main character achieving his or her goal, the plot is not working. Think also of the voyage of the *Titanic* in "Titanic" as an example where the plot works effectively. The ship sinks, and Rose's hope for love becomes a memory rather than a reality. Deploying plot in a story can be a major weakness for directors, so this aspect of the director's idea requires considerable attention.

5. *How do the secondary characters representing the two choices of the premise fit in with the premise?* Are they two distinct groups—helpers and harmers? Is one of the harmers more essential than the others? How? This character, the antagonist, can be the most critical character of all, determining the vigor of the main character's response, the shape of the character arc, and how we feel about the main character at the end. The more powerful the antagonist, the more heroic the sense of our main character at the end. In their nature and actions, secondary characters serve specific purposes in a script. The more they resonate as people rather than story elements, the richer the script will be. Although we experience the story through a main character, secondary characters can help the script seem more credible and compelling.

Let's return to the genre issue at this point. Genre implies the dramatic arc of the film. A thriller is a chase; a police story is about solving a crime and putting the criminal away; a gangster film is the rise and fall of the main character; a science fiction film is a story about the threat of technology to humanity. Some genres are internal. The melodrama is about an interior journey around loss, ambition, or spiritual rebirth. The situation comedy is about values in life and the behavior of the main character (*e.g.*, a man pretends to be a woman to further his ambitions for his career in "Tootsie"). Westerns also tend to be about values, with the pastoral, free past representing the positive and civilization and progress representing the negative. Each genre has a different shape. What is the dramatic arc, and how does it serve the goal of the main character? If the script does not follow genre expectations, do the changes make the script better, fresher, and stronger . . . or the opposite?

Now that you have read the script a second time and taken copious notes, a third reading is necessary to explore dimensions of the script that could yield a director's idea.

Moving Toward Interpretation

Think of this round as the application of text interpretation. A useful approach here is to speculate about the story's potential in the following dimensions:

- Existential
- Psychological
- Sociological
- Political

Each dimension spins the story differently. Let's look at a film such as "Lost in Translation." On a political level we could say the film has a Japanese–American dimension. Films such as Billy Wilder's "One Two Three" put politics and political differences right up front, but in "Lost in Translation" Sofia Coppola does not seem that interested in the political dimensions of a story. What about the sociological dimension of "Lost in Translation"? Is there a class or gender issue at play here? Is there a hierarchy of groups, one over another? Not really. A sociological reading was not important to Sofia Coppola in this film. What about the psychological dimension of "Lost in Translation"? Is this essentially a story of unhappiness or some other character issue? Can the unhappiness of the two main characters be defined in terms of a cause and a cure? Not really. Let's look at the existential dimension, then. Both main characters, the actor and the young photographer's wife, seem to have full lives but are essentially alone. Conversations with their spouses alert us to how alone they feel in their significant relationships. Being in a strange foreign culture with distinctive social mores does not resolve the aloneness of these two characters. Only the friendship each offers the other moves each of these characters away from being absolutely alone. Sofia Coppola has chosen to focus on the existential dimension in her interpretation of the text. She could have chosen any of the other dimensions—psychological, sociological, or political. A different reading, however, would have changed the film considerably.

A second prism available to the director when developing a director's idea is a possible relationship between the narrative and issues of the day. Every time period has recognizable issues of the day. Looking at 2005, for example, large issues of the day would include the role of religion in life, globalization, challenges to the environment, the right to privacy, equality for all (*e.g.*, women's rights in a man's world), and, of course, modernism *versus* tradition. There are many other specific, local issues, but these larger issues are begging for attention on an urgent personal, national, and international level.

If the director is passionate about society, the issues of the day become relevant as a prism for interpreting the script. These issues also give the director a platform for expressing his or her personal beliefs as well as a vehicle for gaining an audience. Issues of the day can focus the director's idea in a particular way. Steven Soderbergh has often used an issue of the day to make his narratives more compelling. "Erin Brockovich" used the prism of women's rights in a man's world to make the main character's journey more compelling to the audience. Power and its partner, corruption, drive the drug story "Traffic." Parenting is at the heart of Soderbergh's revenge story, "The Limey." Considering issues of the day during the text interpretation can help in developing a director's idea.

Voice, which expresses the director's opinions, is another device that can move a director from text interpretation to a director's idea. Voice can in good measure be a reflection of the character of the director. Stanley Kubrick was ambitious, ironic, and passionate in his views of human progress. He differed with technological or scientific views that the human race has progressed. The Coen brothers share Kubrick's skepticism but are far more playful in articulating their voice on the issue. Steven Spielberg also has views on the issue, but being more optimistic in his voice, his narratives seem positively hopeful in comparison to those of Kubrick. "Artificial Intelligence: AI," a Kubrick project directed by Spielberg after Kubrick's death, offers a good example of the clash of two distinct voices. The script developed by Kubrick reflects the critical voice of Kubrick, but the visual style and performances reflect the more optimistic voice of Spielberg.

Directors who are very conscious of the issue of voice and for whom their views supersede any dramatic considerations often opt for voice-oriented story forms—specifically, satire, docudrama, fable, and nonlinear stories. Each of these genres uses distancing strategies such as irony to detach our identification and emotional involvement with the main character. Structure also is used to distance us from the main character. The viewer watches without emotionally identifying with the character. The relationship between the director and the viewer is more direct, as it is not mediated by the viewer's emotional relationship with the main character. Voice is the most direct vehicle for the development of the director's idea.

To say that marketing does not play a role in the development of a director's idea would be disingenuous. Aside from voice, marketing is a most conscious deliberation during development of a director's idea. For the director, it can be the single most influential factor. Sensation sells tickets. Sensation may be generated by plot, by a sexual subtext, by a violent subtext, or by an over-the-top tone or style. Excess and commercialism seem partnered in the work of Quentin Tarantino ("Kill Bill"), Bernardo Bertolucci ("The Dreamers"), John Woo ("Mission Impossible II"), and Adrian Lyne ("Fatal Attraction"). Marketing can be a powerful shaping force in the development of the director's idea.

Choosing the Director's Idea

Now that you have completed a full script analysis and decided which aspect of the story has pulled you into the story, you have five options for choosing the director's idea. Each provides a different pathway; focus on one of the following:

1. *The character arc*—The main character and his or her transformation are the vehicle.
2. *The dramatic arc*—The plot is the driving force. The struggle of the main character and the antagonist determine the direction and shape of the dramatic arc
3. A *subtextual idea*—A narrative can be straightforward *(e.g.,* the romantic nobility of "King Arthur") or complex *(e.g.,* "Silence of the Lambs"). By making the subtext prominent, the character arc and dramatic arc are subsumed by the subtext.

4. *Voice*—The director's ideas about, for example, war (*e.g.*, Malick in "The Thin Red Line"), family values (*e.g.*, Coen brothers in "Raising Arizona"), or racial profiling (*e.g.*, Holland in "Europa Europa") dominate all narrative structures.
5. *Your deepest values in life*—There are filmmakers whose personal ethos is revealed in how they approach the narrative, such as Jean Renoir's humanism in his films; Elia Kazan's contentious framing of class, ethnicity, and intragenerational differences; Roman Polanski's vision of existential aloneness; and Sergei Eisenstein's aesthetic Marxism.

Once your director's idea is defined, you need to conceptualize an approach to directing the actors and a strategy for the camera shots that are in harmony with your director's idea. Remember, the more layered your approach, the more creative and commercial risk-taking is at play.

Index

340

342

Director's idea, 12–23, 52–53, 330–336
   choosing, 335–336
   how works, 41–46
   moving toward interpretation,
      333–335
   overview, 12–15, 330–331
   strategy for reading script, 331–333
   unity of productions, 15–23
"Doctor Zhivago," 100, 193
Doinel, Antoine, 205, 206, 207, 212
Donen, Stanley, 55, 177, 319
Donner, Richard, 28
D'Onofrio, Vincent, 237
Dorff, Stephen, 306, 312
Dorleac, Francoise, 212
"Do the Right Thing," 7, 58
"Double Indemnity," 91, 163, 166, 168,
      170, 173, 323
Douglas, Kirk, 169, 198, 238, 239
Douglas, Melvyn, 176, 183
Dovshenko, Alexander, 123, 147
Downs, Cathy, 137
Dramatic emphasis, 99
"The Dreamers," 335
"The Dreamlife of Angels," 64
Dreiser, Theodore, 123, 151
Dreyer, Carl, 57, 285
Dreyfuss, Richard, 249, 254
"Dr. Jekyll and Mr. Hyde," 90, 93
"Dr. Strangelove," 37, 233, 234, 239,
      242, 320
Ducey, Caroline, 292, 297
"Duel," 248, 254, 256
Dullea, Keir, 236, 242
Dunaway, Faye, 222

E
"Early Spring," 63
"East of Eden," 76–78, 190, 191, 192,
      194, 196, 197, 201, 322
Eastwood, Clint, 4, 7, 58, 110
"Eat Drink Man Woman," 8
Editing, 97–102
   clarity, 98–99
   conflict, 101

continuity, 97
dramatic emphasis, 99
emotional guidelines, 100
main character, 101
new ideas, 99
overview, 97
parallel action, 99–100
story form, 101–102
tone, 100–101
Edwards, Blake, 4
"8 1/2," 57
Eisenstein, Sergei, 4, 10, 118, 122–133,
      143, 147, 193, 234, 238, 286, 321,
      328, 336
"El Cid," 52, 88
"Elizabeth," 90
Elliott, Denholm, 254
Emma, 75
Emmerich, Roland, 261
Emotional guidelines, 100
"Empire of the Sun," 26, 247
"The Enemy Below," 110
Engel, Tina, 264, 270
"The English Patient," 97
"The Enigma of Kaspar Hauser," 64
Ephron, Nora, 175
Epstein brothers, 5
"E.T.," 247, 248, 250, 252, 256
"Europa Europa," 336
European School of acting, 114–119
"Excalibur," 29, 30
"The Exorcist," 28
Exterior stories, 78–80
"Exterminating Angel," 63
Eyes Wide Open, 237, 241
"Eyes Wide Shut," 233, 237, 239,
      240, 241, 242, 243, 244, 304,
      326

F
"A Face in the Crowd," 190, 191, 193,
      301
"Fahrenheit 451," 205
Fairbanks, Douglas, Jr., 150
"Fanny and Alexander," 276

345

Mankiewicz, Joseph, 5, 21, 56, 88, 169, 178
Mann, Anthony, 5, 9, 49, 51, 52, 88, 95, 136, 318
Mann, Michael, 28, 47–48, 80, 95, 254, 319
Mann, Paul, 192, 200
"Man of Marble," 231
"Man on Fire," 7
"The Man Who Loved Women," 206
"The Man Who Shot Liberty Valence," 135, 142
"The Man Who Wasn't There," 84
Marber, Patrick, 79, 114
"Maria Full of Grace," 94
"Marianne and Juliane," 261, 262, 263, 264, 265–267, 268, 269, 270, 272, 321
Marjanovic, Goran, 281
"Marnie," 82
Marshall, Herbert, 178, 183
Marshall, Rob, 39
Marston, Joshua, 94
Martell, Yann, 79
Marx Brothers, 59
Mason, James, 242, 243
Massey, Raymond, 192, 322
"Master and Commander," 83
Mathis, Samantha, 308
Matthau, Walter, 163, 170
Matthis, Samantha, 312
Maugham, Somerset, 78
Mazursky, Paul, 181
McCrea, Joel, 151
McDowell, Andie, 99
McDowell, Malcolm, 242
McLaughlin, Victor, 142, 150
McQ, 7
"Mean Streets," 62
"Meet the Fokkers," 20
Mehta, Deepa, 289
Meirelles, Fernando, 82
Meisner, Sanford, 113, 115
"Memento," 97
Mendes, Sam, 7, 22, 57

"Men in War," 53
"Mephisto," 64
The Merchant of Venice, 75
Mesquida, Roxane, 293, 294
"The Messenger," 7
Meyers, Russ, 290
Michalkhov, Nickolai, 64
Michell, Roger, 8
Milland, Ray, 163, 164, 170, 171, 323
Miller, Arthur, 189
Miller, George, 22
"Miller's Crossing," 84
Mineo, Sal, 141
Minghella, Anthony, 20, 97
"The Missing," 109
"Mission Impossible II," 335
"Modern Times," 55
Modine, Matthew, 237, 242
Monroe, Marilyn, 163, 169, 270
"Monsoon Wedding," 302
"Monster," 302, 303
Montgomery, Robert, 90, 137, 142
Moodysson, Lukas, 274–287, 327, 328
    "A Hole in My Heart," 281–282
    directing actor, 284–285
    directing camera, 285–287
    "Fucking Åmål," 277–278
    "Lilja 4-Ever," 279–280
    overview, 277–278
    text interpretation, 282–283
    "Together," 278–279
Moreau, Jean, 212
Moreau, Jeanne, 290
"The More the Merrier," 149, 150–151, 154, 156, 158, 159
Morgan, Frank, 176
Morgenstern, Danny, 307
Mostel, Zero, 191, 193, 322
"The Motorcycle Diaries," 96
"Mouchette," 61
Mowbray, Alan, 142
"Mrs. Doubtfire," 28, 81
"Mr. Smith Goes to Washington," 21, 178
Müller-Westernhagen, Marius, 265

353

354

355

Wood, Natalie, 189, 191
Wright, Jeffrey, 43
Writing the Short Film, 302
"Wyatt Earp," 76
Wyler, William, 22, 51, 52, 53, 55, 58,
    95, 169
Wyman, Jane, 164

Y
"The Year of the Gun," 28
Yimou, Xiang, 64, 147, 277
"Young Mr. Lincoln," 135, 136

Young perspectives, 80–81
"You've Got Mail," 175

Z
"Z," 82
Zeffirelli, 74
Zemeckis, Robert, 25, 98
"Zero de Conduite," 205
Zinnemann, Fred, 25, 51, 52, 55, 58, 98
Zoncka, Eric, 64
"Zorba the Greek," 22
Zwerling, Darrell, 222

356